THE LOMBARD LAWS

SOURCES OF MEDIEVAL HISTORY

Edited by Edward Peters

THE FIRST CRUSADE: The Chronicle of Fulcher of Chartres and Other Source Materials, ed. Edward Peters

CHRISTIAN SOCIETY AND THE CRU-SADES, 1198-1229. Sources in Translation, Including The Capture of Damietta by Oliver of Paderborn, ed. Edward Peters

THE BURGUNDIAN CODE: The Book of Constitutions or Law of Gundobad Additional Enactments, ed. Katherine Fischer Drew

SELECTED WRITINGS OF ULRICH ZWINGLI, Ulrich Zwingli

FROM ST. FRANCIS TO DANTE: Translations from the Chronicle of the Franciscan Salimbene (1221-88), G. G. Coulton

SCIENTIFIC ACHIEVEMENT OF THE MIDDLE AGES, Richard C. Dales

THE LOMBARD LAWS

*Translated with
an Introduction by*

KATHERINE FISCHER DREW

Foreword by
EDWARD PETERS

PENN

UNIVERSITY OF PENNSYLVANIA PRESS

PHILADELPHIA

CcIRes
DG
511
.L43

ISBN: (Paperbound edition) 0-8122-1055-7

Printed in the United States of America. Editorial production
and design by *Weidner Associates, Inc.*, Cinnaminson, N.J. 08077.

FOREWORD

by Edward Peters

ITALY, THE LOMBARDS, AND LOMBARD LAW

I

On August 13, 554, the Emperor Justinian formally announced the restoration of Roman imperial rule in Italy. For twenty years from his rebuilt capital of Constantinople he had directed a series of wars whose aim was to destroy the kingdom that the Ostrogoths had established in Italy in 491. Nearly all of Justinian's foreign policy, from the Tigris and Euphrates valleys to Gaul, had been directed toward the reconquest of Italy, and in that process Justinian's forces, led by Belisarius and Narses, had destroyed the Vandal kingdom in north Africa, made inroads into Visigothic Spain, and claimed once again naval superiority in the Mediterranean. In 552 Narses destroyed the cavalry of the last Gothic king, Totila, and in 554 the imperial proclamation was issued. Italy was once more to be ruled by the imperial administration; it was to be Empire as usual.

But it was not. Twenty years of warfare had dealt savagely with the towns, the countryside, and the people of Italy, more savagely than the earlier military expeditions of the Visigoths at the beginning of the fifth century, more than the bitter rivalry of military factions at the imperial court in Ravenna in the middle of the century, more than the short-lived kingdom of Odoacer in 476. Certainly the wars undertaken to rid Italy of the Ostrogoths proved far more disastrous than the Ostrogothic occupation itself, which had witnessed a lowering of taxes, the beginnings of the physical restoration of cities, a new air of respect for what Cassiodorus, a Roman official of the great Ostrogothic king Theoderic, called *Romana vetustas*—ancient Roman tradition—and even, among the senato-

rial ranks, a new interest in Roman history. Other parts of the
western half of the Empire had fared worse: Britain was under the
threat of occupation by invading Germanic peoples, and after a
prolonged and at first successful resistance, was lost, probably
during the very years of Justinian's reconquest of Italy. Gaul and
Spain had fallen to the Franks and Visigoths, and the rich provinces of north Africa to the Vandals. Practically alone among the
barbarian invaders, Theoderic insistently maintained his public
respect for Roman institutions, placed Roman officials high in his
court, and acted as a kind of arbiter among the other Germanic
peoples who occupied the other western provinces. Theoderic even
had possessed an official Roman title—*patricius et magister mili-
tum*—conferred upon him in 489 by the Emperor Zeno when he and
his people left the eastern part of the Empire to destroy Odoacer.
King of his own people, Theoderic was nevertheless technically and
legally a servant of the emperor, and in that capacity he governed
the Roman population of Italy for thirty-five years.

In 526 Theoderic died, his carefully maintained rapport with the
Roman senatorial class badly eroded by religious and political differences. A few months before his own death, Theoderic had executed his greatest Roman servant, the philosopher Boethius, on a
charge of treason, and he correctly sensed a renewed effort on the
part of the emperors at Constantinople to reduce his people, just as
he had once, on the emperor's behalf, reduced the short-lived kingdom of Odoacer. After Theoderic's death, rivalries among the
Ostrogoths sharpened Gothic anti-Roman feeling, and the restoration of sound imperial rule in Constantinople itself under Anas-
tasius and Justin I once again awoke imperial ambition to reconquer
the lost western provinces. Justinian's campaign was the result of the
breakup of the fragile Gothic-Roman cooperation and the restoration of the imperial government in the east. Yet the troubled last
years of Theoderic, the short reign of his daughter Amalasuntha,
and the vigorous anti-Roman policies of her successors had already
weakened the economic and political coherence of Italy, even
before Justinian's first invasion in 534. The ensuing wars devas-
tated Italy, and Justinian's official declaration of the restoration of
imperial rule must have had a hollow ring in Italy itself. Italy was
not a tidily restored venerable province of a renewed empire. Most
of it was an empty battlefield.

Upon that battlefield, Roman officials attempted to restore imperial life. Narses, the general to whom the final victory fell, made some efforts in this direction, but his heavy-handed administration made demands upon Italy that could not be met. Not only had plague and famine attended the last years of the Gothic Wars of Justinian, but communications routes had been badly disrupted, agricultural institutions and the population of the countryside had been seriously disturbed and diminished, the administrative classes, particularly the *curialis* class, had disappeared from the cities, and several administrative territories that had long been part of Italy, for example, Sardinia, Corsica, and Sicily, were removed to other divisions of the imperial administration. Ecclesiastical affairs had suffered as well, and upon the Church in Italy fell many of the burdens once easily handled by the Roman civil service. But the Church too was troubled, partly because of the powerful imperial pressure on the Bishops of Rome, and partly because of the rivalry between the sees of Rome and Constantinople. Not even the remarkable series of Popes from Pelagius I (556–561) to Gregory I (590–604) was able to overcome these ecclesiastical difficulties. Finally, the administration of Italy, now formally designated a province by outsiders, civil servants, and soldiers from the Greek east, and the rumors—and facts—of vast amounts of wealth being privately and illegally accumulated by them, could only proclaim reforms; it could not carry them out. The economy and agriculture, the administrative classes and the churchmen, the physical and psychological devastation itself all reflected the troubles of twenty years of war and all too soon began to feel the equally great weight of the demanding, heavy-handed, imperial peace. As a delegation of Romans said to the Emperor Justin II in 567, the tyranny of a Greek eunuch had turned out to be worse than slavery under the Goths.

The dismissal of Narses in 567 did little to change imperial policy in Italy and less to improve conditions in the province itself. The restoration of Imperial Africa, so successful in the sixth century that Africa remained one of the most prosperous provinces of the Empire until the Arab conquests a century later, found no parallel in Italy. Italy was an impoverished province ruled by an administrator controlled from Constantinople. It was not a capital; it was a frontier. In the years 568 and 569 that frontier collapsed.

The last Germanic invasion struck Italy and plunged it once again into war.

The "invasions" of Germanic peoples into the western part of the Roman Empire in the late fourth and fifth centuries were not the holocausts that filmmakers and romantic novelists have often made them out to be. Usually the peoples who entered the Empire without permission numbered among themselves many men who had served as mercenary soldiers in the imperial armies, lived within the frontiers of the Empire for several years, and had already moved far from the old bonds of tribal life—kindred and religion—that had characterized the Germans of the first and second centuries. In many cases, the invaders finally occupied land in the heart of the Empire, where they were vastly outnumbered by the provincial population and frequently given some kind of official or quasi-official status by the imperial government. Of all the invading peoples before 560, only the Vandals, who occupied north Africa, and the Huns imposed their presence purely by military force upon Roman provinces, and both the Vandals and the Huns were eventually destroyed by superior Roman military force. Of the other migrating peoples, the Visigoths were more often the victims of Roman court and military policy than the masters of the provinces in which they finally settled. The Ostrogoths, as we have seen, arrived in Italy with an imperial commission, and their king Theoderic adopted a remarkable policy of pro-Roman conduct. The Ostrogothic kingdom was destroyed by a revived imperial power. The Roman armies and emperors, debilitated as they were, faced with economic and social crisis, and never able to restore the Empire to its old integrity, nevertheless remained capable of causing an enormous amount of difficulty for these early invaders. If the Romans could never fully reconquer their old western provinces, they certainly could, and did, make life very difficult for most of the early Germanic kingdoms that had been precociously carved out of them.

Some Germanic peoples, however, put down deep roots. The Visigoths settled in Spain, safely out of reach of the overextended imperial expeditionary lines. It took a century for the Anglo-Saxons to subdue the resistance in Roman Britain, but subdue it they did. The Franks worked their way slowly south from what is now Belgium, dabbled occasionally in mercenary service, but remained content to drive the Visigoths out of most of Gaul and claim the old province for themselves.

The Lombards, like the Franks and the Anglo-Saxons, were comparative late-comers. They were the last Germanic invaders of the old imperial world until the Vikings in the ninth and tenth centuries, and the last invaders of any kind before the Arabs in the late seventh century. In 568 they entered the debilitated Italy of the post-Gothic War period and overran the initial Byzantine defenses, establishing themselves in the north of the peninsula and in two areas, Spoleto and Benevento, to the east and south of Rome itself. Within two decades, the imperial exarchate ruled only over the northeast, the Duchy of Rome, and the far south of Italy. Justinian's official restoration of imperial rule in Italy had lasted only fourteen years.

II

Only Roman antiquarians and geographers paid much attention to the complicated and highly uncertain distribution of the Germanic peoples beyond their frontiers on the Rhine and Danube. Even Tacitus, the great historian, has been shown to have been more concerned with holding the Germanic peoples up as a mirror to the Romans than with providing an accurate depiction of Germanic life or the cultural differences within the Germanic world. Roman literary sources are less reliable for the Germanic world between the first century B.C. and the third century A.D. than are archaeological discoveries. The Lombards, who may originally have come from Scandinavia, are first attested to in the region of the lower Elbe valley. Archaeologists who have excavated the Lombard urn cemeteries of this and later periods have suggested that Lombard society already recognized the divisions of free warriors, *aldii*, and slaves mentioned in *The Lombard Laws*. By the end of the third century A.D., the cemeteries of the lower Elbe reveal few Lombard traces, suggesting that they had moved on to other lands. Moving south, through central Germany and Bohemia, the Lombards established themselves first north of the Danube, then south of the Danube in the province of Pannonia in the first quarter of the sixth century. Probably both the strong Ostrogothic kingdom in Italy and Byzantine diplomacy served to prevent a deep Lombard penetration of Pannonia until Justinian's Gothic Wars were well underway. The slow Lombard penetration of Pannonia may well have accustomed the Lombards to life within the Roman provincial world, and it was probably there that they learned both the Latin language and the Arian form of Christianity which they preserved until the seventh century. There too, they learned from earlier Germanic settlers of the wealth of the Empire, a lesson that was driven home by their acquaintance with Byzantine diplomacy during their stay in Pannonia. They had entered the world of barbarian kingdoms carved out of the Empire, and they had begun to be influenced by the subtle forces at work in that frontier world.

Among those forces were imperial attempts to create alliances with one or more tribes against others, paying tribute to favored tribes, and fomenting warfare among different tribes. The Avars, a people related to the Huns, had received tribute for a time from the eastern imperial court at Constantinople, and the growth of the Avar power constituted a formidable threat to both the Lombards and their enemies and neighbors the Gepids. In 567, the Lombards, allied with the Avars, destroyed the Gepids, and then, in the next year, the Lombards themselves marched out of Pannonia into Italy. As a result of the destruction of the Gepids and the Lombard migration, the Avars consolidated a vast territory for their own, which they settled until they themselves were destroyed by a Carolingian army late in the eighth century.

In a year of campaigning in Italy, taking cities by force or, more usually, by surrender, the Lombard armies under their king Alboin reached and captured Milan, the former imperial capital. From 568 until Alboin's death in 572 the Lombard conquest of Italy progressed erratically, the king remaining in the north and isolated bands of Lombards under war-leaders penetrating south and even westward into Frankish Gaul. After Alboin's death, the reluctance or inability of the Lombards to establish a successor led to ten years of fragmented rule by Lombard war-leaders called dukes. By the end of the sixth century Italy was divided irregularly between Lombards and imperial occupation forces, with the Duchy of Rome, ruled by a military duke and its bishop, caught uneasily between the two hostile forces. From the pontificate of Gregory I (590–604) to that of Stephen II (752–754), Italy witnessed a century and a half of this balance between Lombard and imperial forces. In 751, however, Lombard pressure finally penetrated the imperial city of Ravenna, and the Lombards won the whole of northern Italy. It was the Lombard triumph against the imperial Byzantine forces that turned their attention once again to the center of Italy and to Rome; faced by such a threat and with no assistance from Constantinople forthcoming, the pope appealed once again to the Franks in Gaul for aid. The successful expeditions of Pepin and Charlemagne precipitated the fall of the Lombard kingdom in 774 and the transformation of the imperial enclave that was papal Rome into the kernel of the later papal state. Lombard law survived in the Frankish north of Italy, however, and after the decline of Carolingian imperial power in the ninth century, Lombard principalities in the south of Italy remained, face to face with their old enemies, the Byzantine forces. Not until the eleventh-century Norman conquest of southern Italy and Sicily did these last Lombard territories fall.

III

The shadow of Justinian looms large over the sixth century and later, not only because of the abortive attempts at reconquest that led to the Gothic Wars and the triumph of city-building that produced the enduring glories of Constantinople, but also through his adaptation and codification of earlier Roman law into the *Corpus Iuris Civilis*, perhaps the most influential legal work the world has ever known. The final version of this great work was promulgated officially in 534, twenty years before the official restoration of imperial rule in Italy. The dismal condition of Italy between 534 and 568, however, did not provide fertile ground for the legal genius of Justinian's compilation, and the *Corpus Iuris Civilis* had to wait until the revival of Roman legal studies in the eleventh century before its full force and majesty began to influence western European law in any substantial way. Italy, like the other western provinces, preserved its own, pre-Justinian Roman law, and it is this vulgar law that plays a role in the history of the relations between the Roman provincials and their barbarian masters between the fifth and eighth centuries. Roman vulgar law in the various forms in which it existed during this period is an important chapter in the history of the shaping of early Italian law.

The "classical" period of Roman law lasted from the late first century B.C. to the middle of the third century A.D. It was marked by the work of eminent individual jurists whose work consisted of increasing the application of Roman law to a bewildering variety of new sorts of cases while at the same time enunciating principles describing the internal consistency of the Roman legal system. They were not philosophers who occasionally considered legal problems; rather they were trained jurists whose attention never wavered from the legal system at hand, whose day-to-day work consisted of advising those involved in legal cases. Their personal authority and prestige were often supported by their high place in imperial councils. The work of these men came to an end in the middle of the third century A.D. From the late third century on, the "postclassical" period, legal thought and legal literature succumbed to the new pressures of imperial bureaucratic service, the changing social and cultural character of the legal profession, and the new needs of an empire in the process of restoration. The anonymity of much of the fourth-century legal literature, the predominance in it of summaries, abridgments, and simplifications of earlier works, and the presence of quickly—and badly—prepared officials in shaping and administering the law parallels in some respects the equally clear tendency in other areas of thought to simplify, abridge, and summarize the contents of older works, from the great scientific encyclopedias to the traditional accounts of Roman history. Legal affairs had come to be handled by the eternally unoriginal routine of bureaucrats; a revival of the rich and complex jurisprudence of the first and second centuries would have been too much to hope for in such a world. The laws most generally applicable to fourth- and fifth-century Roman society were the postclassical remnants and the commands that came from the imperial chancery in the form of edicts and rescripts.

Collections of such edicts comprised, in fact, much of the legal literature of the fourth century. The *Codex Gregorianus* and the *Codex Hermogenianus*, both written around the year 300, contained collections of these imperial laws for handy reference. These books were the predecessors of the later official imperial collections of law, the *Codex Theodosianus* of 438, and ultimately that section of Justinian's *Corpus Iuris Civilis* called the *Code*. Besides these collections there appeared abridgments, with transformations and additions, of works of the jurists of the classical period. Such a work was the *Pauli Sententiae,* produced late in the third century and containing extracts from works attributed to the second-century jurist Paulus. The existence of such works and the disappearance of much earlier legal literature, the irregular training of late imperial legal officials, new influences from the Germanic inhabitants of the empire and ecclesiastical figures, an irregular proliferation of legal literature of enormously varying quality and applicability—all these conditions prevailed in the western, Latin-speaking part of the Roman Empire in the fourth and fifth centuries. It was in part at least in the hope of correcting them that Justinian began his legal reforms in the sixth century.

As we have seen, however, Justinian's reforms came too late to be of much value to the west. There, the continuity of postclassical vulgar law and the new legislation of the Germanic rulers of the western provinces formed a new legal system—or rather a series of systems that contributed heavily to the shaping of European legal history between the fifth and the twelfth centuries. One example of the complex and fascinating way in which some of this law made its way into the Germanic law codes and thus contributed to the process by which the social and mental world of the new inhabitants of the Empire was transformed by the subtle presence of Roman legal thought may be seen in the influence of the *Pauli Sententiae.* This work, composed, as we have seen, late in the third century, contained extracts from the earlier writings of Paulus and other jurists. Beginning in the early sixth century, the rulers of Germanic kingdoms inside the old Empire turned their attention to the legal difficulties of their Roman subjects, and they compiled codes of Roman law for their use. The first of these was the *Breviarium Alaricianum,* or the *Lex Romana Visigothorum,* compiled under the authority of the Visigothic king Alaric II in 506. In the *Breviary* of Alaric, an abridged version of *Pauli Sententiae* appeared, along with other materials from late Roman law, and the influence of Alaric's *Breviary* in southern France and upon the law codes designed for the Roman subjects of barbarian kings in other provinces carried the influence of this single work, although in a much transformed condition, down to the eleventh century. Thus, the law shaped by barbarian rulers for their Roman subjects, as well as individual Germanic law codes that were designed for Romans and barbarians alike, took their "Roman" materials from the legal literature of the fourth and fifth centuries. The magnificent concision and internal consistency of Justinian's *Corpus Iuris Civilis* remained an unknown quantity in those parts of the west that continued to use Roman law. For them, Roman law meant, not the work of Justinian, but that of the anonymous jurists, officials, and lawyers of the postclassical period, transformed by subsequent compilers and augmented by the law codes of the new Germanic rulers.

IV

For the Germanic invaders of the Empire, law played a different role in society from that which it had among the Romans. Roman law was territorial, varied, and applicable to a wide range of social intercourse, much of it wholly outside the experience of the Germanic immigrants. To be sure, much of Roman law was beyond the experience and understanding of many Romans themselves, but even in its transformations of the fourth and fifth centuries, it remained far more complex than Germanic law. Germanic law was personal, not territorial; it "belonged" to each member of a people wherever he or she went. It tended to limit itself to a narrow range of social relations, principally those which would be called torts—injuries—in a modern court. It was not legislated, as was Roman law, but existed as custom, although the very act of writing barbarian laws in Latin must have effected significant social and intellectual changes. The prologues to most codes of barbarian law insist upon the point that the lawgiver, the king, is simply collecting the laws of the people, not making new laws. Finally, the novel experience of the Germanic peoples once they had entered and settled inside the Empire called for a certain amount of borrowing from existing Roman law, and such novel phenomena as the position of the king, for example, influenced the adaptation in some degree of Roman public law, particularly that of treason. The differences between Romans and barbarians had been steadily decreasing from the fifth century, and it is difficult to say which people was more extensively transformed by its experience with the presence and the minds of the other. Certainly, whatever ancient traditions the Germanic peoples had brought with them into the empire were soon transformed by several generations of a different

kind of life among different kinds of people. The transformation of
the barbarian world by migration, literacy, new forms of public
organization, new kinds of landholding, and new pressures on such
traditional institutions as the tribe and the kin-group, the availabil-
ity of new economic resources, and the responses of the Germanic
kingdoms to each other is a first fundamental chapter in the social
and cultural history of Europe.

The Lombards entered Italy at a time when the occupation of
imperial forces elsewhere in the Empire prevented a quick coun-
terattack against the new invaders. The death of Justinian in 565,
the fitful incompetence of his successor Justin II (656–678), the
energetic but unsuccessful rules of Tiberius II (578–582) and
Maurice (582–602), and finally the nadir of imperial rule under
the mad Phocas (602–610) and the prodigious military threat
from the Avars, Slavs, and the restored Persian Empire that occupied nearly the entire reign of Heraclius (610–641) gave the
Lombard leaders an important respite in terms of political organization. In Gaul, the Franks remained too disunited to offer more
than an occasional alliance to the imperial exarch or to the popes
against the Lombards. The Lombards themselves showed a surprising and unpredictable deference to the popes, and this dilemma of
the papacy, well illustrated in the correspondence of Pope Gregory
I (590–604), was not resolved until the Frankish invasions of the
later eighth century. In military and political terms, at least, the
Lombards encountered little of that resistance that the Romans had
used so successfully against the Visigoths and Ostrogoths. Nor did
the Lombards encounter that deeper-rooted social resistance that
an organized provincial population, no matter how remote from
imperial support, might have offered. The devastations of the
Gothic wars and the heavy hand of the imperial restoration debilitated even the social fabric of Italy, leaving little in the way of a
senatorial or curial class that might have led a resistance movement. With the reduction in imperial taxes that accompanied the
Lombard occupation, moreover, even such resistance as might have
been generated lost at least the cause of fiscal oppression, and
many wealthy Romans fled toward, not away from, the new rulers
of northern Italy. Life under the Lombards may well have been pref-
erable to life under the imperial bureaucracy; it was certainly less
expensive.

Not only were the Lombards fortunate in having little serious military and social resistance, but they encountered little institutional or cultural resistance as well. The troubles of the sixth century had reduced not only the civilly active classes of the Empire, but the legal institutions of Italy as well. Justinian's revision came too late, and the twenty years of Gothic wars had done little to impose any regularity or order upon the laws of the Romans. In 508 the Ostrogothic king Theoderic had issued the *Edictum Theoderici*, a much-abbreviated code of law for his Roman and Gothic subjects, based upon the same materials as the *Breviary* of Alaric two years earlier in Gaul. The sixty years between the *Edictum Theoderici* and the arrival of the Lombards had been too full of misery and the disruption of the normal process of social life for there to have been much attention paid to the law itself. The destruction of the Ostrogothic kingdom in 554 may have abrogated Theoderic's *Edictum*, but there was little to substitute for it, little that might have offered some degree of institutional cohesion in the face of the Lombard presence. The leaders of the older imperial society had died off or fled, and many of them had entered the life of religion. Even in the city of Rome itself, which remained under imperial rule, the number of people available to fill the offices of the city was greatly reduced. During the sixth century many of the leading families of imperial Italy died out, either in the wars early in the century, through self-imposed exile to Sicily or north Africa, or through the growing attractions of the religious life. Gregory I himself, after a brief career in the service of the city, as befitted an aristocrat, entered religion around 575.

Thus the Lombards escaped both the shadow of Justinian and the possibility of continued substantial resistance on the part of a diminished and impoverished population. Of all the Germanic invaders of the Empire, with the possible exception of the Anglo-Saxons and the Huns, they may be said to have had a freer hand in politically shaping a new society for themselves than earlier immigrants. The first records of Lombard Italy bear out this freedom. They show hostility to imperial institutions, maintenance of Arian Christianity, indifference to the centralized rule of a king after the death of Alboin, and lack of attention to the fiscal and social institutions of their newly conquered land. The Lombards made no attempts remotely comparable to those of the Ostrogoths earlier to come quickly to terms with the culture or customs of their Roman hosts. Their hostility, indifference, and unpredictability made them a terror to the popes of the late sixth and early seventh centuries and a constant menace to the small expeditionary force that governed those parts of Italy still under imperial control.

In spite of the free hand that Lombard society had at the end of the sixth century, the Lombards did not remain wholly untouched by Roman institutions, however debilitated, for long. Unlike the Anglo-Saxons, they quickly took to that most un-Germanic of Roman institutions, the life of the city. Pannonia during the Lombard presence had remained a part of the complex imperial economic world, and Lombard familiarity with some of the institutions and benefits of the provincial economy may have prepared the invaders of Italy for the extensive participation in the Mediterranean economic world that characterized Lombard society in the seventh and eighth centuries. In spite of the political hostility between Lombards and Byzantines, the Po Valley constituted a major trade route from the Byzantine-held eastern coast of Italy into the Lombard hinterlands, a territory still called Lombardy today. The Lombards also participated in western trade, particularly through the Alpine parts of northern Italy, and with the northern Mediterranean commerce that centered upon Marseilles and the Rhone Valley. Lombard coins, at first gold tremisses (one-third of the Byzantine imperial *solidus*, the great gold coin of the Middle Ages) bearing the likenesses of their enemies the Byzantine emperors, later emerged as the full *solidus*, bearing the likenesses of Lombard kings, and the Lombard gold coinage which lasted far longer than the gold coinage in other parts of the west suggests that the Lombards participated extensively and successfully in the Byzantine economic system. Lombard coins, gold crosses, *fibulae,* shields, and swords have been found far to the north, evidence of the vigorous Lombard role in the trade of the northern Mediterranean, trade which connected east and west in spite of political and religious differences.

Lombard participation in both long- and short-range trade with imperial territories and with other western Germanic kingdoms may well have aided what some historians have called the "orientalization" of much of Italy in the late seventh century, a phenomenon marked by the settlement of large numbers of Greek and

Syrian clergy in Italy and by the momentous but abortive exchange of visits—that of the Emperor Constans II to Italy in 663 and that of the Pope to Constantinople in 710—the last such visits made except for those of the impoverished Byzantine emperors in the fourteenth and fifteenth centuries.

Such a new rapport was also probably instrumental in the conversion of the Lombards from Arianism to orthodox Christianity in the third quarter of the seventh century, a conversion marked by the surprising ecclesiastical synod of Pavia in 679–680, which opened with the reading of a long letter in Greek from the emperor at Constantinople. Behind these social, economic, and religious examples of the changed Lombard presence in northern Italy, of course, there lies the broad spectrum of changes in the Byzantine and Latin worlds: religious disagreement and reconciliation, imperial policies in the north and east of Constantinople, a remarkable series of oriental popes in the late seventh century, and the consequences for the Empire of Justinian's neglect of the eastern frontier —the early seventh-century assaults from the Balkans and Persia and the expansion of Islam in the middle of the seventh century. The Lombards, in invading and conquering much of Italy, had become an integral part of a world in transformation, a world whose principles of operation they had to learn quickly and well.

Each Germanic people that entered the old western provinces of the Roman Empire and settled there had to learn similar lessons, and few succeeded as well as the Lombards. The ferocious Vandals, who swept through Gaul after 406, reached north Africa by the first quarter of the fifth century and, barely a century later, were hardly distinguishable from their Roman neighbors. The more highly Romanized Ostrogoths had counted too much upon the cooperation of their Roman subjects and had underestimated the determination of Justinian to recover Italy. The Visigoths, alternately mauled and starved by the imperial court, found a brief refuge in Spain, where they produced a brilliant and innovative, but curiously perverse and unstable kingdom that went down like tenpins before the Arabs in 711–719. Of all the invaders, the Anglo-Saxons, Franks, and Lombards succeeded best. The Lombards succeeded because of their remarkable ability to adapt to the urbanization of Italy, their economic vitality, and their vigorous attempt to rule a single kingdom with one law for all subjects. We must not be misled by the Lombard defeats at the hands of the Franks late in the eighth century into seeing in Lombard Italy simply one more Germanic society that was unable to develop the political stability and the fusion between their own and Roman culture necessary for survival in the eighth-century world. By the late eighth century, the conditions of political survival had changed, and the Lombards were not the only people who felt the weight of the great Frankish kingdom upon them and were unable to cope with it. As Pepin and Charlemagne were to demonstrate by the book and the sword, the Franks were already on their way to becoming, for however brief a time, the undisputed masters of a new Christian Europe.

V

The experiences of the Lombards in the seventh- and eighth-century Mediterranean world are reflected in their laws, written down in Latin in the seventh and early eighth centuries between 643 and 755. Professor Drew's translation of these laws and her discussion of the important legal aspects of Lombard society make extensive consideration here superfluous. Yet there are dimensions of the Lombard laws that should be noted, not only by students of medieval history but by anyone interested in the role played by the transformation of law in traditional societies. Recent studies on the part of anthropologists of the character of primitive law and a new interest on the part of historians in legal sociology have begun to succeed in freeing early legal history from the restrictive bonds of the formal teaching of law. They have revealed in the study of legal history an important dimension of the history of society. Several characteristics of Lombard law cast considerable light, not only upon the Lombard experience in Italy, but also upon the more general problem of the role of law in the transition of societies from pre-literacy to literacy, from isolation among peoples similar to themselves to contact with wholly different, more complex systems of social organization. In this sense, the study of the Germanic law codes has much to contribute to the comparative history of law and society.

Perhaps the most surprising aspect of such codes as the Lombard laws is the area of social activity that the laws do not touch at all. The life of the Germanic peoples outside the Empire, even the life of those who were strongly influenced by the proximity of the Roman frontier and Roman provincial culture, was far different from the life they led once inside the empire in kingdoms of their own. Little in Germanic experience had prepared them for the complex economic and civil affairs of Italy and Gaul, and such essential concepts as possession, ownership and use of property, legal promises, and legal procedure were different in the two worlds. Sometimes the Roman method seemed superior, and then the Germanic concept, however old and widely accepted, slowly gave way to Roman influence. Sometimes the condition of a Roman law was so confusing to both Romans and Germans that a new hybrid law emerged, often based upon the misinterpretation of a statement that had been itself misunderstood before it got into the late Roman lawbooks. Perhaps more in the case of the Lombards than in that of other Germanic peoples, the necessity of accommodating in Lombard-Roman law a wide variety of social relationships led Lombard kings to a precocious self-consciousness of the changes they were necessarily making in their own law and thus to that remarkable aspect of juridical deliberation that so distinguished Lombard from other German laws. The necessities for legal change contingent upon the Lombards entering the economic community of the Mediterranean, still dominated by the East Roman, or Byzantine, Empire and the remarkable capacity for juridical self-consciousness are but two of the most interesting features of Lombard law. Rothair, whose *Edictum* of 643 is the first of the Lombard law codes, must have known very well the essential reforms that the simple (or rather not so simple) act of writing down the customs of the Lombards, in Latin, in a rough kind of topical order entailed. The problems of dealing with offenses that in many cases must have been unique to the Lombard experience in Italy, and hence not foreseen in the older Lombard customs, and of "renewing, amending, adding that which is lacking and removing that which is superfluous" themselves created not only a very different kind of legal consciousness among the Lombards, but a new kind of legal authority as well. The medium of a written law code changed and expanded by the king and his officials and "our chief men" was a new kind of law, not merely an ancient system of tribal law tidied up.

To what extent does the law of the Lombards emphasize difficulties that had arisen only in Italy? The treatment of the security of travellers, the concern for breaking and entering, the numerous laws touching collective offenses against individuals, the sections on *scandalum*—breach of public peace—and on offenses committed on church property, and the increased scale of payments for the list of minutely detailed personal injuries that appears in many Germanic law codes all reflect the changed character of Lombard society. Sometimes, older Lombard law obviously jarred recent sensibilities; thus the severity of Rothair's penalties for calling a half-free woman a *striga* or a *masca*, witch or vampire, because "it is a thing not to be conceived of by Christian minds as possible that a woman can eat a living man from inside him." Some customs died hard, however, and the blood-feud remained a major institution among the Lombards, just as it did among the Franks. The extensive legislation defining the inferior place of women in Lombard law also deserves particular study. Certainly, as in other codes, the position of women under Lombard law is juridically inferior to that of men, but it may be asked whether the spelling out of these rules did not in itself indicate a changing role, or at least woman's attempt to change her role, in the eyes of the law. Further, to what extent do the laws only attempt to define, rather than describe, the power of women in Lombard society? No reader of the much later heroic saga literature, which, even though it must be used with caution, may illustrate tentatively the distance between formal law and social reality, will remain long under the impression that legal limitations limited the force with which women could influence action and wield power. The inferior place of women in the Germanic law codes has long been a commonplace among legal historians. Should the social historian stop here, or should the questions be asked to what extent do the law codes reflect actual conditions and what means existed for circumventing them?

These are a very few, and not all the most pressing, problems the student of law in a traditional society must face. To be sure, the law codes do not tell us everything, nor do such chronicles as Paul the Deacon's eighth-century *History of the Lombards*. Saints' lives, ecclesiastical documents, chronicles, and law codes all throw particular kinds of light upon these Germanic societies undergoing mental and social change of which they can have been only partly aware. It is unwise to neglect this change and equally unwise to neglect the assistance of anthropology and archaeology in attempting to understand it. The Lombards found Italy as it was, but they did not create it. The greatest historian of early Italy in the English-speaking world, Thomas Hodgkin, once summarized the Lombard legal consciousness in the seventh century:

> And so the Lombard invaders, like children, repeat the lessons which they have learned from their forefathers of the forest and try to fit in their barbarous law terms into the stately but terribly misused language of Latium. Throughout, Roman ideas, Roman rights, the very existence of a Roman population, are not so much menaced or invaded, as calmly ignored. The Code of Rothari, promulgated on the sacred soil of Italy, in a land which had once witnessed the promulgation of the Code, the Institutes, and the Digest of Justinian, is like the black tent of the Bedouin pitched amid the colonnades of some stately Syrian temple, whose ruined glories touch no responsive chord in the soul of the swart barbarian.*

Harsh words, and inaccurate. Neither the Lombards nor the Arabs destroyed the civilizations into which they came in the sixth and seventh centuries. It was the Roman population of Italy, not the Lombards, who complained bitterly over the fiscal policies of the author of the *Corpus Iuris Civilis* and the builder of Constantinople. In their law codes, their practice of allowing Roman advisors to assist the Lombard judges in suits between Lombard and Roman, their occupation of the cities, and their adoption of Latin and orthodox Christianity, the Lombards used what they could of Roman culture, and what they used was largely all that was left. The Bedouin had not destroyed the Syrian temple; he found it, and perhaps later on he used the stones to build a mosque or a garden. Perhaps it is too much to expect that civilizations ought to strike chords of response in the minds of strangers who find them in ruins.

PHILADELPHIA, 1973   EDWARD PETERS

---

* Thomas Hodgkin, *Italy and Her Invaders*, VI (Oxford, 1895), p. 238.

CONTENTS

INTRODUCTION

IMPORTANCE OF THE BARBARIAN CODES

There can be no question that the Germanic barbarians contributed enormously to the emergence of early medieval civilization, even if one may be tempted to rate somewhat higher the contributions of the Roman Empire and the Christian Church. The Germanic contribution, however, is not so easy to trace as is the Roman and the ecclesiastical for the simple reason that, although the barbarians may have had the most profound respect for the art of writing and the products of literacy, they had behind them no long tradition of experience in this area; as a result, the written materials produced by the barbarians themselves, or on their behalf by Roman officials, are not numerous. In contrast, even in the culturally darkest of those transitional centuries between the decay of late Roman civilization and the appearance of a distinctive medieval culture (symbolized by that movement known somewhat misleadingly as the Carolingian renaissance) there continued to be literary materials written by individuals trained in the old Roman tradition (or at least in a somewhat vulgarized form of it); and members of the higher clergy, also trained in the literary tradition, wrote in a relatively voluminous manner on theological subjects and on general matters touching the concerns of the Church.

However, the student who wishes to understand the early Middle Ages faces certain inescapable conclusions. The Roman Empire may never have "fallen," but something certainly happened that caused its virtual disintegration, at least in the west, between the fifth and the eighth centuries. The barbarian invasions were one of the most visi-

1

ble causes of this disintegration, even though the invasions in turn
may have been the result of pressures within and beyond the barbarian world and of internal weaknesses in the Roman Empire. At any
rate, the importance of the Germanic barbarians justifies the most
careful study of whatever sources may be available about them.
These sources include a number of literary works by such Roman
writers as Caesar, Tacitus, Ammianus Marcellinus, Ausonius, Sidon-
ius Apollinaris, Cassiodorus, St. Isidore, and Procopius, as well as a
number of works of somewhat more dubious literary value by individuals of Germanic background, e.g., Jordanes, Gregory of Tours,
the Venerable Bede, Paul the Deacon, Alcuin, and others. The works
of all of these writers have been carefully studied and are available in
a number of modern translations, including translations in English.
But the picture of the Germanic world that emerges from these works
is not at all complete, and the information contained in these writings
is often inconsistent and distressingly contradictory.

To fill out and improve the picture, it is necessary to turn to
materials other than the literary sources. Of increasing importance
for this purpose is the work being done by scholars who are trained to
work with nonliterary materials, the prehistorians, especially the
archeologists. The story of the Germans both before and after their
entry into the Empire has been significantly expanded by the work of
such students.

But although the archeological record can hope to tell us much
about migration routes, settlement patterns, agricultural techniques,
weapons, implements, ornaments, and the like, it is unlikely ever to
provide sufficient evidence to give us a satisfactorily complete view of
the Germanic state and Germanic society. To obtain this we must
turn to another form of evidence left by the Germans themselves, the
evidence of the "barbarian" law codes. The use of a law code to
understand the institutions of any people is of course filled with haz-
ards, and the use of the barbarian law codes may be more dangerous
than the use of most others since none of these codes was a codification of all legal rules and precedents currently in use, as was the
Corpus Juris Civilis for sixth-century Roman law. There is the additional problem that the Germanic codes claimed to be the reduction
to writing of the time-honored customs of the people when it is quite
obvious that frequently the laws represent anything but time-honored

custom—the laws instead have been issued for the purpose, sometimes expressly stated and sometimes not, of modifying customs that no longer fit the needs of a people settling down in contact with a subordinate population enjoying a more sophisticated legal culture.

Scholars have been interested in the barbarian codes since the revival of humanistic studies during the Renaissance, but this interest was much increased by the eighteenth-century Romantic delight in anything that was "Gothic" and by nineteenth-century nationalism. It was primarily the nationalist spirit that led to such large-scale editing projects as the *Monumenta Germaniae Historica*, the best known of the collections of medieval Latin sources. Although the Monumenta edition of the codes has in some cases been modified by contemporary scholarship, nonetheless the most important collection of the barbarian law codes is still to be found in its volumes.

A number of the barbarian codes have been translated into German (in the *Germanenrechte* series of the Akademie für Deutsches Rechtsgeschichte), but only a few of them have been translated into English (see bibliography). It is hoped that this present translation of the Lombard code will add to that corpus of source material needed by students of medieval history and of early social institutions who do not have either the time or the linguistic training to consult the laws in their Latin form.

The remainder of this introduction attempts to place the Lombards in their historical background and to illustrate how the Lombard laws may be used by the historian or by the ethnographer who is interested in medieval institutions as they developed in Italy under Lombard rule.

THE BARBARIAN INVASIONS AND THE GERMANIC KINGDOMS

The Lombards invaded Italy in 568. By this date the Roman and Germanic worlds had been in contact for a long time and the Lombard experience in Italy was influenced by this contact. But although in some ways the Lombard experience was unique and the Lombard state and Lombard society offered some degree of contrast with the other Germanic kingdoms, nonetheless all the Germanic states established within the territory of the West Roman Empire displayed a basic similarity. As background for an understanding of the nature of these Germanic states, it might be well to consider briefly the story of Roman-Germanic relations.

The Germans had been peacefully infiltrating the Roman Empire for centuries before the major invasions of the fifth century. In general, Rome had made no attempt to keep them out so long as they entered individually or in small numbers. In fact, the imperial authorities found the Germans a welcome answer to a number of problems. The most pressing of these problems—and the one earliest apparent—was the problem of recruiting for the Roman army. As early as the second century, when military recruiting in Italy and the more Romanized provinces had become difficult, some Germans were taken into the army. As a result of the population decline caused in part by the catastrophes of the third century (civil war, barbarian invasions, plague, and economic collapse), it then became common to enroll Germans in large numbers.

By the fourth century, the Roman Empire was accustomed to being protected on its frontiers by an army composed largely of barbarians. These barbarians were easily absorbed into those communities where they were given land at the expiration of their term of service or concurrently with their service. Because of the decrease in the Empire's population (especially in the west), great expanses of land lay vacant. Such lands either were granted outright to the Germans or were divided with them according to a system of hospitality whereby a Roman host (*hospis*) divided his land with a barbarian guest (also *hospis*). Since there was plenty of land available and the Empire by this time needed farmers as well as soldiers, the arrangement caused relatively little friction.

By the late fourth century, however, this slow, peaceful penetration no longer answered the Germanic urge for land within the Empire. For some time the barbarians had been piling up along the Rhine-Danube frontier, but the Empire had not as yet been forced to admit whole nations at one time. The pressure on the Germans—already great because of population increase—became much greater in the late fourth century as the Huns appeared out of Asia and began to push westward. The barbarian invasions resulted. The Visigoths crossed the Danube frontier in the late fourth century and, after a long search and much friction with the imperial authorities, finally were allowed to settle in southwest Gaul as federate allies, from which position they later moved into Spain. After the Hun menace had receded, the Ostrogoths crossed the same Danube frontier and, after lengthy negotiations with the East Roman Empire, were "encouraged" to make their home in Italy in the late fifth century.

Meanwhile the Rhine frontier had been breached in the early fifth century, a frontier that had been temporarily denuded of defense because of a struggle over the imperial succession and the necessity of protecting Italy against the Visigoths. A number of Germanic peoples crossed the Rhine River, but the most important of these were the Vandals (who eventually established themselves in north Africa), the Burgundians (who settled in the southeastern part of Gaul), and the Franks (who remained in northeastern Gaul until the late fifth century when the aggressive leadership of Clovis and his sons brought all of Gaul under Frankish control).

By the early sixth century, the Roman Empire in the west had given way to a number of Germanic kingdoms: Anglo-Saxon in Britain, Frankish in Gaul, Visigothic in Spain, Vandal in Africa, and Ostrogothic in Italy. A revival of Roman power would naturally aim at overthrowing these states and restoring their territory to Roman control. Such a revival began under Justinian, the eastern emperor. To Justinian's hope of restoring the old boundaries of the Roman Empire was added the inducement of wresting the western territory from rulers who were for the most part heathen or Arian schismatics (except for the Franks) and restoring it to the true Catholic faith.

Justinian's efforts accomplished only a part of his plan: The Vandals in Africa were defeated, the Ostrogoths in Italy were overthrown, and a small bit of territory in southeast Spain was wrested from the Visigoths. Even this limited conquest did not remain East Roman for long. North Africa, it is true, remained Roman until the Moslem conquest late in the seventh century, but the Spanish territory was soon reoccupied by the Visigoths, and Italy, largely ruined by the long drawn-out war between Ostrogoths and Byzantines, soon attracted another barbarian invasion.

The Lombards, who first became acquainted with Italy by serving as mercenaries in the armies of Justinian, took advantage of the East Roman preoccupation with renewed war with Persia. They had relatively little difficulty in occupying the northern and central parts of Italy—only that area around the city of Ravenna, the Duchy of Rome, and parts of southern Italy and Sicily remained under Byzantine control.

Before turning to the story of the Lombards and their experience in Italy, however, it might be well to look at a composite picture of the Germanic state and Germanic society—a picture based primarily, although not exclusively, on the evidence of the barbarian law codes.

THE GERMANIC STATE AND GERMANIC SOCIETY

The Germanic states were the product of a fusion of Germanic custom and Roman experience, a fusion in which the Roman and Germanic elements differed from place to place. In general, Roman influence tended to be greater in the south and west (Italy, southern Gaul, and Spain) than in the north (Britain and central and northern Gaul). Nonetheless, all of the Germanic states were basically similar, and the picture offered here is a composite one and is not based on any single Germanic kingdom.

In the first century before Christ and immediately thereafter, the comments made by Roman writers about the Germans indicate some uncertainty in the Roman mind about how to interpret the nature of German political life. Whether the king or leader was a ruler with established powers or only a temporary leader elected by the German army in times of stress is not clear, but probably his position lay somewhere between these two extremes. It is certain that the concept of "state" was not well developed and that great power and authority still remained with the kindred. But already the Germans were beginning to pass through an important transition, a transition that was undoubtedly stimulated and speeded up as a result of contacts with Rome. The effect of this transition had been to produce considerable political and social changes among the Germans by the time they established their kingdoms in the fifth and sixth centuries.

By the fifth century, under Roman influence, the Germans had come to regard the state as having certain powers, on the one hand, and certain duties and responsibilities, on the other. This rise in the functions of the state was parallelled by a decline in position of the family. The Germanic family undoubtedly remained very powerful, but in certain areas of activity the family had been superseded by the state. (The term "family" is used here rather than "kin group," since it implies a smaller group of individuals. The Germans of the fifth century did not necessarily live and operate in groups based on the nuclear family alone, but that certainly seems to have been its basic core. The role of the kindred in Lombard society will be discussed in the next section of this introduction.)

The most important area in which the state had increased its authority was in the maintenance of security and the administration of justice. At one time the Germanic family or kin group had almost certainly been the most important if not the only agency for protecting the lives and property of its members and for obtaining redress for offenses committed against them: justice rested primarily on the concept of blood revenge. Since the state was weak, such "revenge" had to be obtained by the offended family. In such a situation the individual alone was quite defenseless; membership in a strong family group was essential. Only through the group did one have "security"—and since only the family could offer security and protection, the possession of landed property could be held securely only by membership in the family. The family property (inherited property as distinguished from land which had been purchased or received as a gift) was possessed or controlled by the head of the family (the "representative" or symbol of the family vis-à-vis other family groups), but this individual's freedom of action in disposing of that property was severely limited. Even after the establishment of the Germanic kingdoms, landed property obtained by a family at the time the estates were first parcelled out could not be disposed of by sale or testament but could only descend within the family according to fixed rules of succession, rules that varied in detail from kingdom to kingdom.

By the fifth century, however, the family group had already lost its role as the sole guarantor of peace and security for its individual members. The state instead had assumed this function. This does not mean that the family organization had completely disappeared; even in the administration of justice the role played by the family was still very important.

For the moment let us look more closely at that transition in juridical life which was taking place at the time the Germans were entering and establishing themselves within the frontiers of the West Roman Empire. The blood feud as a means of securing justice was now formally prohibited by the state (not always successfully, of course), and the state assumed the role of an umpire in disputes between individuals or families. In general, little distinction was made between suits of a civil or criminal nature—or, it might more accurately be said that all offenses were treated as if they were civil offenses. To satisfy the dignity of the offended party, the state intervened to consider the situation and, if the accused were determined guilty, the "punishment" proceeded according to fixed rules. So that there could be no opportunity for further action on behalf of the injured party, the barbarian codes set out in minute detail what "compensation" (or *composition*) would have to be paid by the offending party or his family. These compositions were assessed for all sorts of injuries, from one so minor as striking a man on his little finger to such relatively serious blows to one's pride as pulling his hair, to hitting a man over the head so hard his skull is cracked, or the actual taking of life itself. For all these injuries, a graduated tariff had been fixed so that the quarrelling families could not drag out their contest once the guilt or innocence of the accused party had been established.

In the case of death itself, the value fixed for a freeman's life was known as his *wergeld* or "man value." The amount of the wergeld varied, depending on whether or not a man were Roman or German, or whether he was a member of the clergy or not. But even if he were German, the wergeld might also vary from man to man. Among some of the barbarians (e.g., the Burgundians, Visigoths, and Lombards) the wergeld varied according to the social status of the individual (a matter of birth or appointment, not wealth); in these cases, the wergeld of men and women in the same class was usually the same. Among some of the other barbarians, especially the Franks, the wergeld for all social classes was the same but varied according to sex and to age, individuals (both men and women) in the early prime of life enjoying much the highest wergeld. Even homicide would not occasion the blood feud inasmuch as the price for each homicide was fixed in advance, and once payment for the wergeld had been received, the offended family had no further recourse.

In the case of compositions imposed for injuries not producing death the same situation held. Once the injured party had received his compensation (which frequently included something extra for the doctor's fee), he had to accept the situation as settled once and for all. The role played by the state in bringing about this more peaceful state of affairs was to provide the tribunal and judge before which the case was heard and to ensure that the procedures established by law were properly followed. To compensate the state for its trouble and to provide income for the justices, a fine was normally assessed against the guilty party in addition to the payment of the wergeld or composition.

But how was the accused party brought before the court? How was his guilt or innocence determined, and what happened if he or his family were unable to pay the fixed amount? Procedure in these matters varied somewhat from kingdom to kingdom, but in all the Germanic states a number of justices were appointed, each of whom seems to have presided over a specific territory. This justice might also have other functions—he might be a "duke" or "count" and thus an official with extensive military and administrative duties—but for the moment we will consider his judicial functions only. The justice had beneath him certain lesser officials who exercised minor police functions, who witnessed sales and documents, or who acted as messengers when a suit involved parties residing in the territory of two different magistrates. The minor police officers might lead the chase after a fugitive and they might assist in getting the accused party before the court, but ultimately it was the offended family that was responsible for doing this. The court itself might consist of the justice sitting alone (or two justices, one Roman and one German, as in the case of the Burgundians), or it might consist of a magistrate presiding over a number of "good men" selected from the community (as in the case of the *scabini* of the Franks). In either case, the court heard the charge and then heard the accused's response. The function of the court was not to decide which of the two parties was telling the truth, nor was it to seek out evidence to demonstrate the truth. Rather, the function of the court was to decide what form of proof was appropriate to the case. In most instances, proof was established by oath. The court decided which of the two parties (or both) should be required to furnish proof and how strong the oath must be. Normally the accused was asked to furnish proof by appearing before the court with a certain number of oathtakers or oathhelpers. The number of oathhelpers was determined by the court but usually reflected the reputation of the individual concerned and the seriousness of the crime of which he was accused.

When the oathhelpers appeared before the court, they took their oath on some consecrated object (in the case of the Lombards this was usually the Gospels or weapons). It must be understood that the oathhelpers were not witnesses. They were not giving sworn evidence. They were swearing their willingness to support the plea of their principal, whether he were accuser or defendant. The entire procedure was a very formal one and if, at any point in the process, the oathhelper hesitated or refused to take the oath, the oath was said to be broken and the accused "proved" to be guilty (if the oath were for the defendant); the accuser lost his case if the oath were on his behalf. Among most of the barbarians, it seems that only a man of good reputation was allowed to establish his case by oath in the first place; if the accused were an individual of poorer reputation, he might be put to proof by the ordeal. The Lombards, however, do not seem to have used the ordeal very extensively at all—perhaps only in the case of the unfree. On the other hand, the Lombards still used the judicial duel (the *camfio*) from time to time despite their lawgivers' attempts to discourage that practice.

Whatever the form of proof, if the accused party were determined guilty, the penalty was prescribed by law and consisted of the payment of a certain sum to the injured party or to his family, in addition to the payment of a fine to the state. If the accused were unable to pay the composition (and normally it would seem that he could expect to have the help of his immediate family or larger kin group, although some of the codes, e.g., that of the Lombards, do not specifically state this), he was obliged to work out the sum of the debt in the service of the offended party. In most cases, the size of the composition was not prohibitive and its payment caused relatively little difficulty. In certain very serious cases, however, such as homicide or disloyalty, the sum might be so large as to be impossible of payment; in these cases debt servitude almost certainly followed.

The types of proof and penalty just described applied, almost without exception, to cases involving freemen. In the case of the semifree and slaves, however, the situation might differ. Normally the means of proof remained the same, with perhaps a greater tendency to use proof by ordeal rather than by oath, but the penalty differed. Usually the guilty half-freeman was assessed a fine—a fine that he might pay by himself or with the assistance of his lord, for the half-free were regarded as the lord's legal dependents (their legal position being not unlike that of the women·and minor sons of the family). In the case of slaves a composition might also be assessed, but in this case the slave's lord almost certainly had to pay—unless the master preferred to let his slave pass into the possession of the injured party. In some cases, however (e.g., among the Burgundians), a money composition might be replaced in the case of slaves by so many blows of the lash. With a very few exceptions (e.g., forgery or counterfeiting among the Burgundians and Lombards), a freeman did not receive physical punishment for his crime but simply paid composition. However, in a few instances, such as treason or certain kinds of premeditated murder, the death penalty was imposed.

Thus the role played by the family in maintaining security for its members remained essential: the man without a family had no one to help him bring an offending party before the courts, no one to help support his oath, no one to help him pay the compositions imposed by law on those found guilty of a crime. To be sure, the state had now emerged as a very powerful entity in its own right; for to convene the courts and administer the laws presupposes a considerable administrative organization and to prevent injured families from resorting to the blood feud required considerable prestige on the part of the government, to say nothing of the police force necessary to maintain peace and quiet.

Since the Germanic kingdoms were established in territory that was already occupied (and the Germanic settlers constituted only a minority of the new kingdoms' population), the barbarian kings were required to play a dual role. Toward the Roman population, the Germanic king took the place of the Roman provincial governor. Depending somewhat upon the security of local conditions, the old Roman civil administration remained intact, the Roman provincial administrators serving the barbarian kings in more or less the same fashion that they had earlier served a Roman governor. In this sense the Germanic king had become a Roman magistrate.

But the situation was complicated by the Germanic concept of nation and kingship. In the past, a German's birth had been the most decisive element in his life, determining his family ties and the nation to which he belonged. This "national" consciousness remained strong even after the establishment of the new barbarian states, and it was certainly one factor—albeit not the only one—that slowed down amalgamation between Romans and Germans. From the legal point of view, this strong national consciousness led to the development of what is known as the "personality of law" concept. The "law" by which a man was to be judged was determined by his birth (i.e., by his "nation") rather than by the territory in which he dwelt.

This attitude produced a kind of dual social and legal system in the new Germanic kingdoms, with the king and his administration providing the connecting link between the two. For the Roman part of the population, Roman law remained in force and was administered by magistrates learned in the Roman law. And since the times were uncertain and not all the complexities of the classical Roman law seemed applicable, the barbarian king might issue a revised and simplified version of the Roman law for the use of his judges (e.g., the Visigothic *Breviarium Alaricianum* and the Burgundian *Lex Romana Burgundionum*). Italy, of course, was exceptional in this matter, for, in addition to the Roman population living within the Lombard kingdom, there were also Romans living in the Exarchate of Ravenna (Ravenna and its environs, the Duchy of Rome, the Duchies of Naples and Capua, etc.). The legal needs of such a numerous population justified the retention of a more complex form of the Roman law. Theoretically, this Roman law was to be found in the Corpus Juris Civilis, which Justinian had promulgated in the Italian peninsula following its conquest in 552. Byzantine control lasted such a short time in most parts of the peninsula, however, and contacts with Byzantium were so liable to interruption in the others, that the Corpus Juris Civilis never received universal acceptance by the "Romans" of Italy until the revival of Roman legal studies in the eleventh century. Before that time, what Roman law was followed in the peninsula was based predominantly on the fifth-century compilation, the Theodosian Code.

In all of the Germanic kingdoms, Germanic custom was the rule for the Germanic part of the population. But in the process of taking up land among a more highly sophisticated people, the Germans found that their ancient customs frequently provided no remedy for their grievances, or it prescribed a remedy no longer suitable. Accordingly, most of the new Germanic kingdoms needed new codes of Germanic law, codes available in written form, for the instruction of the judges. Thus, a number of "barbarian codes" were issued, such as those for the Visigoths, Burgundians, Ripuarian and Salian Franks, Ostrogoths, Lombards, and Anglo-Saxons. (There were a number of later Germanic codes issued, but for the most part they did not apply to those kingdoms established within the former boundaries of the West Roman Empire.)

That the barbarian kings were able to operate such a complicated dual system is a tribute to their own dedication and adaptability and to the willingness of the old Roman civil servants to serve under barbarian leadership. The situation was not an easy one. Added to the shifting nature of an imperial policy that tended to play off one barbarian power against another were deep-seated local causes of friction between Romans and Germans. The requirement that many Roman landlords ("hosts") share their estates with a barbarian "guest" undoubtedly was responsible for much ill-feeling; the uncouth manners of the barbarians tended to irritate and outrage the more sophisticated Romans; and the schismatic Arian faith to which most of the barbarians had been converted before their entry into the Empire aroused much natural hostility from the increasingly devout Catholic population, a hostility furthered and organized by the hierarchy of the Western Church under the leadership of the pope.

The barbarian king's position was thus a very difficult one. It is a curious fact that those barbarian kingdoms that went furthest in the direction of compromise and assimilation did not ultimately create a lasting political life, whereas those kingdoms that retained a stronger Germanic flavor and made fewer concessions or none at all to the Roman population were longer lasting. Thus the Ostrogothic and Burgundian kingdoms, which had made significant attempts at assimilation, enjoyed only a relatively brief existence; the Vandal, Lombard, and Visigothic kingdoms had a somewhat longer one; and the Franks and Anglo-Saxons (both nations still heathen at the time of their entry into the Empire), who accorded little if any recognition to the Roman element in their population, gave their names to states that survived from the medieval period to the present time.

But the seeming political success of the Anglo-Saxons and Franks may be misleading. The states that they established disintegrated in the crisis of the ninth and tenth centuries, and the "England" and "France" that emerged by the close of the tenth century were new states—medieval states no longer barbarian. For a more "typical" barbarian kingdom it might be well to look at the Italy of the Lombards.

THE LOMBARD STATE AND LOMBARD SOCIETY

The Lombard Kingdom

There are few historical references to the Lombards before they entered the Italian peninsula in the sixth century. At the close of the fifth century they were living in central Europe in the middle Danube area. Their movements from this time on can be tentatively traced in the works of the sixth-century Byzantine historian Procopius and the late-eighth-century Lombard historian Paul the Deacon.

As allies of the East Roman Empire, some Lombards had participated in the Byzantine conquest of Italy in the early sixth century. The Lombards as a nation, however, did not enter Italy until 568 under the leadership of Alboin, their semilegendary king. Although Italy was then under Byzantine domination, the Lombards had little difficulty occupying most of the northern and central part of the country. Doubtless the Byzantine defensive troops had been largely withdrawn because of a war with Persia in the east and the native Italian population may well have found little to choose between incorporation in a schismatic Germanic kingdom and submission to exorbitant Byzantine taxation.

The only city to hold out against Lombard conquest was the city of Ticinum (Pavia). Paul the Deacon's account of the taking of Pavia (written nearly 200 years after the event) offers some idea of his approach to history:

> The city of Ticinum indeed, after enduring the siege for three years and some months, at length surrendered to Alboin and to the Langobards besieging it. When Alboin

entered it through the so-called gate of St. John from the eastern side of the city, his horse fell in the middle of the gateway, and could not be gotten up, although urged by kicks and afterwards struck by the blows of spears. Then one of those Langobards thus spoke to the king, saying: "Remember sir king, what vow you have plighted. Break so grievous a vow and you will enter the city, for truly there is a Christian people in this city." Alboin had vowed indeed that he would put all the people to the sword because they had been unwilling to surrender. After he broke this vow and promised mercy to the citizens, his horse straightway rose and he entered the city and remained steadfast in his promise, inflicting injury upon no one. Then all the people, gathering around him in the palace which king Theodoric had formerly built, began to feel relieved in mind, and after so many miseries were already confident in hope for the future.*

When it fell, Pavia became the capital of the Lombard kingdom.

Lombard rule in northern Italy was fairly well established by the year 572 when a period of confusion followed the assassination of Alboin. For some twelve years thereafter the Lombards failed to elect a new king. During this interregnum, however, the conquest of Italy continued; but whereas previously the movement had been a national one under the direction of a king who was a military chieftain and the leader of his people, the Lombard nation now broke up into a number of groups, each under the direction of a duke. During this period, a number of semiindependent Lombard duchies were established as Lombard control was pushed further south in the general direction of the city of Rome. Unfortunately, the benevolent spirit displayed by Alboin following the capture of Pavia was either not observed by all of his subordinate commanders or the fiction of Lombard oppression had become too well established by the time of Paul's writing to be overlooked, for Paul later recorded in his history that

after his death the Langobards had no king for ten years but were under dukes, and each one of the dukes held possession of his own city, Zaban of Ticinum (Pavia),

---

* *History of the Lombards*, tr. by William Dudley Foulke, University of Pennsylvania Press, 1972, pp. 80–81.

Wallari of Bergamus (Bergamo), Alichis of Brexia (Brescia), Euin of Tridentum (Trent), Gisulf of Forum Julii (Cividale). But there were thirty other dukes besides these in their own cities. In these days many of the noble Romans were killed from love of gain, and the remainder were divided among their "guests" and made tributaries, that they should pay the third part of their products to the Langobards. By these dukes of the Langobards in the seventh year from the coming of Alboin and of his whole people, the churches were despoiled, the priests killed, the cities overthrown, the people who had grown up like crops annihilated, and besides those regions which Alboin had taken, the greater part of Italy was seized and subjugated by the Langobards.*

The division of political authority resulting from the failure to elect a king, however, weakened the Lombards to the point where outside intervention in Italy threatened; accordingly, in 584 the dukes recognized a limit to their authority by participating in a regal election that put Authari on the Lombard throne. The new king succeeded in establishing some sort of central organization for the Lombard kingdom and secured Theodolinda, the Catholic daughter of the duke of the Bavarians, as his queen. This marriage to Theodolinda proved to be an important one, for she became the ancestress of the so-called Bavarian dynasty of Lombard kings and she also introduced Roman Catholicism among the Lombards. Thereafter Catholicism slowly replaced the Arianism to which the Lombards seem to have been converted while living in the area of the Danube.

The Lombard conquest never extended into the extreme southern part of Italy, and even in the northern and central sections the Lombards did not succeed in establishing a single unified state because of the continued tendency of the dukes to defy the royal control. It was not until late in the Lombard period (in the mid-eighth century) that the Exarchate of Ravenna fell to Lombard conquest, and some land in the vicinity of the city of Rome controlled by the papacy was never secured by the Lombards, although they did hold the duchies of Spoleto and Benevento immediately to the east and south.

---

* Paul the Deacon, pp. 86–93.

After Authari, the next Lombard ruler of significance was Rothair, Duke of Brescia, elected in 636. Rothair was an Arian and, as such, was opposed to Roman influences in his kingdom, although he did tolerate the gradual establishment of the Catholic hierarchy there. Rothair's most important contribution to his kingdom was his attempt to reduce the unwritten customs of his people to a single code of law; his contemporaries, however, were more impressed by his militant leadership of the Lombard armies and the territorial expansion that occurred during his reign.

Rothair's reign was followed by a chaotic period of disputed rule. This period temporarily ended in 662 when Grimwald, Duke of Benevento, succeeded in overthrowing the two brothers who were then contesting the throne. Grimwald was the first of the Lombard kings to combine control of the Lombard kingdom with control over the duchy of Benevento, but even under Grimwald the connection was not so close as it appears, for Grimwald's son, Romwald, governed Benevento independent of his father and relied on his father's backing when the duchy was attacked by the Byzantines. Grimwald justified his usurpation of the Lombard throne by offering the Lombards a strong kingship. During his reign the centralization begun under Rothair was continued and Grimwald issued a brief supplement to the law code that had been issued some twenty-five years earlier.

Grimwald's death was followed by another period of disputed rule. Although several of the kings in the period after 671 were fairly able rulers, none of them continued the legislative precedent set by Rothair and Grimwald until Liutprand was elected king in 712. Liutprand (712–744) was probably the most powerful of the Lombard kings. As a Catholic he favored certain Romanizing influences in the kingdom; as a military leader, he reconsolidated the Lombard conquests in Italy and extended them; and as one of the barbarian rulers of western Europe, he maintained peace and friendship with the Franks with whose ruler, Charles Martel, he concluded an alliance against the Moors who threatened Provence. Finally, as a lawgiver, Liutprand was responsible for an extremely important addition to the Lombard laws. During his reign the centralization of the kingdom reached its highest development by increasing the powers of the royal officials at the expense of those whose interests were local. However, in thus strengthening the royal control it would seem that Liutprand was opposed by those men, especially the dukes, who regarded themselves as hereditary possessors of local administrative, judicial, and military authority.

When Liutprand died in 744, the Lombard kingdom appeared to have been built into a consolidated whole with a sufficiently centralized administration to insure its continuing success for some time in the future. Not only had Liutprand subdued the duchies of Spoleto and Benevento where he installed his own followers, but he had also conquered most of the Exarchate of Ravenna and added its territory to his own; he had expanded the Lombard territory at the expense of the Church lands in the vicinity of the duchy of Rome; and he had even remained on friendly terms with Charles Martel and his son, Pepin, the Frankish mayors of the palace to whom successive popes had appealed in vain for aid against those "most wicked" Lombards.

Yet despite the successes of Liutprand and the seeming strength of the kingdom, and despite the fact that his successors—Ratchis, Aistulf, and Desiderius—were fairly able although not very diplomatic rulers, the fact is that the Lombard kingdom did not long survive. The last Lombard kings proved unable to hold the kingdom together; and upon their final defeat by the Franks in 774, the Frankish ruler, Charlemagne, assumed the Lombard crown.

The basic cause for the failure of the Lombards to establish a lasting state was their failure to develop a concept of royal power that should take precedence over local interests. This weakness was apparent in the activities of the dukes, all of whom—but especially those located in Spoleto and Benevento—regarded their own interests as of more importance than those of the nation. The resulting diffusion of power might be checked during the reign of an especially strong king, but the dukes were always eager to reassert themselves after his death. Behind the tendency toward independence on the part of the dukes was the inability or unwillingness of the Lombards to work out a strong rule of succession. Although a certain tendency toward hereditary succession was certainly present, this never replaced the basically elective nature of the Lombard kingship. As a result, there were long periods of disputed rule followed by the usual compromises necessary to secure election support. Under the circumstances it may be surprising that the Lombards produced as many strong kings as they did.

Despite this fundamental weakness of the Lombard kingdom, its overthrow in the eighth century was the immediate result of a diffusion of political power in Italy among a number of interested parties, the five most important being the Lombard national party under the leadership of the Lombard king, an antiroyal Lombard party under the leadership of the dukes of Spoleto and Benevento, an imperial party under the distant control of the Byzantine Emperor, a Roman party under the leadership of the pope, and a foreign party under the leadership of the Carolingian mayors of the palace and later kings. Alliance between two or more of these various parties shifted constantly in the eighth century, the only thread of continuity being provided by the papal policy which aimed to maintain a relatively equal balance between Lombards and Byzantines. When that seemed no longer possible, the papacy then sought outside help from the Franks.

The Lombard rulers during this period were Ratchis—who issued a supplement to the law code but who was later deposed because of his too-liberal attitude toward the Romans—and his brother Aistulf. When Ratchis retired to Monte Cassino, Aistulf resumed the policy of expansion that had been followed by Liutprand. Faced by renewed Lombard threat, Pope Stephen II crossed the Alps to seek aid from Pepin, now king of the Franks. The way for this action had been prepared three years earlier when Pepin, until then officially only "mayor of the palace," addressed his famous appeal to the pope inquiring whether it were good or ill that there were kings in Gaul who had no royal authority. Stephen II's reply that he who had the power ought to be king lent papal sanction to the setting aside of the Merovingian dynasty and the establishment of the Carolingian—and, in addition, provided the pope with a powerful potential ally. Pepin repaid his debt to the pope in 754 when he invaded Italy with a Frankish army and forced the Lombards to pay tribute to the Franks and to turn over to the papacy certain cities in the exarchate recently conquered by the Lombards and demanded by the pope in his assumed role of temporal successor to the emperor in Italy. When Aistulf delayed in restoring these cities, Pepin invaded Italy again in 756 and this time required the payment of additional tribute and the actual "restoration" of the towns in question. Except for Venetia, the holdings of the Exarchate of Ravenna in northern and central Italy now passed to the control of the pope and would form the basis of the temporal state ruled by the papacy until modern times.

Once this had been accomplished, the Franks withdrew from Italy and were occupied with their own affairs. But the Lombards, though humiliated, had lost little territory. Aistulf was an able king and in the midst of his troubles with the Franks managed to find time to issue law supplements in 750 and 755. Aistulf died in 756, however, and the succession was disputed. Desiderius, Duke of Tuscany, finally secured election, although only after he had obtained the support of the papacy by a promise to cede further territory to the papal states. For a time Desiderius succeeded in placating the papacy, in retaining friendly relations with the Franks, and in regaining some of the territory which had been lost by the Lombard kingdom.

Nonetheless, the popes continued to appeal to the Franks for aid against the Lombards; and in 771 when Charlemagne, successor to Pepin, repudiated his wife, a daughter of Desiderius, it was clear that another conflict between the Franks and Lombards would follow. The Frankish invasion of Italy came in 773, and Pavia fell in the following year, its fall symbolizing the end of the Lombard kingdom; henceforth the Frankish kings wore the famed iron crown of the Lombards. It should be noted, however, that Italy was administered by the Franks as a separate kingdom: Lombard laws and institutions remained in effect although the higher Lombard officials were replaced by Franks.

The Lombard duchies of Spoleto and Benevento in the south retained a measure of independence after 774 and Prince Arichis of Benevento, the son-in-law of Desiderius, considered himself the legitimate successor to the Lombard crown. However, although the failure of the Franks to subdue completely the southern duchies had an important influence on the history of southern Italy, this was not of very great significance in Lombard history, for the Lombard kingdom had always been rooted in the north. The Lombard state had fallen to an alliance between the Franks and the papacy. Primarily because of its own lack of organic unity, it could not match this combination of power. The Lombard nobility failed to support the crown, which it felt was increasing the royal power at the nobles' expense, and consequently the Lombard state presented little effective opposition to the Frankish conquest.

The Lombard Laws

The Lombard laws were issued in written form between the years 643 and 755 under the direction of various Lombard kings. They fall into two major parts, the first and more complete issued in 388 titles by King Rothair in 643 and popularly known as *Rothair's Edict* (although the appellation *Rothair's Code* might be more aptly descriptive). The second major portion of the laws, containing 153 titles, was issued in the years from 713 to 735 by King Liutprand. In addition to these two primary issues, there were a number of shorter supplements. In 668, nine titles were added by King Grimwald; further additions were made by King Ratchis in 745 and 746 and others by King Aistulf in 750 and 755. The laws issued by Rothair seemed to be intended to constitute a complete code of law, for they were arranged in a more or less systematic manner. The later lawgivers were concerned primarily with filling in the gaps left by the earlier codification or in modifying it; accordingly, there was little system or order in the sequence of their titles.

There were no other laws issued during the independent existence of the Lombard kingdom. When the territory came under the rule of the Franks in 775, however, Frankish control was never completely asserted in the southern duchies of Spoleto and Benevento. The dukes of Benevento considered themselves the legitimate successors of Desiderius and two of these princes—Aregis in 774 and Adelchis in 866—issued laws to be enforced within their duchies. These laws issued by Aregis and Adelchis formed a supplement to the Lombard code for use in Benevento.

The Frankish kings allowed Lombard law to remain in force in the Carolingian kingdom of Italy and added a number of their own laws ("capitularies") to form the Lombard code as it was applied from the eighth to the tenth centuries. This supplemented Lombard code remained in effect even after the conquest of Italy by Otto I of the German Roman Empire and was further supplemented by additional titles issued by the emperors from Otto I to Henry II.

By the eleventh century, Lombard law had been considerably modified and supplemented as a result of such legislative activity. It was thus a very attenuated form of Lombard law that was gradually displaced by a revived Roman law—not so much that vulgar Roman law which had had an unofficial existence throughout the Lombard and Frankish periods, but a Roman law based on the more classical civil law of the Corpus Juris Civilis.

Organization of the Lombard State

Since the information provided by Paul the Deacon, the Lombard historian, is primarily concerned with the heroic traditions of the Lombard experience in Pannonia and in Italy, not much information is available in his work about the institutional organization of the Lombard kingdom or about the legal and economic customs of the people. Contemporary Roman writers were likewise preoccupied with the military threat of Lombard conquest or with the attitude of the Lombards to certain religious controversies. For a closer look at the daily lives of the Lombard people we must rely on two other types of material, the physical evidence left behind by the Lombards, which is being studied with ever greater care by archeologists, and the written evidence left in the form of charters detailing gifts and purchases and in the form of legislation.

The number of charters that have survived from the Lombard period are few; nonetheless, their study merits more care than has yet been devoted to them. The laws are our most complete source, and the description of a few important Lombard institutions that follows is based almost entirely on them. It should be kept in mind at all times, however, that laws may describe the unusual rather than the usual condition and that the lawgivers took for granted that their justices and the people were so familiar with basic customs that no reference to them was necessary. The material on Lombard life that follows is intended only to illustrate how the laws may be used; further studies may modify this picture and may contribute greater detail about life in Lombard Italy.

The position of the Lombard king after the establishment of the Lombard kingdom is difficult to determine. He was head of his nation but, since his position depended more on election than on birth, it is hard to define his actual power. His military power was real, and so long as the Lombards remained on a war footing and it was necessary for the entire nation to cooperate in the face of enemies, the Lombard king was an effective military chieftain and the real leader of his people. His political and judicial authority, however, were challenged almost from the beginning by those of his important followers who were given positions of administrative importance in the newly conquered territory. The Lombard method of controlling the countryside was to assign a duke and a number of family groups to a geographical province as it was conquered. Since the king's attention was taken up with further conquests, the dukes tended to become virtually independent rulers on a local scale and they naturally resented any effort on the part of the crown to reassert its own political and judicial jurisdiction.

The result of this development was a dual set of administrative organs in the Lombard kingdom. On the one hand were the dukes who claimed extensive authority and who appointed their own subordinates, and on the other hand was the king who appointed a series of royal officials responsible to himself. This struggle between dukes and king is apparent in the laws, especially in those of Rothair where the duke was actually referred to as a judicial figure. After the time of Rothair, however, royal policy aimed at reducing if not eliminating the power of the dukes and accordingly only the royal officials were mentioned: the *gastald* (most important of the royal administrative-judicial officials); the *schultheis* (a lesser administrative-judicial officer responsible to the gastald); and a host of minor officials—foresters, hundred-men, and messengers—who assisted the higher officials in their work but who did not enjoy judicial powers themselves.

The situation in administrative-judicial matters was paralleled in military affairs. The military authority of the king may well have been the most effective aspect of the royal position at the time of the invasion. The Lombards were at this time fighting "as a nation" and every free Lombard rendered military service. The original military basis of Lombard organization persisted long after the Lombards had settled down to rule and cultivate the Italian countryside in the usual names given to the typical Lombard freeman—for he is always an "army man"—an *exercitalis* (derived from the Latin) or an *arimannus* (derived from the Germanic language of the Lombards). The Lombard freeman owed military service to his nation—this was accepted as a natural privilege and responsibility of freedom. His military service (the type of which was determined by his ability to provide himself with military equipment) was owed on two levels. He was expected to answer the royal summons to serve in the event of a threat to the "national" security and he was also expected to answer the summons of his duke in the event of a threat to local security. Under normal circumstances the interests of these two parties were the same and the Lombard freeman followed his duke to serve in the royal army. On occasion, however, the interests of the two parties were opposed. The numerous periods of civil strife in Lombard history indicate that many freemen regarded their loyalty to the duke as taking precedence over their loyalty to the king. Certainly this dilemma contributed to the internal weakness of the Lombard kingdom.

The royal policy that aimed to increase the centralization of the kingdom at the expense of the ducal authority was stoutly resisted. The northern dukes were more or less effectively controlled by the crown after the beginning of the seventh century, but the southern dukes (of Spoleto and Benevento) successfully defied the extension of royal authority and assumed the role of the crown for themselves within their territory. When the Lombard king was individually strong—as, for instance, was true in the case of Rothair and Liutprand—the royal policy of centralization was relatively successful and the Lombard kingdom seemed well on its way toward consolidation. That this centralization was not completely effective, however, is abundantly clear, for as soon as the controlling hand of Liutprand was removed in the eighth century, the dukes immediately began to pursue a foreign policy of their own aimed at personal aggrandizement—even if at the expense of the Lombard kingdom as a whole. This revolt of the dukes was aided by the military support of their followers, some of whom were ordinary freemen of the duchy and some of whom were those *fideles* (*gasindii*) bound by special oaths of loyalty to their lords.

The Judicial System

Despite the ducal pretensions, the dispensation of justice was fundamentally a prerogative of the Lombard king. The king himself could act to settle legal disputes among his subjects, but ordinarily suits were heard and disposed of by the king's judicial officials and only in cases of lasting dissatisfaction (and within prescribed limits) would these suits be appealed to the king.

The theoretical justification for royal control of the judicial system may well have developed from the combination of two concepts: the idea that every man's person and property constituted a special domain protected by a peace which it was an offense to violate, and the attitude that the kingdom was in effect the personal domain of the king and as such it was protected by a peace the violation of which was an offense against the royal power. To breach this royal peace was to commit an offense that the Lombards termed *scandalum*. A number of the laws specifically state that a particular fine is to be imposed in order to avert the *faida* (the blood feud) and hence prevent a breach of the peace or scandalum. The penalty for breaking the peace increased the closer the violence came to the person of the king: hence the commission of scandalum in the city where one of the king's officials was present was definitely breach of the royal peace but it was a less serious breach of that peace than the commission of scandalum in the city where the king himself was present. Nonetheless, any violent act was a form of scandalum and was thus an offense against the public peace as well as an offense against the injured individual or family. The royal courts therefore considered two offenses when they judged any violent act or any act that might lead to violence in retaliation, and accordingly the penalty, the compensation, was divided between the two offended parties: the royal court (the fisc) and the private party.

The lower Lombard courts were those presided over by the schultheis (*sculdahis*) whose court was associated with a small territorial jurisdiction that is not named in the laws. All suits were to be brought first before the schultheis and, if the matter were a relatively minor one, the case would be decided then and there. If, however, the schultheis decided that it was out of his jurisdiction, the matter was referred to the court of the gastald (*gastaldius* or *iudex*), and if the case were so serious that even this magistrate hesitated to render a decision, the parties were referred to the king. A number of regions each presided over by a schultheis were grouped to form the judicial territory presided over by the gastald: this territory was called the *civitas*, a region that may or may not have coincided with the old Roman subdivision of the same name.

These royal officials (king, gastald, schultheis) acting in their judicial capacity were assisted by the lesser royal officials, the "hundredmen" (*centini, degani*), and perhaps also by the foresters (*saltarii*). These lesser royal officials do not seem to have had the power to render judicial decisions, however; they performed police duties and acted as agents or representatives (*missi*) of the gastald or schultheis when called upon to do so. The Lombard courts were not attended by the freemen of the community sitting in the capacity of doomsmen; rather the Lombard courts were presided over by the royal magistrate who announced judgment in accordance with accepted custom as codified in the Lombard Laws.

The Lombards normally used two methods of judicial proof: *compurgation* and *trial by combat*. Proof by compurgation was the more usual method of procedure, although in certain more serious cases trial by combat was employed, either because of the nature of the case or at the request of the accusing party. That the method of proof by combat (the camfio) was passing out of favor and was somewhat distrusted as a means of providing justice is indicated by several of the laws of Rothair and of Liutprand.

The method of compurgation followed by the Lombards resembled that in use among the other barbarians. It was a method of proof or of defense that rested not upon the presentation of material witnesses but upon one's personal standing in the community or upon the reputation of his family. Thus, depending on rank and upon the seriousness of the accusation, one had to counteract the charge against him with a certain number of oathtakers or oathhelpers (*sacramentales*) consisting of those who knew the defendant best— either his near relatives or fellow freemen of the community, men of good reputation. If these oathtakers, who were known to be men of integrity in the community, were willing to offer oath for the defendant, the community as a whole (represented by the king's official, the judge), must accept the purity of the defendant's oath also.

A man accused of some offense was expected to appear before

the court with a certain number of oathhelpers, the number varying from three to twelve, depending upon the seriousness of the charge. The oath might be taken on the Gospels or upon weapons that had been blessed for this purpose. The charge was considered proved against the accused man when the oath of the accused and his oathhelpers was imperfect or broken.

Proof by ordeal does not seem to have been used very extensively by the Lombards, perhaps never in the case of freemen. There is, however, some indication that the ordeal was used as a means of proof among the slaves.

Among the Lombards the role of the state remained almost exclusively the passive one of providing the court presided over by a royal magistrate. Since the Lombard concept of law did not distinguish between disputes of a civil nature and offenses of a criminal nature, the man guilty of a "crime" could be "brought to justice" only by the institution of a suit for damages brought against him by the injured party.

Conviction of crime in the courts ordinarily did not result in physical punishment, but rather a fine (composition) was imposed; part of this fine (usually half) went to the injured party in the form of damages. As among the other Germanic peoples, this system of requiring the payment of compensation to the injured party was a substitute for the older system of the blood feud where obtaining justice was a strictly family matter. By the time the Lombard laws were reduced to writing, however, the state had become strong enough to prohibit the blood feud (the faida) or at least to limit its frequency.

Compensation was sometimes assessed in kind (e.g., when the injury was to a man's crops or animals) but more frequently in coin. Compensation for personal injury might be referred to as wergeld or composition. The wergeld was the value placed on a man's life and varied with his legal status. In a case such as that involving a man's death, the killer was required to pay wergeld to the relatives or heirs of the man killed, this payment being made to satisfy them and to avert the feud. Composition was the sum paid by the guilty party for offenses other than homicide.

The compensation required in case of injury was based not only on the degree of incapacity caused thereby, but also on the nature of the injury, for some relatively minor injuries might nonetheless be serious blows to the personal dignity of the person offended. A con-

siderable portion of Rothair's Edict (Titles 41 to 125) is taken up
with a schedule of fines to be paid in each of a long number of injuries. Ordinarily, the composition to be paid varied with the quality of
the person injured: an injury to a freeman involved a larger payment
than a corresponding injury to an *aldius* (half-freeman) or to a personal or household slave (*servus ministerialis*), and such an injury to
an aldius or household slave likewise involved a larger payment than
a corresponding injury to an agrarian slave (*servus rusticus*). The
person to whom the compensation was paid also varied depending
upon the legal competence of the person injured. Ordinarily only the
person who was in his own legal power (*selpmundius*) was entitled to
receive composition. In case of an injury to a woman, the composition was paid to her husband or other legal guardian (*mundwald*); in
the case of a minor, to his guardian; in the case of an aldius or freedman, to his patron (*patronus*); and in the case of a slave, to his lord.
It was generally the case that the person legally responsible for the
injured party was the one to receive the composition. However, this
was not always true, for in certain specified cases it was the injured
party himself—even though he were a person not legally competent
—who received the composition, and this exception was even in rare
cases extended to the slaves.

With few exceptions, the compositions imposed in the Lombard
code varied from half a solidus to 1200 solidi. The composition of
twenty solidi seems to mark a division between what might be called
the more and less serious cases: those compositions up to and including twenty solidi were for the most part those imposed for injuries to
various parts of the body that did not result in death or permanent
injury and those imposed in specific cases of petty theft. If an
offender were unable to pay the fine of twenty solidi or less, he was to
be handed over to the injured party to serve as a debt slave until such
time as the sum of the debt was worked out. If, however, the fine
involved was a larger sum, the guilty man was turned over to the
injured party to serve permanently as a debt slave.

Social Classes

The social and economic organization of the Lombard kingdom
must be inferred from references in some of the laws. At the top of

the social scale were the Lombard freemen whose status was reflected in the amount of their wergeld. Two classes of such freemen were clearly distinguishable, their status being determined, it would seem, by whether or not they possessed land. The landholders (who belonged to the "first" class) had a wergeld of 300 solidi; the landless freemen (the lesser men, *minores homines*) had a wergeld of 150 solidi. Another distinguishing characteristic in social rank was added by service to the king, but how much such service increased a man's wergeld is not clear. The right to possess land and the right to render military service were among the prerogatives of the freemen and even though some of them must have been relatively poor, a great gulf separated them from the lesser classes of society.

All Lombard freemen above the age of eighteen were legally competent. In addition to his own legal independence, the Lombard freeman might enjoy the right of legal protection (*mundium*) over a number of other persons: his wife and unmarried daughters, minor sons, *aldii*, and slaves. The Lombard freeman to whose household these legal incompetents belonged represented these persons in all matters: he appeared for them in court and paid out and received composition in their stead. Free women were not legally competent, although they had rights protected at law; they belonged to the same social class as the men of their families, and the value placed on their lives was the same. These persons—husband, wife, unmarried daughters, minor sons, and other dependents—formed the basic Lombard family under the legal representation of the husband. The composition of that group referred to in the laws as the "near relatives" is nowhere precisely defined but for purposes of inheritance the right to inherit extended to relatives in the seventh degree. The near relatives were called upon when the family group was incomplete—especially if it lacked an adult male head or competent heirs—or they might be among the oathhelpers who appeared in court with a plaintiff or defendant. A more extensive discussion of the relationship between the family and this larger kin group follows later.

The next lower class in the Lombard state was that of the half-free (aldii). Racially speaking, the ranks of the aldii must have been quite mixed. It is almost certain that at least a portion of the population that inhabited Italy prior to the Lombard conquest was retained on the land as half-free agricultural workers, although certainly not all of the conquered Roman population was reduced to the status of aldii, as was once the generally accepted belief. But in addition to Roman elements in this class, there were also a number of persons of Germanic birth, including some Lombards. It was possible to raise persons from the rank of slave to that of aldius by an act of partial manumission, and since there were non-Lombard Germans among the slaves as the result of capture in war and Germanic Lombards among the slaves as the result of the operation of the laws on debt servitude, persons of these racial origins must have found their way into the ranks of the aldii. The value of the aldius (usually described as *pretium* although occasionally as wergeld) was sixty solidi. The aldius was not legally competent; that is, he could not enter into legal transactions in his own name, and he might not ordinarily give and receive compositions. The patron of the aldius, although occasionally referred to as patronus, was usually called *dominus* or lord.

The lowest social class in the Lombard kingdom was that of the slaves. There was quite a difference, however, between the household or personal slaves (servi ministeriales) on the one hand, and the agri-cultural slaves (servi rustici) on the other. The value (pretium) of the household slaves varied between twenty-five and fifty solidi, depending upon training. The pretium of the agricultural slaves varied ordinarily between sixteen and twenty solidi, depending upon training—but one should note the major exception of the master swineherd whose value was fifty solidi. Slaves, of course, were not legally competent and the laws made no attempt to interfere between the slave and his lord. However, the schedule of tariffs for injuries did contain a set of compositions to be applied in cases of injury to a slave by someone other than his lord. These compositions were to be paid to the slave's lord and were compensation for the damage done to the lord's property. Nonetheless, there is no reason to think that the lot of the slaves was especially hard and the high value placed on the life of a trained slave indicates that he held an impor-tant position in the Lombard economy. There must furthermore have been no special stigma attached to slavery for the schedule of high fines in the laws working in conjunction with the laws on debt slavery resulted in the reduction to slavery (sometimes temporary, sometimes permanent) of many respectable members of society.

Slaves could be manumitted by any one of a number of methods. A slave could be completely freed and given the full legal privileges of a freeman; he could be freed but remain under the legal protection of his former lord; or he could be accorded something resembling "half-freedom"—i.e., he could be raised to the status of an aldius.

The Lombard Family and Familial Institutions

The Lombard family consisted of a man and wife and their descendants and dependents. Sons became legally competent at eighteen and presumably they then no longer formed a part of the direct legal community under their father's protection (mundium). In many cases, however, adult sons continued to live with their parents, probably even after marriage, inasmuch as the Lombard laws did not allow the sons to force a division of the family property during the father's lifetime. However, voluntary division of the property before the father's death must have been common since the laws carefully set forth the respective shares of father and sons in the event of such a division. Adult sons could of course also acquire property by inheritance from someone other than their father, they could obtain land by gift or purchase, or, in the event of marriage, they might gain control over the sometimes extensive properties of their wives. In such cases, the son or sons set up independent households and became the heads of families of their own.

The possession of property thus seems to be the key to the composition of the family. Property was essential to the continuation of the family and the Lombards, like the other Germans, regarded family property as the rightful possession of the family, not to be dissipated by sale or testament by him who controlled it at any one time. This property was not owned in common by all the members of the family, however, for it was divided among the heirs according to law upon a man's death—that is, the heirs normally did not hold it in common. Of course, any property other than family property that a man acquired he might dispose of in any way that he wished.

When a girl married, she normally passed from her father's legal control to that of her husband. Since the right of legal protection over a woman and her property was a valuable property right, marriage was an important familial institution and was carefully regulated in the Lombard laws. A summary of the legal aspects of the marriage relationship offers a fairly broad glimpse of this institution as it was known to the Lombards.

Marriage was essentially a contract entered into by the bridegroom (supported or not by his relatives) and the relatives of the girl. The marriage consisted of two ceremonies. The first of these ceremonies was the betrothal, at which time the terms of the marriage contract were agreed upon. The bridegroom promised to pay a certain sum (called the *meta*) to the bride's relatives for the transfer to him of the girl's mundium or right of legal protection.

The next step after betrothal was the marriage ceremony proper —heavy fines being provided if either the bridegroom or the relatives of the girl should deliberately delay this ceremony for more than two years. Although any unfaithfulness on the part of the girl during the period of the betrothal was punished as adultery, the girl nonetheless during this time remained in the legal protection of her own family since her mundium had not yet been transferred to her husband-to-be. At the time of the marriage, the bridegroom completed the payment of the meta and the girl's relatives (usually her father or brother) formally handed her over to her husband, a handing over known as tradition (*traditio*), thereby transferring her mundium from her own family to her husband. Henceforth the husband, instead of her family, was legally responsible for his wife (and he also had control of her property, although he could not sell it or dissipate it without the consent of the woman and her relatives).

At the time of the marriage, the girl's father was expected to bestow a "gift" upon the newly married couple (the *faderfio*), and on the morning following the wedding night the husband was expected to bestow a gift upon his wife (the morning gift—*morgengab* or *morgincap*). These gifts might well have been of very considerable size and the woman seems to have had some claim to both as part of her separate property which in the event of her death passed to her heirs rather than to her husband.

The form of marriage just described was not the only form of marriage known to the Lombards. If, for one reason or another, the bridegroom had not paid for the bride's meta at the time of the marriage, the marriage was nonetheless recognized as socially and morally binding on the part of bride and groom—however, the girl's mundium remained with her family, her children were legally protected by the mother's family rather than by the father's, and her family rather than her husband was heir to any property she might have.

The Lombard man might also enter into one or more unions outside of marriage and such unions, although definitely inferior to marriage, were legally recognized inasmuch as the children of such unions enjoyed a guaranteed (albeit subordinate) place in the father's inheritance. Such children born outside a legal marriage were described as "natural" children to distinguish them from "illegitimate" children (the offspring of prohibited [illegal] unions who had no claim at all on the family inheritance).

Although daughters might inherit the family property in the absence of sons, women were never recognized as legally competent and their property was administered by whoever held their mundium. But even if not legally competent, the Lombard woman enjoyed considerable protection at law. Her husband or mundwald might not dissipate her property nor might he seriously mistreat her. A husband could put his wife aside only if she were guilty of adultery or of plotting against his life—putting her aside for any other cause subjected him to loss of his wife's mundium and the payment of a very large fine.

In addition to his wife, unmarried daughters, and minor sons, a man's legal community included also his dependents. The right or responsibility for controlling the marriage of these dependents was just as important as the right to control the marriage of his daughters. Consequently, the laws covered these marriages also.

Free women were not allowed to marry slaves, but a freeman might marry a slave woman. To make this a legal marriage, however, he must purchase the woman (if she belonged to another lord) and free her in the formal public ceremony known as *gairethinx* (literally, the "spear assembly"). Thereafter the woman and her children were free and the children were the father's legitimate *fulborn* heirs. If the man did not marry the slave woman but nonetheless had children by her, these children were slaves of the mother's lord unless the father purchased the children and formally freed them—whereupon they were classed as his natural children and as such were eligible for a share of the inheritance.

Although a free woman might not marry a slave, she might marry a semifree aldius. If the woman's mundium remained with her relatives, then her children were free and remained under the protection of the mother's family. If the aldius (or more likely his lord) purchased the woman's mundium, then her children were aldii of the father's lord unless after the father's death the woman's relatives repurchased her mundium and purchased the mundium of her children also. A freeman might marry an aldia, but if he did not formally free her, then his children by her were counted as natural and not legitimate.

In marriages between aldii and slaves, the children seemed to follow the status of the more lowly of their parents. For example, if an aldia married a slave, then the aldia lost her own liberty and her children were slaves of the father's lord. If, on the other hand, an aldius married a female slave, then their children were slaves of the mother's lord. Quite obviously, these provisions were of no great importance when the aldii and slaves belonged to the same lord—but when the dependent husband and wife belonged to different lords, then such careful provisions were necessary to prevent disputes over whom the children belonged to. These provisions covered the situation even when slaves belonging to different lords married. After the slave father's death, the mother slave might leave and return to the household of her own lord—but her children remained as slaves of the father's lord. The aldius of one lord might marry the aldia of another. If the man's lord paid for the woman's mundium, then the children were *aldii* of the father's lord. If the father's lord did not acquire the woman's mundium, then the children were aldii of the mother's lord.

Just as the importance of the family required detailed provisions for marriage, so it also required detailed provisions for inheritance. When the laws were first codified by Rothair in the seventh century, disposition of the family property was controlled entirely by the customs of inheritance. By the eighth century, however, certain modifications in the inheritance laws had taken place as the result of either ecclesiastical influence or the influence of Roman law.

The basic inheritance laws provided that property should pass according to a prescribed formula to a man's legitimate and natural descendants. If there were no claimant available among these heirs, the family property passed to other members of the kin group. According to law, persons within the seventh degree of relationship (from a common male ancestor) might be considered for the inheritance in the absence of more immediate heirs. Should no heirs be available even within this expanded kin group, the property passed to the king.

Among the important changes taking place in the inheritance laws between the seventh and eighth centuries was an improvement in the position of women. At the earlier time they were not allowed to inherit the family property even if no sons were available. By the later period, daughters were allowed to inherit in the absence of sons (but since they were not legally competent, their mundium passed to the closest male kin). Another important change taking place in the inheritance laws was to admit the validity of certain testamentary bequests. A man might favor one of his sons over the others (within carefully fixed limits), and he might also by testament leave a part of his property to a daughter or daughters even if he had sons. And finally, the most extensive use of the testament seems to have been in connection with gifts left to the church.

The Role of the Church

Since the Lombards were Arians at the time of their conquest of Italy and the native Italian population was Catholic, there was for a time a dual ecclesiastical order in the Lombard kingdom. According to Paul the Deacon:

> Then Arioald, after he had held the sovereignty over the Langobards twelve years, departed this life, and Rothari, of the race of Arodus, received the kingdom of the Langobards. And he was brave and strong, and followed the path of justice; he did not, however, hold the right line of Christian belief, but was stained by the infidelity of Arian heresy. The Arians, indeed, say to their own ruin that the Son is less than the Father, and the Holy Spirit also is less than the Father and the Son. But we Catholics confess that the Father and Son and Holy Spirit are one and the true God in three persons, equal

> in power and the same in glory. In this time there were
> two bishops throughout almost all the cities of the king-
> dom, one a Catholic and the other an Arian. In the city
> of Ticinum too there is shown, down to the present
> time, the place where the Arian bishop, who had his seat
> at the church of St. Eusebius, had a baptistery, while
> another bishop sat in the Catholic Church. . . .*

So, if we can believe Paul, there was a time when both Arian and
Catholic bishops resided in the capital Pavia. Perhaps the presence of
both is partly responsible for the failure of the Lombard clergy to
exert much control over Lombard policies since neither could allow
his competitor to play a more influential role than he himself.

The clergy does not seem to have played a direct role in Lombard political life nor does it seem to have exercised any direct influence over Lombard legislation. Since members of the clergy were not
subject to Lombard law but were subject to Roman law, there was no
provision in the Lombard laws for offenses committed by or against
them and no wergeld was set for members of the clergy. When the
Lombard lawgiver stated that he was issuing his laws with the consent of his nobles, his *fideles*, and sometimes even with the consent of
all Lombard freemen, he never specifically mentioned members of
the clergy as being among those present at the assembly. Although
the church was certainly an increasingly important institution in the
Lombard kingdom (as evidenced by its influence over the use of
testaments, the role of the clergy in administering the ordeal, the
role of the church in certain forms of manumission, the recognition that the church building enjoyed a peace which it was scandalum
to violate, and the use of the square in front of the church as a place
where public witness of gifts and exchanges might take place), members of the clergy played no such visible role at the Lombard court as
would have been found among the Franks, the Visigoths, and even
the Anglo-Saxons. Doubtless, continued political hostilities between
the Lombards and Rome were to a significant degree responsible
for this condition.

---

* Paul the Deacon, pp. 193–95.

CONCLUSION

A number of problems have been encountered in this translation. The language of the text is not classical Latin and a number of Germanic words appear; hence, a considerable difficulty has been met in attempting to find English words to translate accurately the meaning of some of the passages. In·general, an attempt has been made to render everything into English, although this has at times forced awkward phrases into the translation. No English equivalent for the Lombard half-freeman was found, however, and the Latin form *aldius* has been retained; no English equivalent for the sworn follower was found, and therefore the Latin form *fidelis* has been kept. The Latin *mundium*—the right of legal protection over someone not competent at law—has also been retained.

Only a few of the most important and interesting Lombard institutions and customs revealed in the laws have been described in this introduction. In the code there is to be found additional material on much else: on the Lombard method of distraint and use of sureties, on contracts and sales, on the highly personal attitude toward crime and the exaggerated sense of personal dignity felt by the Lombards, on their attitude toward Christianity and the city of Rome, on the subject of witchcraft and sorcery, on the influence of Roman law on Lombard law, and much more. In many respects the Lombards seem only a stage removed from barbarism, but in many other respects they show themselves to have learned a great deal as a result of their earlier contact with the Byzantine Empire and their later contacts with the people of Italy. Perhaps the process of Italian unification would not have been so long delayed had the Lombards not fallen before the Franks. Nonetheless, although the Lombard kingdom fell, Lombard influences were to be felt in Italy for many centuries thereafter.

I. Rothair's Edict[1]

The most noble Rothair, king of the Lombards, together with his principal judges, issues this lawbook in the name of the Lord.

In the name of the Lord, I, the most noble Rothair, seventeenth king of the Lombards, [issue this lawbook] with the aid of God in the eighth year of my reign and in the thirty-eighth year of my life, in the second indiction, and in the seventy-sixth year after the happy arrival of the Lombards in the land of Italy, led there by divine providence in the time of King Alboin, my predecessor. Issued from the palace at Pavia.

The collection which follows makes evident how great was and is our care and solicitude for the welfare of our subjects; for we recognize that it is not only the numerous demands of the wealthy which should carry weight, but also the burdensome trials of the poor are important. Therefore, trusting in the mercy of Almighty God, we have perceived it necessary to improve and to reaffirm the present law, amending all earlier laws by adding that which is lacking and eliminating that which is superfluous. We desire that these laws be brought together in one volume so that everyone may lead a secure life in accordance with law and justice, and in confidence thereof will willingly set himself against his enemies and defend himself and his homeland.

In these matters our concern for the future assures us that what we do here is useful and so we have ordered the names of the Lombard kings, our predecessors, and from what family they came, to be noted down here insofar as we have ascertained them from the older men of the nation.

The first king was Agilmund, from the family of the Gugings.
The second was Lamisio.
Leth was third.
Gildioch, son of Leth, was fourth.
Godioch, son of Gildioch, was fifth.
Sixth was Klaffo, son of Godioch.
Seventh was Tato, son of Klaffo. Tato and Winigis were sons of Klaffo.
Eighth was Wacho, son of Winigis, nephew of Tato.
Ninth was Walthari.
Tenth was Audoin, from the Gaugus family.
Eleventh was Alboin, son of Audoin, who, as mentioned above, led the nation into Italy.
Twelfth was Klep, from the Belios family.
Thirteenth was Authari, son of Klep.
Fourteenth was Agilulf, a Thuring from the family of the Anawas.
Fifteenth was Adalwald, son of Agilulf.
Sixteenth was Arioald, from the Kaup family.
In the name of God, I, Rothair, son of Nanding, from the family of the Harode, am the seventeenth king, as stated above. Nanding son of Notzo, Notzo son of Alamund, Alamund son of Alaman, Alaman son of Hiltzo, Hiltzo son of Weilo, Weilo son of Weo, Weo son of Frocho, Frocho son of Facho, Facho son of Mammo, Mammo son of Obthora.

Here End the Names of the Kings

Here Begin the Titles of the Laws

1. On him who plots against the life of the king.
2. On him who takes counsel with the king regarding the death of another.
3. On him who attempts to flee outside the province.

4. On him who invites enemies within the province.
5. On him who hides a spy.
6. On him who raises a revolt in the army.
7. On him who abandons his colleague during a battle.
8. On him who commits a breach of the peace (scandalum) in the assembly.
9. On him who accuses a man before the king.
10. Concerning the freeman who plots against the life of another man.
11. On plots involving death.
12. Concerning several men who kill someone.
13. Concerning him who kills his lord.
14. On murder.
15. Concerning him who violates a sepulchre.
16. On him who finds a man's corpse in a river.
17. On him who is making his way to the king.
18. On him who, armed, throws himself upon someone who is making his way to the king.
19. On him who enters a village with an armed following.
20. On him who holds his duke in contempt.
21. On him who refuses to go out with the army.
22. On him who refuses to aid his duke in the accomplishment of justice.
23. Concerning the duke who mistreats one of his men.
24. Concerning the gastald who mistreats one of his men.
25. On him who seeks back his property from someone else.
26. On him who blocks the way to a free woman or girl.
27. On him who blocks the way to a freeman.
28. On him who blocks the way to a man or woman slave.
29. On him who blocks a field or meadow or any enclosure to another man.
30. On him who throws a freeman from his horse.
31. On him who in disguise does violence to a freeman [i.e., concerning the *walopaus*].
32. Concerning the freeman who has been found at night in another man's courtyard.
33. Concerning the slave who has been found at night in another man's courtyard.

34. On him who in anger shoots an arrow into another man's court-yard.

35. On him who breaks the peace [commits scandalum] in a church.

36. On him who breaks the peace [commits scandalum] in the palace when the king is present.

37. Concerning the freeman who breaks the peace [commits scandalum] in a district (*civitas*) where the king is present.

38. Concerning the slave who breaks the peace [commits scandalum] in a district (civitas) where the king is present.

39. Concerning the freeman who breaks the peace [commits scandalum] in another district (civitas).

40. Concerning the slave who breaks the peace [commits scandalum] in another district (civitas).

41. On beating a freeman.

42. On binding a freeman.

43. On hitting a freeman.

44. On him who wounds another man in a fight.

45. Concerning the composition for various injuries.

46. On him who hits another man on the head.

47. On him who hits another man on the head so that the bones are broken.

48. On gouging out eyes.

49. On cutting off noses.

50. On cutting off lips.

51. Concerning the front teeth.

52. Concerning the molar teeth.

53. On cutting off ears.

54. Concerning facial injuries.

55. Concerning injuries to the nose.

56. Concerning injuries to the ears.

57. Concerning arm wounds.

58. Concerning injuries to the arm.

59. Concerning injuries to the chest.

60. On injuries to the hip.

61. About the number of wounds.

62. On cutting off hands.

63. Concerning first fingers [thumbs] of the hand.

64. Concerning second fingers.
65. Concerning third fingers.
66. Concerning fourth fingers.
67. Concerning fifth fingers.
68. On cutting off feet.
69. Concerning big toes.
70. Concerning second toes.
71. Concerning third toes.
72. Concerning fourth toes.
73. Concerning fifth [little] toes.
74. Concerning all these wounds and injuries.
75. On the death of a child in its mother's womb.
76. On the half-free (aldii) and household slaves (servi ministeriales).
77. On injuries to aldii or household slaves.
78. On aldii or household slaves who have been beaten.
79. On him who strikes an aldius or household slave upon the head.
80. Concerning injuries to the face.
81. On gouging out eyes.
82. On cutting off noses.
83. On cutting off ears.
84. On cutting off lips.
85. On knocking out teeth.
86. Concerning molar teeth.
87. Concerning broken arms.
88. On cutting off hands.
89. Concerning first fingers [thumbs] of the hand.
90. Concerning second fingers.
91. Concerning third fingers.
92. Concerning fourth fingers.
93. Concerning fifth fingers.
94. On broken hips.
95. On cutting off feet.
96. Concerning first [big] toes.
97. Concerning second toes.
98. Concerning third toes.
99. Concerning fourth toes.
100. Concerning fifth toes.

101. Concerning injuries to the chest.
102. On piercing arms and legs.
103. Concerning field slaves (servi rusticani).
104. Concerning injuries to the face.
105. On gouging out eyes.
106. On cutting off noses.
107. On cutting off ears.
108. On cutting off lips.
109. Concerning teeth.
110. On piercing arms and legs.
111. Concerning injuries to the chest.
112. On breaking arms, hips, or legs.
113. On cutting off hands.
114. Concerning first fingers [thumbs].
115. Concerning second fingers.
116. Concerning third fingers.
117. Concerning fourth fingers.
118. Concerning fifth fingers.
119. On cutting off a field slave's feet.
120. Concerning first [big] toes.
121. Concerning second toes.
122. Concerning third toes.
123. Concerning fourth toes.
124. Concerning fifth toes.
125. On beating field slaves.
126. On crippling limbs.
127. Concerning wounds and injuries inflicted on aldii and field slaves.
128. He who struck the blow shall seek the doctor.
129. On killing aldii.
130. On killing household slaves.
131. Concerning the household slave who is an understudy.
132. On killing tenant slaves (servi massarii).
133. On the killing of ox plowmen.
134. On the killing of a field slave subordinate to the tenant slave (massarius).
135. On killing herders.
136. On killing cattleherds, goatherds, or oxherds.

137. On killing the child of a tenant slave.
138. Concerning the case of a man killed by a tree cut down by several men.
139. On the use of poison.
140. Concerning the freeman or free woman who administers poison.
141. Concerning the use of poison.
142. Concerning the man or woman slave who administers poison.
143. Concerning the man who seeks revenge after accepting composition.
144. Concerning the master builders from Como (*magistri comacini*).
145. On the hiring of master builders from Como.
146. On arson.
147. Concerning the brand of fire which has been carried farther than nine feet.
148. Concerning the fire made beside the road.
149. On burning a mill.
150. On destroying a mill.
151. On building a mill on someone else's property.
152. On the death of a borrowed or hired worker.
153. Concerning degrees of relationship.
154. On legitimate and natural sons.
155. No one may give his natural sons the same status as his legitimate sons.
156. Concerning natural sons whose mothers are the slaves of someone else.
157. Concerning the child of a natural son.
158. On the survival of a legitimate daughter and a natural son.
169. On just causes for disinheriting a son.
160. On the survival of legitimate daughters, legitimate sisters, and natural sons.
161. On the disposition of the sisters' guardianship (mundium) between legitimate and natural sons.
162. On the death of a natural son.
163. Concerning the man who plots a relative's death.
164. Concerning the man who accuses his nephew of being born in adultery.

193. Concerning the free girl who follows another man's slave outside the country.
194. Concerning the man who has intercourse with a woman slave belonging to someone else.
195. Concerning offenses against a girl.
196. On adultery.
197. On witchcraft.
198. Concerning the man who charges a girl in the guardianship (mundium) of someone else with some offense.
199. Concerning the widow who returns to her father's house.
200. On killing women.
201. On killing free women.
202. Concerning women who conspire in the death of their husbands.
203. Concerning women who kill their husbands.
204. On the legal competence of women.
205. On the rape of aldiae.
206. On the rape of freedwomen.
207. On the rape of female slaves.
208. On abducting another man's aldia.
209. On abducting a woman slave.
210. Concerning seeking refuge at the king's court with an abducted woman.
211. On marriage with another man's wife.
212. Concerning the man who discovers his wife in adultery.
213. On adultery.
214. Concerning the man who marries a free girl without the consent of her family.
215. Concerning the death of a girl who is betrothed.
216. Concerning the aldius who marries a free woman.
217. Concerning the aldia who marries a slave.
218. Concerning the aldius who marries an aldia.
219. Concerning the aldius who marries a slave.
220. Concerning the woman slave who marries a slave belonging to someone else.
221. Concerning the slave who marries a free woman.
222. Concerning the man who marries his own slave.

255. On the discovery of thefts through an informer (*proditor*).
256. Concerning the slave who commits a theft while in flight.
257. Concerning the free woman who attempts to steal.
258. Concerning the aldia or female slave who attempts to steal.
259. Concerning the freeman who orders his boy or slave to steal.
260. Concerning articles found along the road.
261. Concerning the slave, married to another man's woman slave, who steals.
262. Concerning the slave who, while in flight, gives property to anyone.
263. On thefts committed by several men.
264. Concerning freemen or slaves who try to flee outside the country.
265. Concerning ferrymen.
266. Concerning ferrymen who knowingly transport thieves.
267. Concerning ferrymen who transport fugitive bondsmen.
268. Concerning ferrymen who knowingly transport fugitive freemen.
269. Concerning the bondsman who flees to another man.
270. Concerning the man who does not wish to return another man's fugitive bondsman.
271. Provision for the situation where the king's court does not wish to return another man's fugitive bondsman.
272. On taking sanctuary in a church.
273. On slaves who flee within the country.
274. Concerning the man who keeps a fugitive bondsman for more than nine nights without notifying his lord.
275. Concerning the bondsman who seeks refuge with someone else.
276. Concerning the man who knowingly receives a fugitive bondsman.
277. Concerning anger (*aistan*).
278. On violation of someone else's courtyard.
279. Concerning a band of field slaves.
280. Concerning the sedition of field slaves.
281. On theft and the penalty therefor.
282. Concerning theft of firewood.
283. Concerning theft of cut wood.

284. On entry into a man's garden.
285. On fences.
286. On fence boards.
287. On fence poles.
288. On plows.
289. On lead bells.
290. On yokes.
291. On reins.
292. On grape vines.
293. On poles that support vines.
294. Concerning cutting down vines.
295. On vine shoots.
296. Concerning stealing grapes.
297. On animals at pasture.
298. On halters.
299. On nets.
300. On cutting trees.
301. On chestnut, hazel-nut, pear, or apple trees.
302. On olive trees.
303. Concerning the man or animal that impales himself on another man's fence.
304. Concerning the horse or other domestic animal that impales itself [while jumping] into another man's enclosure.
305. Concerning the man who makes a ditch around his field.
306. On wells.
307. On weapons.
308. On taking weapons without consent.
309. On wild animals.
310. On animal traps.
311. Concerning men killed by trapped animals.
312. On finding wounded animals.
313. On hiding found animals.
314. How long animals belong to the hunter.
315. On domesticated stags.
316. Concerning the trapping of someone else's stag.
317. On domesticated birds.
318. On bees.
319. On taking bees from a marked tree.

355. On plowing over someone else's seeded field.
356. On reaping someone else's meadow.
357. Concerning the man who fetters his animal in someone else's field.
358. No one shall deny fodder to those who are traveling.
359. On oaths.
360. On pledges and sureties.
361. Concerning the man who gives pledges.
362. Concerning the man who dies after naming oathhelpers and surety.
363. On broken oaths.
364. Concerning the man who confesses a crime.
365. Concerning the debts of a dead father.
366. On disputes between creditors and debtors.
367. On foreigners (*waregang*).
368. On duelling.
369. On royal cases.
370. Concerning slaves of the king who commit murder.
371. Concerning other cases involving the king's slaves.
372. Concerning slaves of the king who steal.
373. Concerning slaves of the king who violate a courtyard.
374. On the killing of a schultheis (sculdahis).
375. Concerning property acquired by the gastald (gastaldius).
376. Concerning him who tries to kill another's aldia or woman slave because she is a witch.
377. On striking out a freeman's one eye.
378. On free women who are involved in a breach of the peace (scandalum).
379. On destroying a hut on another man's land.
380. Concerning taking one's animals secretly from another man's enclosure.
381. Concerning the charge of cowardice.
382. On him who knocks down a freeman.
383. On him who drags a freeman by his beard or hair.
384. Concerning broken arms, thighs, or legs.
385. Concerning the guardianship (mundium) and debts of a girl.
386. Concerning the present laws.

387. On him who accidentally kills a freeman.
388. We decree these things.

[HERE BEGIN THE LAWS]

[*On him who plots against the life of the king.*]
  1. That man who conspires or gives counsel against the life of the king shall be killed and his property confiscated.

[*On him who takes counsel with the king regarding the death of another.*]
  2. He who receives counsel from the king concerning another's death or kills a man by the king's order, shall be entirely without blame. Neither he nor his heirs shall suffer any payment or trouble at any time from that one [the man conspired against] or his heirs. For since we believe that the heart of the king is in the hand of God, it is inconceivable that anyone whose death the king has ordered could be entirely free of guilt.

[*On him who attempts to flee outside the province.*]
  3. He who tries to flee outside of the country shall be killed and his property confiscated.

[*On him who invites enemies within the province.*]
  4. He who invites or introduces enemies into our land shall be killed and his property confiscated.

[*On him who hides a spy.*]
  5. He who hides a spy (*scamaras*) within the land or gives him provisions shall either be killed or shall pay 900 solidi as composition to the king.[2]

[*On him who raises a revolt in the army.*]
  6. That one who while on campaign raises a revolt against his duke or against him appointed by the king to command the army, or that one who raises a revolt in any part of the army, shall be killed.

[*On him who abandons his colleague during a battle.*]
  7. He who during a battle with the enemy abandons his com-

rade or makes him *astalin*, that is, betrays him and does not remain with him, shall be killed.

[*On him who commits a breach of the peace (scandalum) in the assembly.*]

8. He who creates a disturbance (scandalum)[3] in the council or other assembly shall pay 900 solidi as composition to the king.

[*On him who accuses a man before the king.*]

9. If in the presence of the king one man accuses another of an offense which would involve the loss of his life, then the accused may offer satisfactory oath and clear himself. If in such a case the man [accused] is present together with him who accused him of the offense, then the accused may refute the charge, if he can, by means of the *camfio*,[4] that is, by judicial duel. If the accusation is proved against him, he shall lose his life or pay such an amount as composition as pleases the king. If the charge is not proved against him, and it is recognized that he has been accused wrongfully, then he who accused him and was not able to prove it shall pay the amount of his wergeld[5] as composition, half to the king and half to him charged with the offense.

[*Concerning the freeman who plots against the life of another man.*]

10. If any freeman plots against another man's life and that one does not die as a result, then the plotter shall pay twenty solidi as composition.

[*On plots involving death.*]

11. On plots involving death. If freemen without the king's consent plot another man's death, but that one does not die as a result of the agreement, then each of them shall pay twenty solidi as composition, as stated above [Rothair 10]. But if that one [conspired against] dies as a result of the plot, then the doer of the deed shall pay the victim's wergeld, according as he is valued, as composition.

[*Concerning several men who kill someone.*]

12. If two or three or more freemen commit a homicide together, and wish to associate themselves so that as one they may

pay composition for that one [the man killed] according as he is valued, such an agreement is permitted to them. If one of them separates himself from the others and is not able to clear himself as the law provides, namely, [he is not able to prove] that he inflicted none of the blows against that man who was killed, then he is as guilty as the others who paid the composition. If he does clear himself, however, he shall be free of blame in connection with the homicide. If [he is accused of being] in the counsel [of the conspirators], he shall pay twenty solidi as composition, as stated above [Rothair 10], unless he can clear himself of involvement in the conspiracy.

[*Concerning him who kills his lord.*]

13. He who kills his lord (*dominus*), shall be killed himself. The man who tries to defend this murderer who killed his lord shall pay 900 solidi as composition, half to the king and half to the relatives of the dead man. And he who refuses aid in avenging the man's death, if his aid is sought, shall pay fifty solidi as composition, half to the king and half to the man to whom he refused aid.

[*On murder.*]

14. On murder (*morth*).[6] If anyone secretly kills a freeman or a man or woman slave, if one or two persons commit the homicide, he or they shall pay 900 solidi as composition.[7] If more than two were involved, each shall pay the wergeld of the man killed, if he was a native-born freeman, according to his rank (*in angargathungi*). If it was a slave or freedman who was killed, each shall pay composition according to his value. If they plunder the dead body, that is, if they commit *plodraub*, each shall pay eighty solidi as composition for this.

[*Concerning him who violates a sepulchre.*]

15. On grave breaking (*crapworfin*).[8] He who breaks into the grave of a dead man and despoils the body and throws it out shall pay 900 solidi to the relatives of the dead. And if there are no near relatives, then the king's gastald[9] or schultheis[10] shall exact this penalty and collect it for the king's court.

[*On him who finds a man's corpse in a river.*]

16. On despoiling the dead (*rairaub*). He who finds a human corpse in a river or beside it and despoils the body and hides it shall

pay eighty solidi as composition to the relatives of the dead man. If he found and stripped the body, however, and immediately after made it known to those in the vicinity that he did it for the sake of reward and not for the purpose of robbery, then he shall return those things which he had found on the body and no further guilt shall be imputed to him.

[*On him who is making his way to the king.*]

17. If one of our men wishes to come to us, let him come in safety and return to his home unharmed; let none of his enemies presume to cause any injury or harm to him on the journey. It shall be done thus in order that he who hastens to come to the king may come openly and receive no injury or damage of any sort on that journey while coming to the king and returning. He who does cause such injury shall pay compensation as is provided below in this code [Rothair 148].

[*On him who, armed, throws himself upon someone who is making his way to the king.*]

18. He who, in order to avenge some injury or damage, attacks with arms one of his enemies who is on his way to the king, shall pay 900 solidi, half to the king and half to him who bore the injury.

[*On him who enters a village with an armed following.*]

19. He who falls upon another with armed hand in order to vindicate some injury, or who leads an armed band containing up to four men into a village, shall die for his unlawful presumption or shall at least pay 900 solidi as composition, half to the king and half to him who was wronged. Each of those with him, if freemen, shall pay eighty solidi as composition, half to the king and half to him who was wronged. And, in addition, if they have burned houses in that village or killed any man there, then they shall pay composition, according as the damage is assessed, to him whose houses were burned or whose relative or slave was killed.

[*On him who holds his duke in contempt.*]

20. If any soldier refuses to go to his duke for justice, he shall pay twenty solidi as composition to the king and to his duke.[11]

[*On him who refuses to go out with the army.*]

21. Anyone who refuses to go out with the army or with the

guard shall pay twenty solidi as composition to the king and to his duke.

[*On him who refuses to aid his duke in the accomplishment of justice.*]

22. Any soldier who refuses aid to his duke when that one is pursuing justice, shall pay twenty solidi as composition to the king and to the duke.

[*Concerning the duke who mistreats one of his men.*]

23. If a duke treats his men unjustly, the gastald shall aid the injured man. The gastald shall find out the truth and bring [the case] to justice in the presence of the king or at least before the duke.

[*Concerning the gastald who mistreats one of his men.*]

24. If any gastald treats his man contrary to reason, then the duke shall aid the injured man and find out the truth.

[*On him who seeks back his property from someone else.*]

25. If anyone attempts to obtain his property from another soldier, and that one does not return it to him, then he shall go to his duke. And if the duke or the judge appointed for that place by the king will not serve him with truth and justice, then he [the duke or judge] shall pay twenty solidi as composition to the king and to him who brought the case, and the case shall continue.

[*On him who blocks the way to a free woman or girl.*]

26. On road-blocking (*wegworin*),[12] that is *orbitaria*. Anyone who places himself in the road before a free woman or girl, or inflicts some injury upon her, shall pay 900 solidi as composition, half to the king and half to her who suffered the injury or to him who is her legal guardian [who holds her mundium].[13]

[*On him who blocks the way to a freeman.*]

27. Anyone who blocks the road to a freeman shall pay him twenty solidi as composition, provided no physical injury was caused. But he who causes injury shall pay twenty solidi as composition to him before whom the road was blocked and he shall also pay compensation for any wounds or injuries that he inflicted according to the schedule provided below [Rothair 43–128].

[*On him who blocks the way to a man or woman slave.*]

28. Anyone who blocks the road to another's man or woman

slave or to his *aldius* or freedman shall pay twenty solidi as composition to that one's lord.

[*On him who blocks a field or meadow or any enclosure to another man.*]

29. He who in defense closes his field or meadow or other enclosure to any man by placing himself so that it cannot be entered is not guilty as is that one who blocks the road to a man simply walking along, because [in this particular case] he is protecting his own property.

[*On him who throws a freeman from his horse.*]

30. On throwing someone from his horse (*marahworfin*).[14] He who intentionally throws a freeman from his horse to the ground by any means shall pay the aggrieved party eighty solidi as composition. And if he causes that one some injury, he shall in addition pay composition for the injuries as is provided in this code [Rothair 43–128].

[*On him who in disguise does violence to a freeman (i.e., concerning the* walopaus).]

31. Concerning him who in disguise does violence (the walopaus).[15] He who unjustly does violence to a freeman as a walopaus shall pay the injured party eighty solidi as composition. A walopaus is one who secretly puts on another's clothing or disguises his head or face.

[*Concerning the freeman who has been found at night in another man's courtyard.*]

32. If a freeman is found in someone else's courtyard at night and does not willingly give his hands to be bound, he may be killed and no compensation may be sought by his relatives. But if he gives his hands to be bound and they have been bound, he still must pay eighty solidi for himself, because it is not consistent with reason that a man should silently or secretly enter someone else's courtyard at night; if he has some useful purpose, he should call out before he enters.[16]

[*Concerning the slave who has been found at night in another man's courtyard.*]

33. If a slave is found at night in someone else's courtyard and

does not give his hands [to be bound], he may be killed and no compensation may be sought by his lord. But if the slave holds out his hands and they have been bound, he may free himself [i.e., his lord may free him] with a payment of forty solidi.

[*On him who in anger shoots an arrow into another man's courtyard.*]

34. That one who in anger shoots an arrow or hurls a lance into another's courtyard from outside of the wall and wounds someone within the yard shall pay twenty solidi as composition. In addition, he must pay composition for any wounds or injuries inflicted as provided in this code [Rothair 43–128].

[*On him who breaks the peace (commits scandalum) in a church.*]

35. On breach of the peace (scandalum). He who creates a disturbance (scandalum) in a church shall pay forty solidi to that venerable place in addition to [the composition paid] him who suffered the wounds or injuries. The abovementioned forty solidi shall be collected by the schultheis or judge of the district and laid on the holy altar of that church where the offense occurred.

[*On him who breaks the peace (commits scandalum) in the palace when the king is present.*]

36. He who dares to create a disturbance (scandalum) within the king's palace when the king is present shall lose his life unless he can redeem his life from the king.

[*Concerning the freeman who breaks the peace (commits scandalum) in a district* (civitas) *where the king is present.*]

37. The freeman who creates a disturbance in that district (civitas)[17] where the king is present, although he does not strike a blow, shall pay twelve solidi to the king's palace [i.e., the royal fisc]. But he who raises a disturbance and also strikes a blow, shall pay twenty-four solidi to the fisc.[18] In addition, he shall pay composition for any wounds or injuries which he caused as provided below [Rothair 43–128].

[*Concerning the slave who breaks the peace (commits scandalum) in a district* (civitas) *where the king is present.*]

38. The slave who creates a disturbance in a district where the

king is present, shall pay six solidi to the royal fisc. And if he also strikes a blow, then he shall pay twelve solidi to the fisc in addition to paying composition for the wounds or injuries as provided in this code.[19]

[*Concerning the freeman who breaks the peace (commits scandalum) in another district* (civitas).]

39. The freeman who dares to create a disturbance in another district [where the king is not present] but does not strike a blow shall pay six solidi to the royal fisc. That one who does, however, strike a blow shall pay twelve solidi to the fisc in addition to paying composition for the wounds or injuries that he inflicted as provided in this code [Rothair 43–128].

[*Concerning the slave who breaks the peace (commits scandalum) in another district* (civitas).]

40. The slave who creates a disturbance in another district [where the king is not present] shall pay three solidi to the royal fisc. That one, however, who inflicts wounds or injuries shall pay six solidi to the fisc in addition to paying composition for the wounds or injuries to him who suffered them.

[*On beating a freeman.*]

41. Concerning the beating of a freeman. If anyone, by himself or with the aid of someone else, plans an ambush against some freeman who is simply standing or walking along unprepared, and if they seize him disgracefully and beat him without the king's command, then, since they treated the man shamefully and with derision, they shall pay as composition half of the wergeld which they would have paid had they killed him.

[*On binding a freeman.*]

42. Concerning the binding of a freeman. He who binds a freeman without the king's command and without cause shall pay as composition an amount equal to two-thirds of the wergeld which would have been paid in case of the man's death.

[*On hitting a freeman.*]

43. Concerning the hitting and wounding of a freeman. He who, in the course of a sudden quarrel, strikes a freeman and causes him some injury or wound, shall pay to him three solidi as composi-

tion for one blow, six solidi for two blows, nine solidi for three blows, twelve solidi for four blows. If, however, more blows were suffered, the blows [in excess of four] are not to be counted and the injured man must be content.

[*On him who wounds another man in a fight.*]

44. He who hits another man with his fist shall pay him three solidi as composition. He who strikes another on the ear shall pay six solidi.

[*Concerning the composition for various injuries.*]

45. In the matter of composition for blows and injuries which are inflicted by one freeman on another freeman, composition is to be paid according to the procedure provided below and the blood-feud (faida[20]) shall cease.

[*On him who hits another man on the head.*]

46. He who hits another man on the head so that the skin which the hair covers is broken shall pay six solidi as composition. If he strikes two blows, he shall pay twelve solidi as composition. If there are three blows, he shall pay eighteen solidi. If there are more blows than this number, they are not to be counted but compensation shall be paid for three only.

[*On him who hits another man on the head so that the bones are broken.*]

47. He who hits another man on the head so that the bones are broken shall pay twelve solidi as composition if one bone is broken. He shall pay twenty-four solidi as composition if two bones were broken; thirty-six solidi for three. If there are more broken than this, they are not to be counted. And the one bone should be such that the sound it makes against a shield [can be heard] a distance of twelve feet away along the road; and this measure, indeed, should be taken by the foot of a medium-sized man, not by the hand.[21]

[*On gouging out eyes.*]

48. On gouging out eyes. In the case where someone gouges out another man's eye, composition shall be computed as if for death *angargathungi,* that is, according to the rank of the person: he who strikes out the eye shall pay half of the wergeld as composition.

[*On cutting off noses.*]

49. On cutting off noses. He who cuts off another man's nose shall pay half of that one's wergeld as composition.

[*On cutting off lips.*]

50. On cutting off lips. He who cuts off another man's lip shall pay sixteen solidi as composition. And if one, two or three teeth are thereby exposed, he shall pay twenty solidi as composition.

[*Concerning the front teeth.*]

51. Concerning the front teeth. He who knocks out another man's tooth—one of those which appear when smiling—shall pay sixteen solidi as composition for one tooth. If two or more of such teeth which appear in smiling are knocked out, the composition shall be computed according to this assessment for each one.

[*Concerning the molar teeth.*]

52. Concerning the jaw teeth. He who knocks out one or more molars shall pay eight solidi as composition for each tooth.

[*On cutting off ears.*]

53. On cutting off ears. He who cuts off another man's ear shall pay him a fourth part of his wergeld as composition.

[*Concerning facial injuries.*]

54. Concerning blows on the face. He who strikes and wounds another man's face shall pay him sixteen solidi as composition.

[*Concerning injuries to the nose.*]

55. Concerning blows on the nose. He who strikes and wounds another man's nose shall pay him sixteen solidi as composition provided [the nose] heals so that only a scar remains.

[*Concerning injuries to the ears.*]

56. Concerning blows on the ear. He who strikes and wounds another man's ear shall pay him sixteen solidi as composition if the ear heals.

[*Concerning arm wounds.*]

57. Concerning arm wounds. He who strikes another man on

the arm so that the arm is pierced shall pay sixteen solidi as composition.

[*Concerning injuries to the arm.*]
58. He who strikes another man on the arm so that it is not pierced shall pay him eight solidi as composition.

[*Concerning injuries to the chest.*]
59. He who strikes someone else on the chest [and inflicts a wound] shall pay him twenty solidi as composition.

[*On injuries to the hip.*]
60. Concerning blows on the hip. He who inflicts a wound on another man's hip in such a way that it is pierced shall pay sixteen solidi as composition. If, however, the hip is not pierced, he shall pay eight solidi as composition.

[*About the number of wounds.*]
61. On the number of blows. If it happens that there is more than one blow, they should be counted up to three, and for each of such blows, composition should be calculated as above. If there are more than three blows, no additional composition should be paid for them.

[*On cutting off hands.*]
62. Concerning cutting off hands. He who cuts off another man's hand shall pay the injured party as composition half of the wergeld at which he would have been valued if he had been killed. And if it appears that the hand has been paralyzed although not cut off from the body, then the perpetrator of the deed shall pay the injured party a fourth part of his wergeld as composition.

[*Concerning first fingers (thumbs) of the hand.*]
63. Concerning first fingers [thumbs]. He who cuts off the thumb from another man's hand shall pay that one as composition a sixth part of the wergeld at which he would have been valued if he had been killed.

[*Concerning second fingers.*]
64. Concerning second fingers. He who cuts off the index

finger from another man's hand shall pay sixteen solidi as composition.

[*Concerning third fingers.*]

65. Concerning third fingers. He who cuts off the middle finger from another man's hand shall pay five solidi as composition.

[*Concerning fourth fingers.*]

66. Concerning fourth fingers. He who cuts off another man's ring finger shall pay eight solidi as composition.

[*Concerning fifth fingers.*]

67. Concerning fifth fingers. He who cuts off another man's little finger shall pay sixteen solidi as composition.

[*On cutting off feet.*]

68. On cutting off feet. He who cuts off another man's foot shall pay half the wergeld of the injured party as composition. If the foot is crippled although not completely cut off, the doer of the deed shall pay the injured party a fourth part of his wergeld as composition.

[*Concerning big toes.*]

69. About big toes. He who cuts off another man's big toe shall pay him sixteen solidi as composition.

[*Concerning second toes.*]

70. About second toes. He who cuts off the second toe of another man's foot shall pay him six solidi as composition.

[*Concerning third toes.*]

71. He who cuts off a third toe of the foot shall pay three solidi as composition.

[*Concerning fourth toes.*]

72. He who cuts off a fourth toe shall pay three solidi.

[*Concerning fifth (little) toes.*]

73. He who cuts off a fifth toe of the foot shall pay two solidi as composition.

[*Concerning all these wounds and injuries.*]

74. In the case of all wounds and injuries mentioned above, involving freemen as they do, we have set a higher composition than

did our predecessors in order that the faida, that is the blood feud, may be averted after receipt of the abovementioned composition, and in order that more shall not be demanded and a grudge shall not be held.[22] So let the case be concluded and friendship remain between the parties. And if it happens that he who was struck dies from the blows within a year, then the one who struck the blow shall pay composition according to the quality of the person (angargathungi).

[*On the death of a child in its mother's womb.*]

75. Concerning the death of a child in its mother's womb. If a child is accidentally killed while still in its mother's womb, and if the woman is free and lives, then her value shall be measured in accordance with her rank, and composition for the child shall be paid at half the sum at which the mother is valued. But if the mother dies, then composition must be paid for her according to her rank[23] in addition to the payment of composition for the child killed in her womb. But thereafter the feud shall cease since the deed was done unintentionally.

[*On the half-free (aldii) and household slaves (servi ministeriales).*]

76. Concerning the half-free (aldii)[24] and the household slaves (servi ministeriales).[25] We call those "household slaves" who have been taught, nourished, and trained in the home.

[*On injuries to aldii or household slaves.*]

77. He who strikes another's aldius or household slave so that the wound or bruise is apparent shall pay one solidus as composition for one blow. He who strikes two blows shall pay two solidi. He who strikes three, three solidi. He who strikes four shall pay four solidi. If, however, more blows than this were endured, they shall not be counted.

[*On aldii or household slaves who have been beaten.*]

78. He who strikes another's aldius or household slave on the head so that the bones are not broken shall pay two solidi composition for one blow. He who strikes two blows shall pay four solidi; in addition he shall pay for the work lost and for the doctor's fee.[26] If, however, he inflicts more blows than this against the head, they shall not be counted.

[*On him who strikes an aldius or household slave upon the head.*]

79. He who strikes another's aldius or household slave on the head so that one or more bones are broken shall pay four solidi as composition, and in addition he shall pay for the work lost and for the doctor's fee.

[*Concerning injuries to the face.*]

80. Concerning blows on the face. He who strikes another's aldius or household slave on the face shall pay two solidi as composition.

[*On gouging out eyes.*]

81. On gouging out eyes. He who gouges out the eye of another's aldius or household slave shall pay half of the sum (pretium) at which he would have been valued had he been killed.[27]

[*On cutting off noses.*]

82. On cutting off noses. He who cuts off the nose of another's aldius or household slave shall pay eight solidi composition in addition to a payment for the work lost and for the doctor's fee.

[*On cutting off ears.*]

83. On cutting off ears. He who cuts off the ear of another's aldius or household slave shall pay two solidi composition in addition to a payment for the work lost and for the doctor's fee.

[*On cutting off lips.*]

84. On cutting off lips. He who cuts off the lip of another's aldius or household slave so that the teeth can be seen shall pay four solidi composition in addition to a payment for the work lost and for the doctor's fee.

[*On knocking out teeth.*]

85. On knocking out teeth. He who knocks out one or more of the teeth (those which appear in smiling) of another's aldius or household slave shall pay four solidi composition for one tooth. If several teeth were knocked out, moreover, composition shall be calculated in accordance with this amount.

[*Concerning molar teeth.*]

86. On molars. If anyone knocks out the molar teeth, he shall pay two solidi as composition for one molar; if he knocks out more than one, composition shall be reckoned in accordance with this sum.

[*Concerning broken arms.*]

87. On broken arms. He who breaks the arm of another's aldius or household slave shall pay six solidi composition in addition to a payment for the work lost and for the doctor's fee.

[*On cutting off hands.*]

88. On cutting off hands. He who cuts off the hand of another's aldius or household slave shall pay half of that one's value (pretium) as composition.

[*Concerning first fingers (thumbs) of the hand.*]

89. About first fingers [thumbs]. He who cuts off the thumb of another's aldius or household slave shall pay eight solidi as composition in addition to a payment for the work lost and for the doctor's fee.

[*Concerning second fingers.*]

90. He who cuts off the second finger of that one's hand shall pay six solidi as composition.

[*Concerning third fingers.*]

91. He who cuts off the third finger, that is the middle one, shall pay two solidi as composition.

[*Concerning fourth fingers.*]

92. He who cuts off the fourth finger shall pay two solidi as composition.

[*Concerning fifth fingers.*]

93. He who strikes off the fifth finger shall pay four solidi as composition.

[*On broken hips.*]

94. On broken hips. He who breaks the hip bone or shin bone

of another's aldius or household slave shall pay three solidi composition in addition to a payment for the work lost and for the doctor's fee.

[*On cutting off feet.*]

95. On cutting off feet. He who cuts off the foot of another's aldius or household slave shall pay half of that one's value (pretium) as composition.

[*Concerning first (big) toes.*]

96. About big toes. He who cuts off the big toe of another's aldius or household slave shall pay four solidi as composition in addition to a payment for the work lost and for the doctor's fee.

[*Concerning second toes.*]

97. He who cuts off the second toe of another's aldius or household slave shall pay two solidi as composition.

[*Concerning third toes.*]

98. He who cuts off a third toe shall pay two solidi as composition.

[*Concerning fourth toes.*]

99. He who cuts off a fourth toe shall pay one solidus as composition.

[*Concerning fifth toes.*]

100. He who cuts off a fifth toe shall pay one solidus as composition.

[*Concerning injuries to the chest.*]

101. About blows against the chest. He who wounds another's aldius or household slave in the chest, either piercing it with an arrow or striking a blow with any kind of weapon, shall pay six solidi as composition in addition to a payment for the work lost and for the doctor's fee.

[*On piercing arms and legs.*]

102. On puncturing arms and legs. He who punctures the arm or leg of another's aldius or household slave shall pay three solidi as composition in addition to a payment for the work lost and for the

doctor's fee. He who strikes [an arm or leg] but does not puncture it shall pay one solidus as composition.

[*Concerning field slaves (servi rusticani).*]

103. Concerning field slaves (servi rusticani).[28] He who strikes another man's field slave on the head so that the skin is broken shall pay one solidus for one blow, or two solidi for two blows, in addition to a payment for the work lost and for the doctor's fee. More blows shall not be counted. Moreover, he who breaks one or more bones shall pay three solidi as composition; more breaks will not be counted.

[*Concerning injuries to the face.*]

104. Concerning blows on the face. He who wounds another man's field slave on the face shall pay one solidus as composition.

[*On gouging out eyes.*]

105. On gouging out eyes. He who gouges out the eye of another man's field slave shall pay as composition to his lord half of the sum (pretium) at which that one would have been valued had he been killed.

[*On cutting off noses.*]

106. On cutting off noses. He who cuts off the nose of another man's field slave shall pay four solidi as composition in addition to a payment for the work lost and for the doctor's fee.

[*On cutting off ears.*]

107. On cutting off ears. He who cuts off the ear of another man's field slave shall pay two solidi as composition in addition to a payment for the work lost and for the doctor's fee.

[*On cutting off lips.*]

108. On cutting off lips. He who cuts off the lip of another man's field slave so that the teeth are exposed shall pay three solidi as composition.

[*Concerning teeth.*]

109. About teeth. He who knocks out a tooth (one of those which appear in smiling) of another man's field slave shall pay two solidi as composition for one such tooth, and one solidus for a

molar. Moreover, he who knocks out more teeth shall pay a composition calculated from the amount for one tooth.

[*On piercing arms and legs.*]
110. On puncturing arms and legs. He who punctures the arm or leg of another man's field slave shall pay two solidi as composition. However, he who strikes the blow but does not puncture the limb shall pay one solidus as composition in addition to a payment for the work lost and for the doctor's fee.

[*Concerning injuries to the chest.*]
111. On blows against the chest. He who wounds another man's field slave in the chest shall pay three solidi as composition in addition to a payment for the work lost and for the doctor's fee.

[*On breaking arms, hips, or legs.*]
112. On breaking arms, hips, or legs. He who breaks the arm, hip, or leg of another man's field slave shall pay three solidi as composition in addition to a payment for the work lost and for the doctor's fee. And if the break has not healed within a year and the slave has not been restored to health, then he who broke the bone shall pay as composition to his lord a fourth part of the sum at which the slave is valued.

[*On cutting off hands.*]
113. On cutting off hands. He who cuts off the hand of another man's field slave shall pay half of his value as composition to his lord.

[*Concerning first fingers (thumbs).*]
114. About first fingers [thumbs]. He who cuts off the thumb of another man's field slave shall pay four solidi as composition.

[*Concerning second fingers.*]
115. He who cuts off the second finger shall pay three solidi as composition.

[*Concerning third fingers.*]
116. He who cuts off the third finger shall pay one solidus as composition.

[*Concerning fourth fingers.*]
117. He who cuts off the fourth finger shall pay one solidus as composition.

[*Concerning fifth fingers.*]

118. He who cuts off the fifth finger shall pay two solidi as composition in addition to a payment for the work lost and for the doctor's fee.

[*On cutting off a field slave's feet.*]

119. On cutting off a field slave's feet. He who cuts off the foot of another man's field slave shall pay half of that one's value as composition.

[*Concerning first (big) toes.*]

120. About big toes. He who cuts off the big toe of another man's field slave shall pay two solidi as composition.

[*Concerning second toes.*]

121. He who cuts off a second toe shall pay one solidus as composition.

[*Concerning third toes.*]

122. He who cuts off a third toe shall pay one solidus as composition.

[*Concerning fourth toes.*]

123. He who cuts off a fourth toe shall pay half a solidus as composition.

[*Concerning fifth toes.*].

124. He who cuts off a fifth toe shall pay half a solidus as composition.

[*On beating field slaves.*]

125. On beating field slaves. He who strikes another man's field slave one blow (which is *pulslahi*[29]) shall pay half a solidus as composition if the wound or bruise is apparent. If he strikes up to four blows, he shall pay up to two solidi as composition. More than four blows shall not be counted.

[*On crippling limbs.*]

126. On crippling limbs. If in the case of the abovementioned blows and injuries suffered by aldii or household slaves or field slaves or aldiae or female slaves, the hand or foot or limb which was struck or hit is crippled although not entirely cut off, then composition shall be paid in the same manner as if it had been entirely cut off.

[*Concerning wounds and injuries inflicted on aldii and field slaves.*]

127. All blows and injuries which occur among the aldii as well as household slaves or field slaves and aldiae or female slaves shall be settled by the procedure outlined above. If, however, there is any doubt that they may recover or be healed quickly, then the lord shall receive half of the assessed price of the blow. Payment of the remaining half shall be suspended until it is known whether the servant will recover from his injuries within one year. If he dies from the blows within a year, composition shall be paid to his lord as is provided below [Rothair 129–37], and the amount which had already been received for the blow shall be reckoned as part of the composition for the dead man.

[*He who struck the blow shall seek the doctor.*]

128. Concerning him who struck the blow. He who struck the blow should seek the doctor; if he has neglected to do this, the man struck or his lord should find the doctor. And he who broke the head or struck the abovementioned blows shall pay for the work lost and an amount for the doctor's fee as adjudged by learned men.

[*On killing aldii.*]

129. On killing aldii. He who kills an aldius shall pay sixty solidi as composition.

[*On killing household slaves.*]

130. On killing household slaves. He who kills another's household slave—one who has been trained or taught as above—shall pay fifty solidi as composition.

[*Concerning the household slave who is an understudy.*]

131. In the case of another household servant who is found to be subordinate to him [i.e., to the household slave (servus ministerialis) mentioned in the preceding law] but is nevertheless called a *ministerialis*: whoever kills such a one shall pay twenty-five solidi as composition.

[*On killing tenant slaves* (servi massarii).]

132. On killing tenant slaves (servi massarii).[30] Whoever kills another's tenant slave shall pay twenty solidi as composition.

[*On the killing of ox plowmen.*]

133. On killing ox plowmen (*bovulci*). Whoever kills another man's slave ox plowman, one with his own house,[31] shall pay twenty solidi as composition.

[*On the killing of a field slave subordinate to the tenant slave* (massarius).]

134. Concerning the field slave who is under a tenant slave (massarius). Whoever kills another man's field slave who is under a tenant slave shall pay sixteen solidi as composition.

[*On killing herders.*]

135. On killing herders. He who kills another man's swineherd —one who is a master (*magister*) and who has two or three or more learners (*discipuli*) under him—shall pay fifty solidi as composition. He who kills a less important swineherd shall pay twenty-five solidi as composition.

[*On killing cattleherds, goatherds, or oxherds.*]

136. Whoever kills a cattleherd, goatherd, or oxherd who is a master shall pay twenty solidi as composition. Moreover, he who kills one of the learners who are following [such a master] shall pay sixteen solidi as composition. We speak here of those herders who serve freemen and who have their own houses.

[*On killing the child of a tenant slave.*]

137. On killing the small child of a chief field slave. He who accidentally kills the small child of a tenant slave (massarius) or of another slave shall have it decided by the judge according to the child's age or according to whatever profit he was able to produce: and thus composition is to be paid.

[*Concerning the case of a man killed by a tree cut down by several men.*]

138. Concerning the case of a man killed by a tree cut down by several men. If two or more men cut down a tree, and another man coming along is killed by that tree or it causes some damage, then those who were cutting the tree, however many they were, shall pay composition equally for the homicide or for the damage. In the case where one of those cutting the tree is killed by the tree, then, if there were two colleagues, half of the wergeld shall be assessed to the dead

man and the other half shall be paid by his colleague to the relatives [of the dead man]. And if there were more than two men involved, an equal portion shall likewise be assessed to the dead man and to those who still live: each shall pay an equal share of the total wergeld, the feud ceasing since it happened without design.

[*On the use of poison.*]

139. On the use of poison. The freeman or free woman who mixes poison intending to give it to someone to drink shall pay twenty solidi as composition, just as in the case of him who plots the death of someone else.

[*Concerning the freeman or free woman who administers poison.*]

140. If a freeman or free woman gives another poison in his drink but that one does not die, he who gave the poison shall pay as composition a sum equal to half the wergeld at which that one would have been valued had he been killed.

[*Concerning the use of poison.*]

141. Whoever gives another poison in his drink and that one dies shall pay as composition a sum equal to the full wergeld of the dead man in accordance with his rank.

[*Concerning the man or woman slave who administers poison.*]

142. If a man or woman slave gives someone poison and that one does not die, then the slave's lord shall pay as composition a sum equal to half of the wergeld at which he who got the poison is valued. And in every case, the value of the man or woman slave shall be counted in the amount of the composition and the slave shall be killed. And if the one who received the poison dies, then the slave's lord shall pay the full wergeld as composition. The value of the slave shall, however, be counted in the amount of the composition, and he or she shall thereafter be killed. And there shall be no redemption or pardon from death for the slave.

[*Concerning the man who seeks revenge after accepting composition.*]

143. Concerning the man who seeks revenge after accepting composition. If a freeman or slave is killed and composition paid for

the homicide and oaths offered to avert the feud, and afterwards he who received the composition tries to avenge himself by killing a man belonging to the associates from whom he received the payment, we order that he repay the composition twofold to the relatives of the freeman or to the slave's lord. In like manner concerning him who tries to avenge himself after accepting compensation for blows or injuries, he shall restore that which he accepted in double amount. In addition, he shall pay composition, as provided above, if he has killed the man.

[Concerning the master builders from Como (magistri comacini).]

144. Concerning the master builders from Como (magistri comacini).[32] If it happens that someone is killed by some material or by a stone falling from a house being constructed or restored, according to an agreed contract, by a master builder with his helpers, the man to whom the house belongs shall not be required to pay compensation but the master builder (magister comacinus) and his helpers shall pay composition for the homicide or for the damage. Since, according to the accepted agreement, the master is to be well paid, he not undeservedly should be responsible for damages.

[On the hiring of master builders from Como.]

145. Concerning the hiring of master builders. If anyone seeks out and hires one or more master builders from Como (magistri comacini) to work by the day alongside his own slaves in the making of a house or home for himself, and if it happens by some chance that one of the [hired] builders is killed in connection with [the building of] that house, no compensation shall be required from him whose house it is. But if a piece of wood or stone falls from the building and kills some stranger or causes him injury, liability shall not rest upon the builders but he who hired them shall be responsible for the damages.

[On arson.]

146. On arson. He who deliberately and with evil intent burns another man's house shall pay as composition a sum three times the value of the house and all its contents. Let restoration be made according to the value of the burned house and its contents as determined by men of good faith from the vicinity. And if any controversy

arises over what was burned up inside the house, the man who suffered the loss shall state under oath what it was he lost: all these things shall be restored threefold by him who deliberately committed this evil deed.

[*Concerning the brand of fire which has been carried farther than nine feet.*]

147. Concerning a brand of fire carried more than nine feet from the hearth. He who carries a brand of fire more than nine feet from his hearth and thereby causes some damage to his own or to another man's property shall render compensation singlefold (*ferquido*),[33] that is, he shall pay the value of the damage alone as compensation since he did it unintentionally. If the damage occurs to himself or to someone else within nine feet from the hearth, he shall not be liable for compensation.

[*Concerning the fire made beside the road.*]

148. He who makes a fire beside the road should extinguish it before he goes away and not leave it negligently. If, after his departure, someone sustains damage or injury from that fire, he who made it and left it negligently shall pay the amount of the damage which has been adjudged to have been sustained as composition. And this [liability] is to be reckoned from that hour when the fire was left up to the same hour of the next day or night, that is, for twenty-four hours. But if it happens that the fire crosses over an open road or a stream and causes damage, no compensation shall be required from him who left the fire.

[*On burning a mill.*]

149. On burning a mill. He who deliberately and with evil intent burns another man's mill shall pay as composition a sum equal to three times the value of the property and its contents.

[*On destroying a mill.*]

150. Concerning destruction of a mill. He who destroys another man's mill or breaks his dam without the authorization of a judge shall pay the owner of the mill twelve solidi as composition. If he had appealed to the judge and the judge delayed in deliberating the case or gave permission to the wrong party to overturn the mill then he [the judge] shall pay twenty solidi composition to the king's

fisc, having been compelled to do so by one of the royal officials (the *stolesazo*).[34]

[*On building a mill on someone else's property.*]

151. He who builds a mill on someone else's land and cannot prove it his own shall lose the mill and all his work, and that one shall have it whose land or river bank it is; for everyone must know that that which belongs to another man is not his own.

[*On the death of a borrowed or hired worker.*]

152. Concerning the death at work of a hired laborer. If anyone seeks out and hires workmen and it happens by chance that one of them drowns or is struck by lightning or is killed by a tree blown down by the wind, or dies a natural death, the man who sought out and hired the laborer shall not be liable for damages because the workman did not die by the action of the man who hired him or by his men. If one of the workmen is killed or injured by someone, however, then he who was responsible for the death or injury shall pay composition.

LAWS REGARDING LEGITIMATE CHILDREN[35]

[*Concerning degrees of relationship.*]

153. On degrees of relationship. All relationship should be counted to the seventh degree when determining what relative or heir should succeed through kinship and degree. And he who desires the succession must be able to give the names of all his related ancestors. If the litigation should be brought before a royal court, he who seeks the inheritance may offer oath with his legitimate oathhelpers[36] to this effect: the deceased is our kinsman and we are related to him in the following manner.

[*On legitimate and natural sons.*]

154. On legitimate and natural sons. If anyone leaves a legitimate son who is *fulborn*, and one or more natural sons, the legitimate son shall take two-thirds of the property of the father, the natural son(s) one-third. If there are two legitimate sons, the natural sons shall have a fifth part of the inheritance no matter how many natural sons there may be. If there are three legitimate sons, the natural sons shall have a seventh part. If there are five legitimate sons, the natural

sons shall have an eleventh part. If there are six legitimate sons, the natural sons shall have a thirteenth part. If there are seven legitimate sons, the natural sons shall have a fifteenth part. If there are more legitimate sons than this, moreover, the substance of the father shall be further divided in accordance with this arrangement.

[*No one may give his natural sons the same status as his legitimate sons.*]

155. No one may raise his natural sons to the same status as his legitimate sons unless the legitimate sons, after reaching legal age, give their consent to their father. Sons reach legal age when they are twelve years old.

[*Concerning natural sons whose mothers are the slaves of someone else.*]

156. In the case of a natural son who is born to another man's woman slave, if the father purchases him and gives him his freedom by the formal procedure (*thingaverit*),[37] he shall remain free. But if the father does not free him, the natural son shall be a slave to him to whom the mother slave belongs. But if the father purchases the son and legally transfers ("things") to him any property, he shall have that property.

[*Concerning the child of a natural son.*]

157. If a child is the son of a natural son, that is, of a *threus*,[38] he shall not be heir to anything unless it is legally transferred ("thinged") to him. If nothing has been legally given to him, nevertheless he shall remain free.

[*On the survival of a legitimate daughter and a natural son.*]

158. If anyone leaves one legitimate daughter and one or more natural sons and other near relatives or heirs, the substance of the dead man shall be divided equally into three parts: the legitimate daughter is to receive four-twelfths, that is, a third part; the natural sons four-twelfths, that is, a third part; and the near relatives or heirs four-twelfths, that is, a third part. If there are no near relatives, then the king's fisc shall receive their four-twelfths.

[*On the survival of legitimate daughters and natural sons.*]

159. If anyone leaves two or more legitimate daughters and

one or more natural sons and other near relatives as above, the daughters are to receive six-twelfths, that is, one-half; the natural sons four-twelfths, that is, one-third; and the legitimate relatives two-twelfths, that is, one-sixth. If there are no near relatives, the king's fisc shall receive that two-twelfths.

[*On the survival of legitimate daughters, legitimate sisters, and natural sons.*]

160. If anyone leaves one or more legitimate daughters and one or more legitimate sisters and one or more natural sons, the daughters and sisters shall share equally among themselves six-twelfths of the property, that is, one-half; the natural sons shall receive four-twelfths, that is, one-third; and the legitimate relatives—or the king's fisc if there are no legitimate relatives—shall receive two-twelfths, that is, one-sixth. Moreover, with regard to the guardianship (mundium)[39] of the abovementioned women, the natural sons shall receive one part and the legitimate heirs or the king's fisc two parts.

[*On the disposition of the sisters' guardianship (mundium) between legitimate and natural sons.*]

161. On division of the right of guardianship (mundium) between legitimate and natural sons. If a man leaves legitimate and natural sons as well as legitimate and natural sisters, the legitimate sons shall receive two-thirds of the sisters' mund and the natural sons one-third.

[*On the death of a natural son.*]

162. If a man leaves legitimate sons and two or more natural sons, and if it happens that one of the natural sons is killed, then the legitimate brothers shall receive two-thirds of the composition for the one killed and the natural brothers shall receive the remaining one-third. Furthermore, the property of the dead man shall revert to the legitimate brothers, but not to the natural sons. We order this in order to postpone the faida, that is, to avert the blood feud.[40]

[*Concerning the man who plots a relative's death.*]

163. If anyone plots the death of a relative, that is, if a brother plots or advises in the death of his brother or [a nephew] in the death of his uncle (the uncle on his father's side), or [a cousin in the death] of his cousin, and that one plotted against does not leave sons,

[the plotter] may not be an heir of him against whose life he conspired but the other near relatives shall succeed. And if [the murdered man] does not have other near relatives or legitimate sons, then the king's fisc shall succeed. Moreover, with respect to the life of this murderer it shall be in the power of the king to judge as he chooses. The near and legitimate relatives shall have any property which the murderer leaves, or, if there are no such relatives, that property shall be added to the property of the king's fisc.

[*Concerning the man who accuses his nephew of being born* in *adultery.*]

164. Concerning the man who charges that his nephew was born in adultery. If any of the relatives—the *barbas*, who is the paternal uncle, or any of the [other] near relatives—maliciously claims that his nephew or other relative was born as the result of an adulterous union and is not the child of his claimed father, then he who is so accused shall call forth his free oathhelpers and offer oath that he is a legitimate son and therefore his property belongs to him legally and should not pass to the other [the accuser] by law. If he can do this, he shall have and enjoy his property because it would be grave and unjust that such a cause should be settled by a duel between the two men.[41]

[*Concerning the man who claims the guardianship (mundium) of another man's wife.*]

165. If anyone says regarding another man's wife that the right to her mundium (guardianship) belongs to him and not to her husband, then he who has her as a wife shall offer oath with his twelve legal oathhelpers to the effect that he had legally acquired the mundium of that woman from its former possessor and it ought not to belong to the other. If he is able to do this, he shall have and enjoy her mundium. For it seems to be unjust that such an important case should be settled by a duel between the two men.

[*Concerning the husband suspected of killing his wife.*]

166. Concerning the husband suspected of killing his wife. If it is suspected that a husband has killed his wife, we decree that the husband may clear himself with his legal oathhelpers by swearing that he was not involved in the death of that woman, either through

himself or through any personal substitute; and then he shall be absolved of this crime. For it seems to be unreasonable and absurd that such a case should be settled by a duel between two men.

[*On brothers who remain in the common house.*]

167. Concerning brothers who remain in the common house. If brothers remain in the common house after the death of their father and one of them while a personal follower of the king or of a judge acquires some property, that property shall be his henceforth without dividing with his brothers. But he who acquires something while on campaign with the army shall hold it in common with the brothers who are left in the common house. If anyone makes a formal gift (gairethinx) to one of the abovementioned brothers, he to whom it was given shall have it henceforth [without sharing it with the other brothers].

If one of the brothers takes a wife and gives her a marriage portion (meta)[42] from the common property, then when another of the brothers also takes a wife, or when [the common property] is divided, something shall be given to him [or the other brothers] in the same quantity as that which the [first] brother took for his wife's marriage portion. Moreover, with regard to the paternal or maternal property which has been left, they shall divide it equally among themselves.

[*On the disinheritance of sons.*]

168. On disinheritance of sons. A man may not legally disinherit his son without proper reason, nor may he legally transfer to another that which ought legally to go to the son.

[*On just causes for disinheriting a son.*]

169. On just causes for disinheriting a son. We decree that these are just causes for disinheriting a son: when a son plots or advises against the life or family ["blood"] of his father, when he strikes his father deliberately, or when he sins with his stepmother, that is, with his *noverca*. [If a son does any of these things] he may justly be disinherited by his father.

[*A son may not legally alienate his property while his father is still alive.*]

170. Likewise, just as it is not lawful for a father to disinherit

his son without just cause or reason, so it is not lawful for a son to give away or alienate his property by any means while his father is alive, unless the son leaves legitimate sons or daughters or natural sons for whom he may provide according to law.

[*Concerning the man who despairs of his life because of illness.*]
171. If anyone, either because of age or other infirmity, despairs of ever having children and therefore transfers his property to someone else, and if afterwards it happens that he begets legitimate children, then the whole *thinx*,[43] that is the gift which was made before the children were born, is broken and the one or more legitimate sons who were born afterwards shall be the heirs of their father in all things. If, moreover, there were one or more legitimate daughters or one or more natural sons born after the gift had been made, they shall have their rights, just as provided above, as if nothing had been given to anyone else. And he who was given the property shall have only such an amount as the near relatives or the king's fisc would have received if the property had not been transferred.

[*On the transfer of title* (thinx), *which is a gift.*]
172. On the transfer (thinx) which is a gift. If anyone wants to give his property to another, he should not make the gift (gairethinx) secretly but in the presence of freemen. He who makes the gift and he who receives the gift (*gisel*)[44] should be freemen in order that no controversy may arise in the future.

[*Concerning the man who disposes of his property by legally giving it to someone else.*]
173. If anyone gives his property to someone else and says that this gift will become the latter's inheritance (*lidinlaib*),[45] that is, the giver says he will leave the property to the other man on the day of his death: afterwards the donor may not maliciously dispose of that property but he should enjoy it reasonably. If it becomes necessary that [the donor] must sell his land with or without its bondsmen or that he must offer it as a pledge, then he ought first to say to him to whom he had promised the property: "Behold you see that I, compelled by necessity, must give up these things. If it seems fitting to you, help me and thus preserve this property for yourself." Then if he [the receiver of the *thinx*] does not want to help, those things which

[the owner] thereafter transfers to another [because of necessity] shall be firmly and incontestably his who received them [as a purchase or a pledge].

[No one may transfer to another man that gift (thinx) which he first offered to someone else.]

174. On gifts previously made. It is illegal for a donor to transfer to one man that gift (thinx) which he had earlier given to another, provided that he who had received the gift has not done such blameworthy things to his donor as some ungrateful sons are known to have done to their parents, and for which they may be disinherited, as is written in this code [Rothair 169]. Whatever the donor leaves on the day of his death, he who received the gift shall claim as his right: and he shall pay the donor's debts to his creditors and collect [from his debtors]. And that which the donor had placed in trust as a pledge may be reclaimed from trust by the receiver of the gift when he repays the debt.

[Concerning reciprocal gifts (launigild).]

175. On reciprocal gifts (*launigild*).[46] If a man gives his property to someone else and afterwards he who made the gift seeks a reciprocal gift (launigild) in return, then he who received [the gift] or his heirs—if he cannot swear that [a return gift] had been provided—shall return [the gift] singlefold (ferquido), that is, in the same amount as it was on the day it was given. But if he does so swear, he shall be absolved.

[Concerning lepers.]

176. On lepers. If anyone is afflicted with leprosy and the truth of the matter is recognized by the judge or by the people and the leper is expelled from the district (civitas) or from his house so that he lives alone, he shall not have the right to alienate his property or give it to anyone. Because on the day that he is expelled from his home, it is as if he had died. Nevertheless, while he lives he should be nourished on the income from that which remains.

[On the movement of freemen and their families.]

177. Concerning freemen who are allowed to move. Any freeman, together with his family (*fara*),[47] has the right to go wherever he wishes within our kingdom provided that this privilege has been

given to him by the king. If a duke or any other freeman gives him some property and the recipient does not wish to remain with him [the duke or other freeman] or his heirs, the property shall revert to the donor or to his heirs.[48]

[*Concerning betrothal and marriage.*]

178. On betrothal and marriage. If anyone betroths a free girl or woman and, after the betrothal has been made and the agreement signed [Rothair 362], the husband neglects to claim his betrothed for two years and delays in carrying out the nuptials: after the two-year period has passed, the father or brother or whoever has the woman's guardianship may require that the [groom's] surety[49] complete that marriage portion (meta) which had been promised on the day of the betrothal. After this the woman's relatives may give her to another husband, provided he is a freeman. And the marriage portion which had been [demanded and] paid shall be in the control of the girl or woman because the betrothed man neglected to take her to wife within the prescribed period of time, or delayed deliberately, except for some unavoidable cause.

[*Concerning the husband who charges his wife with adultery.*]

179. If a man accuses his betrothed of committing adultery after the betrothal, her relatives may legally clear her with the support of their twelve oathhelpers. After she has been cleared, the man shall receive his betrothed as was first provided in the betrothal agreement. But if, after she has been cleared, he fails to take her to wife, the betrothed man shall be liable to pay a double portion, that is, double the amount which was agreed upon when the betrothal was made. If the relatives cannot clear her of this crime in the manner mentioned, then the betrothed man shall receive back those things which he gave and she shall suffer the punishment for adultery provided in this code [Rothair 211–13].

[*Concerning the girl who becomes a leper after her betrothal.*]

180. Concerning the girl who becomes a leper after her betrothal. If it happens that after a girl or woman has been betrothed she becomes leprous or mad or blind in both eyes, then her betrothed husband shall receive back his property and he shall not be required to take her to wife against his will. And he shall not be guilty in this

event because it did not occur on account of his neglect but on account of her weighty sins and resulting illness.

[*On marriage.*]

181. On marriage. If a father gives his daughter to a husband or a brother gives his legitimate sister, the bridegroom must be content with that amount of the father's or mother's property which the father or brother gave him on the day of the carrying out (traditio)[50] of the nuptials. He should not seek more.

[*Concerning the rights of a woman and the disposition of her guardianship (mundium) after the death of her husband.*]

182. On the rights of the widow. If anyone has given his daughter or other relative in marriage and it happens by chance that her husband dies, then the widow shall have the right, if she wishes, to go to another husband, provided he is free. Moreover, the second husband who wishes to marry her should give, from his own property, for her marriage portion to him who is the nearest heir of the first husband half of that amount which was offered when the first husband betrothed her. If the heir does not wish to accept this amount, then the woman shall have it together with [her first husband's] morning gift (*morgengab*)[51] and that which she brought with her from her own relatives, that is, her father's gift (*faderfio*).[52] Her relatives then have the right to give her to another husband where both they and she desire it, and the relatives of the first husband shall not have her mundium because they refused their consent: therefore her mundium shall return to the near relatives who first gave her to a husband. And if there are no legitimate relatives, then her mundium shall belong to the king's fisc.

If she is a woman who does not wish or is not able to have another husband, then she shall be in the power of that one to whom her mundium belongs. And if that one provides inadequately for her or treats her ill and it is proved, then it is lawful that she should return to her relatives. If she does not have relatives, then she shall find refuge at the king's court and her mundium shall be in the king's power.

[*On the delivery in marriage (traditio) of a girl.*]

183. On the marriage of a girl or woman. If anyone purchases

the mundium of a free woman or girl and she is handed over to him as wife, and if afterwards the husband dies, then the woman ought to go to another husband, to her relatives, or to the court of the king. In such an event the heirs of the first husband should receive half of the marriage portion as established above, and she should be handed over again by hand (*per mano*) in similar manner as she was handed over to her first husband. For without this handing over, none of the things we speak of is fully established.

[*Concerning nuptial gifts.*]

184. On nuptial gifts. If, when a father hands over his daughter to another as wife or a brother hands over his sister, one of his friends gives something to the woman and the gift is accepted, then that gift will be under the control of the man who has acquired her mundium since the husband must make the return gift (launigild) himself if one is required.

[*Concerning incestuous and illegal nuptials.*]

185. On incestuous and illegal nuptials. No man may take to wife his stepmother, that is the woman who was the later wife (*matrinia*) of his father, nor his stepdaughter (*privigna*) who is the *filiastra*, nor the sister-in-law who was his brother's wife. If the woman consented, then the man who took her to wife shall pay 100 solidi to the king's fisc as composition for his guilt, and he shall be separated from her immediately, having been forced to do so by the king. The woman shall keep half of her property and the other half shall go to the king's fisc. The pair shall sustain this punishment because they consented to celebrate illegal nuptials and, as has been said, they shall be separated immediately.

[*On the man who forcefully seizes a woman.*]

186. On violence. If a man violently seizes a woman and takes her unwillingly to wife, he shall pay 900 solidi, half to the king and half to the woman's relatives. And if she does not have relatives, then the entire 900 solidi shall be paid to the king's fisc. The woman then has the right to choose who shall have in his power her mundium, together with all the property legally belonging to her. The woman shall choose as she wishes whether this shall be her father, if she has one, a brother, an uncle, or the king.

[*On the forceful seizure of free women.*]

187. On the forceful seizure of free women. If anyone takes a wife by force, he may pay composition, as above, and then acquire her mundium.[53] But if by chance it happens that, before he has acquired the right to her guardianship, she dies, then her property shall return to her relatives and the man who took her to wife by force must pay composition for her death. Her composition shall be assessed as if for a man of like blood, that is, as if the husband had killed her brother. He shall thus be compelled to pay composition for her death either to her relatives or to him to whom her mundium belongs.

[*Concerning the girl or woman who goes to a husband without the consent of her relatives.*]

188. If without the consent of her relatives a free girl or widow goes to a husband who is a freeman, then the husband who received her to wife shall pay twenty solidi as composition for the illegal intercourse (*anagrip*)[54] and another twenty solidi to avert the feud. If she dies before he has acquired her guardianship, then the property of that woman shall revert to him who has her mundium in his possession, but no liability shall be assessed against the man who presumed to take her. The husband, however, shall lose the woman's property since he neglected to acquire her mundium.

[*On fornication.*]

189. On fornication. If a free girl or woman voluntarily has intercourse with a freeman, her relatives have the right to take vengeance on her. If it is agreed between both parties that he who fornicated with her take her to wife, he shall pay twenty solidi as composition for his offense, that is, for the illegal intercourse. If it is not agreeable that he have her to wife, then he must pay 100 solidi as composition, half to the king and half to him to whom her mundium belongs. If the relatives neglect this or do not wish to take vengeance on her, then the king's gastald or schultheis shall take her to the king and he shall render judgment as is pleasing to him.

[*Concerning him who marries the girl or woman betrothed to another man.*]

190. On those who marry women betrothed to someone else.

He who takes to wife, with her consent, the girl or widow betrothed to someone else, shall pay twenty solidi as composition for the illegal intercourse to the relatives of the woman or to him to whom her mundium belongs. He shall pay another twenty solidi to avert the feud, and then he may acquire her mundium at an agreed price. Moreover, he must pay him who had betrothed the woman and whom he has treated disgracefully double the amount of the marriage portion established at the time of betrothal. After the betrothed man has accepted the double payment as composition, he should be content and nothing more should be required of the surety in connection with this case.

[*On abducting a woman betrothed to another man.*]

191. On the abduction of a woman betrothed to another. He who abducts the girl or widow betrothed to someone else shall be liable to pay 900 solidi, half to the king and half to the relatives of the girl, or to him to whom her mundium belongs. Then if it is so agreed, the abductor may acquire her mundium. Moreover, the offender shall pay as composition to the betrothed man in whose disgrace or scorn he acted an amount equal to double the marriage portion set on the day the betrothal agreement was made. Additional blame shall not be imputed to the surety or to the abductor by the betrothed man, but he should be content with the receipt of the double compensation.

[*Concerning the girl who has been betrothed by her father, brother, or relatives.*]

192. Concerning those relatives who, after betrothing a girl to one man, enter into a secret agreement with another man. If a father has betrothed his daughter, or a brother has betrothed his sister, or any of the relatives have betrothed their female relative to some man, and if afterwards for some strange reason they enter into a secret agreement with someone else, or consent to another man's taking the woman to wife forcefully or with her consent, then those relatives who gave their consent to the fraudulent agreement shall pay him who had betrothed the girl compensation as above, that is, double the marriage portion which was agreed to on the day of the betrothal. Afterwards the betrothed man may not seek more from the prosecution of them or their sureties.

[*Concerning the free girl who follows another man's slave outside the country.*]

193. If a free girl follows another's slave outside of the country, the slave's lord and the girl's relatives are equally obliged to pursue them. If the slave and the girl are found, they shall both be punished as provided by law, but no guilt shall be incurred by the slave's lord.

[*Concerning the man who has intercourse with a woman slave belonging to someone else.*]

194. If any man has intercourse with a native woman slave, he shall pay twenty solidi as composition to her lord. If he fornicates with a Roman woman slave, he shall pay twelve solidi as composition.

[*Concerning offenses against a girl.*]

195. Concerning offenses against a girl. If anyone who possesses the mundium of a free girl or woman—with the exception of her father or brother—plots against the life of that girl or woman or tries to hand her over to a husband without her consent or voluntarily consents that someone do her violence, or if he plans one of these offenses and it is proved, he shall lose her mundium and the woman shall have the right to choose between two things. She may choose whether she wishes to return to her relatives or whether she wishes to commend herself—together with the property which legally belongs to her—to the king's court so that he may have her mundium in his control. And if the man who possesses her mundium denies this offense, he may clear himself [by oath]; and if he clears himself, he shall keep her guardianship as before.

[*On adultery.*]

196. On adultery. If he who possesses the mundium of a free girl or woman—with the exception of her father or brother—[unjustly] charges her with having committed adultery, he shall lose her guardianship and she shall have the right to choose whether she wishes to return to her relatives with her property or to commend herself to the court of the king who will then have her mundium in his control. If the man denies the offense of which he is accused, he may clear himself by oath, if he can, and he shall have her guardianship as before.

[*On witchcraft.*]

197. On witchcraft.[55] If he who possesses the guardianship of a free girl or woman—with the exception of her father or brother—[unjustly] accuses her of being a witch (*striga*) or enchantress (*masca*), he shall lose her mundium as above and she shall have the right to choose whether she wishes to return to her relatives or to commend herself with her own property to the court of the king, who will then have her mundium in his control. If the man denies that he accused her of this crime, he may clear himself [by oath], and if he clears himself, he shall have her guardianship as before.

[*Concerning the man who charges a girl in the guardianship (mundium) of someone else with some offense.*]

198. Concerning him who accuses the girl in the mundium of someone else of having committed an offense. If anyone accuses the girl or free woman in someone else's mundium of being a harlot or witch, and if it is clear that he spoke against her in uncontrolled wrath, he may then offer oath with twelve oathhelpers to the effect that he accused her of the offense of witchcraft in wrath and not with any certain knowledge. For making such an unfounded accusation, he shall pay twenty solidi as composition and he shall not be held further liable. But if he perseveres in his charge and says that he can prove it, the case shall be determined by the camfio, that is, by duel, according to the judgment of God. If he proves his charge by combat, then she shall be guilty and punished as provided in this code [Rothair 189 and 376]. But if he who accused her of the offense is not able to prove it, he shall be compelled to pay as composition an amount equal to the wergeld of that woman as determined by the status to which she was born.

[*Concerning the widow who returns to her father's house.*]

199. Concerning the widow who returns to her father's house. If a father has given his daughter to a husband, or a brother has given his sister, and if it happens that the husband dies and the father or brother redeems her mundium, as provided above [Rothair 183 and 215], then she may return to the home of father or brother and find there her other sisters. If afterwards the father or brother dies while she is in the home with one or more other sisters, and if they divide

the property of the father or brother with the other relatives or with the king's fisc, the widow who had returned to the home of father or brother shall keep her morning gift and marriage portion as before. The father's gift (faderfio)—the other gifts which the father or brother gave her when she went to her husband—shall be held in common with the other sisters. And the one or more other sisters may take [from the father's or brother's property] an amount equal to that which the father or brother gave to the relatives of the dead husband in return for releasing the widow's mundium. The rest of the property of the father or brother shall be divided in equal manner, as provided in these laws [Rothair 158–60]. If the widow remains alone in the house, she shall succeed as an heir to the portion allowed her by law [Rothair 158].

[*On killing women.*]
200. On killing a woman. If a husband kills his innocent wife who had not legally deserved to die [Rothair 202, 211, 212], he must pay 1200 solidi as composition, half to the relatives who gave her to her husband and from whom he received her mundium, and half to the king. This shall be enforced by one of the king's officials and composition shall be paid as provided above. If the man had had children by that woman, they shall have the morning gift and the father's gift of their dead mother. If he had not had children by her, her property shall revert to the relatives who gave her to the husband. And if there are no relatives then this composition and the above-mentioned property shall belong to the king's fisc.

[*On killing free women.*]
201. On deliberately killing a free woman. He who kills a girl or free woman for any reason shall pay 1200 solidi as composition, half to the relatives or to him to whom her mundium belonged, and half to the king. If she does not have relatives, then the entire composition shall belong to the king's fisc. [This is the law] provided he killed her with evil intent, that is, deliberately.

[*Concerning women who conspire in the death of their husbands.*]
202. If a woman conspires in the death of her husband, acting either through herself or through a substitute, the husband has the

right to do with her what he wishes, and he may likewise do what he wishes with the woman's property. If the woman denies the charge, her relatives may clear her either by oath or through the camfio, that is, by duel.

[*Concerning women who kill their husbands.*]

203. The woman who kills her husband shall be killed. If there are no children, the man's relatives shall have his property.

[*On the legal competence of women.*]

204. No free woman who lives according to the law of the Lombards within the jurisdiction of our realm is permitted to live under her own legal control, that is, to be legally competent (selpmundia) [see note 13 above], but she ought always to remain under the control of some man or of the king. Nor may a woman have the right to give away or alienate any of her movable or immovable property without the consent of him who possesses her mundium.

[*On the rape of aldiae.*]

205. On the rape of aldiae. He who rapes another man's aldia, that is, one who was born of a free mother,[56] shall pay forty solidi as composition.

[*On the rape of freedwomen.*]

206. On the rape of freedwomen. He who rapes another man's freedwoman, that is, one who has been set free, shall pay twenty solidi as composition.[57]

[*On the rape of female slaves.*]

207. On the rape of female slaves. He who rapes another man's female slave shall pay twenty solidi as composition.

[*On abducting another man's aldia.*]

208. On abduction. If anyone has abducted another man's aldia and taken her into another man's courtyard and her lord or relatives have pursued them; and if the owner of the courtyard blocks the way and does not permit the lord or relatives to vindicate her or to drag him [who abducted her] without, then he who blocked the way shall pay forty solidi as composition, half to the king and half to him to whom the aldia belongs.

[*On abducting a woman slave.*]

209. On abducting a woman slave. If anyone has abducted another man's female slave and led her away into another man's courtyard and her lord or relatives have followed; and if the owner of the courtyard blocks the way and does not permit them to vindicate her, then he who blocked the way shall pay twenty solidi as composition, half to the king and half to him to whom the woman slave belongs.

[*Concerning seeking refuge at the king's court with an abducted woman.*]

210. On abduction and refuge at the king's court. If any man abducts another man's aldia or woman slave and leads her to the king's court, and her lord or any of his friends or slaves follow, and if the king's gastald or agent blocks the way, that royal agent shall pay forty solidi as composition for the aldia or twenty solidi for the woman slave out of his own property to him to whom the aldia or woman slave belongs.

[*On marriage with another man's wife.*]

211. On marriage with another man's wife. If a freeman or slave takes another man's wife and associates her with himself in marriage, then both shall be killed if both consented [to the union].

[*Concerning the man who discovers his wife in adultery.*]

212. Concerning the man who discovers his wife in adultery. He who finds another freeman or slave having intercourse with his wife shall have the right to kill them both. And if he kills them, nothing shall be required of him.

[*On adultery.*]

213. On adultery. If anyone accuses another of having had intercourse with his wife, he who is charged with the crime shall clear himself either by oath or by combat. If it is proved against him, he shall lose his life.

[*Concerning the man who marries a free girl without the consent of her family.*]

214. He who takes to wife a free girl without the advice and consent of her relatives shall pay twenty solidi as composition for the

seizure, as above, and another twenty solidi to avert the feud. Concerning her mundium, moreover, [let it be arranged] just as it is agreed and the law allows [Rothair 183, 225], provided nevertheless both man and girl are free.

[*Concerning the death of a girl who is betrothed.*]

215. On the death of a girl who is betrothed. If anyone betroths a girl or widow, and by chance she dies before her mundium has been handed over by her father or by anyone else who possesses it, the marriage portion given by the betrothed man shall be returned to him in the same amount as he gave. But her other property belongs to him who possesses her mundium because she died before the actual handing over.

[*Concerning the aldius who marries a free woman.*]

216. On the aldius who marries a free woman. If any man's aldius takes to wife a free woman (one who is folkfree)[58] and acquires her mundium, and if after children are born the husband dies, then if the woman does not wish to remain in that house and her relatives want to bring her back to them, they may return the price which had been paid for the woman's mundium by him to whom the aldius belonged. She may then return to her relatives without the morning gift or any of her husband's property but with any property which she brought with her from her own relatives, if there was any. And if the woman had children and they do not wish to remain in their father's house, they may leave the paternal property by purchasing their own mundium at the same rate as was paid for the mundium of their mother. They may then go freely wherever they wish.

[*Concerning the aldia who marries a slave.*]

217. On the aldia who marries a slave. The aldia or freedwoman who enters another man's house to a husband and marries a slave shall lose her liberty. But if the husband's lord neglects to reduce her to servitude, then when her husband dies she may go forth together with her children and all the property which she brought with her when she came to her husband. But she shall have no more than this as an indication of her mistake in marrying a slave.

[*Concerning the aldius who marries an aldia.*]

218. On the aldius who marries an aldia. If any man's aldius

takes an aldia or freedwoman to wife, and if there are children from this union, the children shall follow the legal status of the father and shall be aldii like their father.

[*Concerning the aldius who marries a slave.*]

219. If an aldius takes to wife the female slave of his own [lord] or of some other lord, their children shall be the slaves of him to whom the mother slave belongs.

[*Concerning the woman slave who marries a slave belonging to someone else.*]

220. If any man's female slave enters another man's house and takes a slave there as husband, then when the husband dies she shall take nothing with her from that house except that which she brought with her.

[*Concerning the slave who marries a free woman.*]

221. The slave who dares to marry a free woman or girl shall lose his life. With regard to the woman who consented to a slave, her relatives have the right to kill her or to sell her outside the country and to do what they wish with her property. And if her relatives delay in doing this, then the king's gastald or schultheis shall lead her to the king's court and place her there in the women's apartments among the female slaves.

[*Concerning the man who marries his own slave.*]

222. On marrying one's own woman slave.[59] If any man wishes to marry his own woman slave, he may do so. Nevertheless he ought to free her, that is, make her worthy born (*vurdibora*), and he ought to do it legally by the proper formal procedure (gairethinx). She shall then be known as a free and legal wife and her children may become the legal heirs of their father.

[*Concerning the man who dies without heirs.*]

223. Concerning the man who dies without heirs. If a man dies without heirs and his property passes to the king's fisc, anyone who has given a gift to the dead man or made him a loan shall not have the right to seek it back. Because after the property passes to the king's hand, all transactions come to an end and terminate without penalty or appeal.

[*On manumission.*]

224. On manumission. He who wishes to free his own man or woman slave shall have that right if it pleases him. He who wishes to make his slave folkfree and a stranger to himself, that is, legally independent (*haamund*),[60] ought to do it thus. The lord shall first hand the servant over to the hand of another freeman and confirm it by formal action (gairethinx). And the second man shall hand the servant over to a third in the same manner, and the third shall hand him over to a fourth. And this fourth man shall lead him to a place where four roads meet and give him arrow and whip,[61] and say: "From these four roads you are free to choose where you wish to go." If the act is done thus, the former slave will then be legally independent and completely free. Afterwards his patron will not have the right to require any liability of him or of his children. And if he who is made legally independent dies without legal heirs, the king's fisc shall succeed him, not the patron or his heirs [Rothair 158–60, 171].

(II). It shall be likewise concerning the slave who becomes *inpans,* that is, him who has been set free at the king's command: he shall live according to that same law as he who becomes legally independent.

(III). If, moreover, the former slave has been made folkfree and given the choice of the four roads, but has not been made legally independent and therefore is not a stranger, he shall live with his patron as with a brother or other related free Lombard. And if this one who was made folkfree does not leave legitimate sons or daughters [when he dies], his patron shall succeed him, as is provided hereafter [Rothair 225].

(IIII). He who wishes to raise his slave to the status of an aldius should not give him the choice of the four roads.

These are the four kinds of manumission. The possibility of future difficulty requires that the manner in which the man or woman has been freed should be recorded in a charter of freedom. If the charter has not been executed, however, nevertheless the former slave's freedom remains in effect.

[*Concerning the children of freedmen.*]

225. On the children of freedmen. If the freedman who has

been made folkfree leaves legitimate sons, they shall be his heirs; if he leaves daughters, they shall have their legal share [Rothair 154, 158–60, 171]. If he leaves natural sons, they shall also have their legal share [Rothair 154, 158–60, 171]. But if he dies without heirs but while still alive made provision according to Lombard law for his personal property, that is, for his hand tools ([h]andegawere) and his weapons (angawere), then he to whom he left it shall have that property. But the property which he possesses through the gift of a benefactor—if he has not obligated it during his freedom—shall return to the patron or his heirs. If he has acquired any gift while in the service (gasindium)[62] of the duke or in the service (obsequium) of private men, that property shall revert to the giver. Concerning the other property, if, as has been said, he does not leave heirs or make provision for it while alive, the patron shall succeed him just as if he were a relative.

[On the law by which freedmen shall live.]

226. All freedmen who have obtained freedom from their Lombard lords ought to live according to the law of their lords and benefactors in the status which has been granted to them by their lords.

[On purchases and sales.]

227. On purchases and sales. If any man buys land, whether it is land to build on or for a servile holding (casa mancipiata), and holds it in person for five years, and if after this time the seller or his heirs contest the sale and claim that they had only temporarily conveyed[63] the property but had not sold it, then they [the seller or his heirs] must offer written documents wherein the first man requested merely to lease [the land]. If they do not have such documents, the purchaser shall do nothing, but he should offer an oath, the strength of which is determined by the value of the money with which he bought the property. [If he can offer such an oath], he should not lose the property to the other by law [Rothair 359, 365] but he is permitted to possess incontestably that which he bought.

[On possession.]

228. On possession. If anyone charges that another's movable or immovable property is possessed illegally and the possessor denies

it, we decree as follows. If he has had possession of it for five years, then he who possesses it should deny [the charges] by oath or defend himself by combat, if he can.

[*Concerning him who sells another man's property.*]

229. Concerning him who maliciously sells another man's property. He who knowingly sells another man's property—either male or female slaves, or other property—and this is discovered and proved shall restore it eightfold.[64] He who sells it unknowingly shall offer oath [to the effect] that he sold the property believing it to be his own; he shall then return the person or object together with any output which may have been produced.

[*Concerning bondsmen who are lepers.*]

230. On bondsmen who are lepers. If anyone buys a bondsman and afterwards he turns out to be a leper or mad, then the seller, if he is accused, shall offer oath alone that he did not know of this infirmity when he sold the bondsman. [And if he can so swear], he shall not be further liable.

[*On the purchase of a female slave.*]

231. Concerning the purchase of a female slave. If any man purchases a female slave and afterwards another man comes along and says that she is his, they both should return to the seller. If the seller cannot clear himself, he should offer oath that he did not know of the fraud nor did he enter into collusion with anyone. He should then return the price which he received on the day when he sold her, and the woman slave should be restored to her proper lord. And if the woman slave had children after the sale, then that one who first sold her and could not clear himself should purchase her children, however many there may be, and turn them over to her lord. However many children there are, they shall follow their mother. If the seller has died without legal heirs and the property of the seller has passed to the king's fisc, there shall be no appeal; provided, however, that he [the purchaser] offers oath to the effect that he bought her of him whose property has passed to the king's fisc.

[*On the purchase of a horse.*]

232. On purchase of a horse. If anyone has bought a horse without knowing the seller, and if some man comes along who says

that the horse is his, then let the man who bought the horse, if he cannot produce the seller or does not know him from whom he bought it, offer oath that he is neither a thief nor a colleague of thieves, but had purchased the horse with his own money. In addition, he shall add in his oath that if at any time [in the future] he comes upon the seller, he will not deny it. After he has offered such an oath, he shall return the horse and be content. That one, moreover, who claimed the horse as his own, shall take it on condition that if it is recognized, when the man appears who made the sale, that he claimed it with evil intent, then the horse shall be returned ninefold[65] to him to whom it was sold.

[*On purchases from slaves.*]

233. On purchases from slaves. A slave may not sell or emancipate land, bondsmen, or any other property without the consent of his lord. He who buys from a slave shall lose the price he paid and also restore the property to its rightful owner.

[*On sales made by tenant slaves (massarii).*]

234. About the tenant agricultural slave (massarius) [see note 30 above]. The massarius with regard to his own property—his ox, cow, horse, or smaller animal—has the right to give away or accept them in association with someone else [i.e., with the consent of his lord]. He may not sell them unless it is for the benefit of the holding (casa) and only to the extent that the sale will profit the holding and not diminish it.

[*On sales made by an aldius.*]

235. Concerning the aldius. It is not lawful for an aldius or anyone who has not been made legally independent (amundius) to sell either land or bondsmen without the consent of his patron, nor may he set any free.

[*On digging out boundary markers.*]

236. On digging out boundary markers. The freeman who destroys an old boundary marker, and this is proved, shall pay eighty solidi, half to the king and half to him on whose boundary the marker had been set.

[*On slaves who dig out boundary markers.*]

237. Concerning slaves who dig out boundary markers. If any

man's slave destroys an old boundary marker, he shall be killed
unless he is redeemed for forty solidi.

[*On marked trees.*]

238. On marked trees. If a freeman cuts down or destroys a
tree on which marks designating boundaries have been made, he shall
pay eighty solidi, half to the king and half to him whose tree it was.
And if a slave does this on order from his lord, the lord shall also pay
eighty solidi as composition.

[*Concerning the slave who cuts down a marked tree.*]

239. If a slave on his own authority cuts down a tree marking
established boundaries, he shall be killed unless he is redeemed for
forty solidi.

[*Concerning the man who marks trees in someone else's wood.*]

240. On marking trees in the wood of another man. He who
deliberately makes new marks in the form of notches or carvings in
another man's wood and is not able to prove the wood his own shall
pay forty solidi as composition, half to the king and half to him
whose wood it is.

[*Concerning the slave who marks trees in someone else's wood.*]

241. Concerning slaves who mark trees. If a slave without the
order of his lord makes notches or carvings [on the trees] in someone else's wood, his hand shall be cut off. But if he does it by order of
his lord, the guilt shall be attributed to his lord, as above.

[*Concerning the illegal minting of coins.*]

242. He who mints gold or strikes money without the king's
command shall have his hand cut off.[66]

[*On forged charters.*]

243. On forged charters. He who forges a charter or other kind
of document shall have his hand cut off.

[*Concerning the man who illegally climbs over the walls of a fortification or town.*]

244. He who goes out or enters through the wall of a fortification (*castro*) or city without the consent of the officials shall, if he is
a freeman, pay twenty solidi to the king's fisc. If, moreover, he is an

aldius or a slave, he shall pay ten solidi to the king's fisc. If he has committed theft therein he shall pay composition in accordance with the penalty for theft as is provided in these laws [Rothair 253–62].

[*On pledges.*]

245. On pledges and debts.[67] He who has a debtor shall demand his debt from him once, twice, and even three times, and if then the debtor has not returned or paid composition for the debt, he [the creditor] may take a pledge as surety from those properties which can be pledged.

[*Concerning the man who takes pledges before demanding payment of a debt.*]

246. On taking pledges before demanding payment. If anyone presumes to take a pledge from another man for any debt or cause whatever before [the debt] has been demanded of the debtor three times, the pledge which was taken before the demand shall be returned ninefold to the possession of its owner.

[*A man shall not take pledges on behalf of another man.*]

247. No one may take pledges on behalf of another with the exception of him who is found to be *gafans*, that is, he is a near relative co-heir who, as it happens, has come for the inheritance.

[*Concerning the man who takes pledges by mistake.*]

248. If anyone by mistake takes a man or woman slave as a pledge, we decree that after he recognizes that he has taken the pledge mistakenly he should immediately release him or her. If the slave's lord charges him, then he should offer oath that he did it by mistake and not with evil intent, that he believed that he had taken a pledge from his debtor. He shall then be without penalty. But if he has struck or used violence against the pledge, he should pay composition just as is provided in these laws [Rothair 76–128]. If he does not dare offer oath to the effect that he took the pledge by mistake, then he must return the pledge eightfold.

[*On herds of mares or pigs.*]

249. On taking mares or pigs as pledges. He who, without the king's command, takes away a herd of mares or pigs as pledges, shall be killed unless he pays 900 solidi as composition, half to the king

and half to him whose pledge he took. The men who were with him, if they were freemen, shall each pay eighty solidi as composition, half to the king and half to him from whom the pledges were taken. If the accomplices were slaves following their lord, their composition shall be included in the composition of their lord; for the blame is the lord's not the slaves' who followed their lord.

[*Concerning the man who takes broken horses or trained oxen as pledges.*]

250. He who, without the king's consent, takes broken horses or oxen or cows trained to the yoke [as pledges] shall return them ninefold.

[*Concerning what can be done if a debtor does not have any property except horses or oxen.*]

251. If a freeman is a debtor and has no property other than broken horses or oxen or cows trained to the yoke, then he who seeks the debt [from him] should go to the schultheis and state his case, namely, that his debtor has no property other than that noted above. The schultheis shall then take the oxen or horses and place them with the creditor until justice has been done to him. If the schultheis delays in doing this, he shall pay twelve solidi to the king's fisc. When justice has been done, the pledge will be restored.

[*A man shall not take a holding owing tribute* (casa ordinata tributaria) *as a pledge for any debt.*]

252. It is not lawful that anyone take a holding owing tribute (casa ordinata tributaria) as a pledge for any debt—only male and female slaves, cows, or sheep. Indeed, the pledge which the creditor takes should be kept safe in his care for the prescribed time: twenty days in cases between those persons who live within 100 miles of one another. If within these twenty days the debtor does justice and returns the debt but does not redeem his pledge and after the twenty days have passed one of the pledges, a bondsman or domestic animal, dies or kills a man or does damage or goes elsewhere, then the debtor shall assess the damage to his own loss since he had neglected to redeem his pledges. But if within the twenty days the man or woman slave dies or the domestic animal perishes or kills a man or

does some other damage, then he who took the pledges shall be responsible for the damage and shall make satisfaction to their owner. If the creditor and debtor live more than 100 miles from one another, then the pledge should be guarded for sixty days.

[On theft.]

253. On theft. If a freeman commits a theft and is taken in the act, which is called *fegangi,*[68] and if the theft involves more than ten *silequae,*[69] he shall return that stolen ninefold and pay eighty solidi composition for such guilt, or [if he cannot pay] he shall lose his life.

[Concerning slaves who commit thefts.]

254. If a slave commits a theft and is taken in the act in a theft involving up to ten seliquae, it shall be returned ninefold by him [by his lord?], and in addition he [i.e., his lord?] shall either pay forty solidi as composition for the guilt or the slave shall be killed.

[On the discovery of thefts through an informer (proditor)*.]*

255. If anyone discovers a theft through a way-pointer (*proditor*)[70] or informer, then he who committed the theft shall restore it ninefold.

[Concerning the slave who commits a theft while in flight.]

256. If a slave commits a theft or does some damage while he is in flight, and if in his flight he goes out of the country and does not return, then the slave's lord shall restore half of that which the slave took or of the damage which he caused. If the slave returns to his lord's control, however, his lord shall return the amount which he took in full, the penalty for theft not applying in this case since the slave was in flight[71] [when he committed the offense].

[Concerning the free woman who attempts to steal.]

257. If a woman who is folkfree is taken in theft, then the amount which she took shall be returned ninefold by her [by the holder of her mundium?]. Other penalty, however, shall not be demanded by him who sustained the injury, but let shame be reflected on her who did this disgraceful deed [cf. Rothair 253, Liutprand 146].

[Concerning the aldia or female slave who attempts to steal.]

258. If an aldia or woman slave is taken in theft, her lord shall pay a ninefold composition for the theft in addition to forty solidi for her guilt.

[Concerning the freeman who orders his boy or slave to steal.]

259. If a freeman orders his boy or slave to commit a theft and the theft is discovered, then a ninefold composition shall be made [to the owner] and another such amount shall be paid to the king's fisc, for it is dishonest and contrary to reason for a freeman to be involved in theft or to give his consent to it.

[Concerning articles found along the road.]

260. He who finds an article of gold or of clothing or anything else along the road and raises it above his knees without making known [that he had found it] or without taking it to the judge shall return it ninefold.

[Concerning the slave, married to another man's woman slave, who steals.]

261. If a slave, while he has to wife the woman slave belonging to another lord, commits a theft while supporting the woman and her children, slaves who belong to another lord, then the slave alone [i.e., his lord?] shall pay composition for the whole theft which he committed and no blame shall be imputed to the injury of the woman or her children [i.e., to their lord?]. This provision applies should the woman or the children not have gone with the father to commit the theft, for if they have, a similar penalty shall be applied to them [to their lord?].

[Concerning the slave who, while in flight, gives property to anyone.]

262. If a slave while in flight commits any properties to another man [for keeping] and afterwards their true owner seeks them back, if he who received the properties refuses [to give them up] and it is found out, then he [who received the properties from the slave] shall return them as if they had been stolen.

[On thefts committed by several men.]

263. If several men, whether free or slave, commit a theft together they may, if they wish, clear themselves together [cf.

Rothair 12] and return the theft eightfold. He who separates himself from the others shall pay composition by himself according to the law, that is, he must pay a ninefold composition for the theft.

[*Concerning freemen or slaves who try to flee outside the country.*]

264. The judge or other resident within the boundaries of our state who apprehends a freeman or slave, trying to flee outside the country, should hold him and keep safe the property which he carried with him. The apprehender should immediately send notice to the judge of the place from which the fugitive had fled in order that he may claim him. And this official shall pay two solidi for the fugitive in order that he and the properties that he took with him may be returned. If the fugitive flees from his bonds, then he who held him shall offer oath that he did not let him go with evil intent but intended to guard him with all possible means. After such an oath has been given, he should return any properties that he took [from the fugitive]; the compensation for apprehending the fugitive ought not to be sought but the apprehender should not suffer further blame. If the fugitive does not allow his hands to be tied and he is killed, nothing shall be required [for his death] but the properties which he carried with him should be returned. If that one who tried to take the fugitive is killed by him, nothing should be required [of the fugitive's lord].

[*Concerning ferrymen.*]

265. Concerning boatmen who provide a ferry across a river. If anyone accuses a boatman of transporting a fugitive or thief across a river and the boatman denies it, we decree that the ferryman may offer oath alone that he did not know that he transported a fugitive or thief; and he shall be absolved from any blame.

[*Concerning ferrymen who knowingly transport thieves.*]

266. The boatman who knowingly transports a thief with stolen goods shall be considered as an accomplice of the thief and he shall pay composition with him for the theft. In addition, he must pay twenty solidi to the king's fisc.

[*Concerning ferrymen who transport fugitive bondsmen.*]

267. The boatman who knowingly transports fugitive bondsmen, and it is proved, shall search for them and return them together

with any properties taken with them to their proper owner. If the fugitives have gone elsewhere and cannot be found, then the value of those bondsmen together with the sworn value of the property which they carried with them shall be paid by that ferryman who knowingly transported the fugitives. In addition, the ferryman shall pay twenty solidi as composition to the king's fisc.

[*Concerning ferrymen who knowingly transport fugitive freemen.*]

268. The boatman who carries a fugitive freeman across, recognizing him to be a fugitive, shall lose his life or pay as composition a sum equal to his wergeld, because after the boatman has recognized that the man is in flight and yet he is unable to hold him, he ought to run ahead and proclaim that the man is in flight.

[*Concerning the bondsman who flees to another man.*]

269. If any man's bondsman flees to another man and the bondsman's lord, having followed, peacefully asks that he be returned in grace and if the bondsman is returned in grace and the lord nonetheless punishes him for his guilt, then the lord shall pay twenty solidi as composition to that one from whose courtyard he took the servant. If the lord denies that he inflicted such punishment for the bondsman's guilt, he may offer oath alone on the gospels and be absolved from payment of composition.

[*Concerning the man who does not wish to return another man's fugitive bondsman.*]

270. If the man to whom someone else's bondsman has fled does not return him after a second or third request, then he shall be forced to restore the bondsman and in addition pay as composition another servant of the same value as the first is adjudged to be.

[*Provision for the situation where the king's court does not wish to return another man's fugitive bondsman.*]

271. The king's court. If a man's bondsman takes refuge at the king's court and the king's gastald or other official fails to return him after the second or third request, we order that the king's official return the bondsman and in addition be required to give another of the same value from his own property to the lord whose bondsman be

delayed in returning. If the bondsman's lord received him back in grace from the king's court and afterwards inflicted punishment upon the bondsman because of his guilt, he shall pay forty solidi as composition to the king's court whence he took him.

[*On taking sanctuary in a church.*]

272. The church. If a man's bondsman takes refuge in a church or in a priest's house and if the bishop or priest who is in charge of the place fails to return him in grace after the third request, we order the bishop or priest to return that bondsman together with another of the same value from his own property, as above. If the bondsman was returned in grace and afterwards his lord inflicted punishment upon him because of his guilt, the lord shall either clear himself as above or shall be liable to pay forty solidi to the church. This shall be exacted by one of the king's officials and the payment turned over to that holy place which sustained the injury.

[*On slaves who flee within the country.*]

273. He who seizes his fleeing slave in the courtyard of another man shall not be blamed because he seized his property in another man's courtyard. If he to whom the court belongs, or any of his men, takes the bondsman from his lord's hand or blocks the way to him, that one who followed his slave within may not create a disturbance (scandalum) [Rothair 8, 34–40, 277] in that courtyard. If he does create it, he shall pay composition as is provided in this code.

He who blocked the way in the interest of the slave or took the bondsman from his lord's hand shall be liable to punishment. If by chance the bondsman dies or runs away, then he who took him from his lord's hand shall return another bondsman of the same value. If the bondsman is found, he shall be returned, and his lord shall not be compelled after such annoyance to receive him in grace if he does not wish to do so.

[*Concerning the man who keeps a fugitive bondsman for more than nine nights without notifying his lord.*]

274. If any man keeps a fugitive bondsman in his house for more than nine nights without notifying his lord and if thereafter the bondsman commits some evil deed or dies or runs away, then he who kept him and neglected to send for his lord shall return that bonds-

man or his value to his lord and furthermore he who had him longer than [this period of time] shall pay the composition imposed for any damage caused by the bondsman.

[*Concerning the bondsman who seeks refuge with someone else.*]

275. He who receives the fleeing bondsman who belongs to another man shall immediately notify his lord in writing or by means of some reputable man in order that [the lord] may receive him back in grace. If [the lord] does not want to take him back and delays and the bondsman then flees elsewhere, no blame shall fall on that one who received him first in his house. But he who receives a bondsman and does not notify his lord shall return that bondsman together with a payment for the work lost, and in addition he shall pay the composition for whatever damage the bondsman caused.

[*Concerning the man who knowingly receives a fugitive bondsman.*]

276. He who knowingly receives a fugitive bondsman or gives him provisions or shows him the road and the fugitive flees on, shall seek after him. If he does not find him, he shall pay the value of the bondsman together with the value of the property which he carried with him. If he does find him, he shall return the bondsman together with a payment for the value of his lost work.

[*Concerning anger* (aistan).]

277. Concerning anger. He who enters the courtyard of another man in a state of rage *(haistan),*[72] that is, with hostile spirit, shall pay twenty solidi as composition to him whose courtyard it is.

[*On violation of someone else's courtyard.*]

278. On violation of another man's courtyard. A woman is not able to commit breach of a courtyard, which is *hoberos,* for it is foolish to think that a woman, free or slave, could commit a forceful act with arms as if she were a man.[73]

[*Concerning a band of field slaves.*]

279. Concerning a band of field slaves. If a band of slaves enters a village armed for the purpose of committing some evil deed and if any freeman from our jurisdiction places himself at their head, then that freeman shall either be killed or he must pay 900 solidi as composition, half to the king and half to him who suffered the injury.

Each of the slaves who were in the band with that one shall pay forty solidi, half to the king and half as above.

[*Concerning the sedition of field slaves.*]

280. On seditious acts committed by field slaves. If, for any reason, rustics (*homines rusticani*) associate together for plotting or committing seditious acts such as, when a lord is trying to take a bondsman or animal from his slave's house, blocking the way or taking the bondsman or animal, then he who was at the head of these rustics shall either be killed or redeem his life by the payment of a composition equal to that amount at which he is valued. And each of those who participated in this evil sedition shall pay twelve solidi as composition, half to the king and half to him who bore the injury or before whom he presumed to place himself. And if that one who was trying to take his property endures blows or suffers violence from these rustics, composition for such blows or violence shall be paid to him just as is stated above, and the rustics shall suffer such punishment as is noted above for this presumption. If one of the rustics is killed no payment shall be required because he who killed him did it while defending himself and in protecting his own property.

[*On theft and the penalty therefor.*]

281. On theft and its penalty. He who steals wood from another man's wood lot shall pay six solidi as composition to him to whom the wood lot belongs.

[*Concerning theft of firewood.*]

282. He who steals a piece of wood or a shingle from a house under construction shall pay six solidi as composition.

[*Concerning theft of cut wood.*]

283. He who steals some of the cut wood in the courtyard or on the road to a house under construction shall pay six solidi as composition. If, moreover, he steals it and scatters it in the forest, he shall pay an eightfold composition.

[*On entry into a man's garden.*]

284. On gardens. He who enters or leaps into another man's garden for the purpose of committing a theft shall pay six solidi as composition. If, however, he is seeking his own property and does not do any damage, he shall not be guilty.

[*On fences.*]
285. On broken fences. He who breaks another man's fence (which is called *idertzon*) shall pay six solidi as composition.

[*On fence boards.*]
286. On fence boards (*axegias*). He who takes one or two of the boards from a board fence shall pay one solidus as composition.

[*On fence poles.*]
287. On fence poles (*sepe stantaria*). He who takes a pole from a fence made of poles shall pay one solidus as composition. He who takes the crosspole shall pay three solidi as composition.[74]

[*On plows.*]
288. On plows. He who deliberately destroys another man's plow or furrow breaker shall pay three solidi as composition. He who steals it shall return it eightfold.

[*On lead bells.*]
289. On lead bells (*tentinni*). He who steals the lead bell from a horse or ox shall pay six solidi as composition.

[*On yokes.*]
290. On yokes. He who steals a yoke shall pay six solidi as composition.

[*On reins.*]
291. On reins. He who steals the lines from yoked oxen shall pay six solidi as composition. If a thief takes a small object for which a composition of six solidi or less has been provided in this code, he shall not be held as taken in the act of theft (*figangit*), but shall pay composition only, as is provided.

[*On grape vines.*]
292. On grape vines. He who destroys a vine by taking more than three or four vine stalks shall pay six solidi as composition.

[*On poles that support vines.*]
293. On poles that support the vine. He who takes a supporting pole from a vine shall pay six solidi as composition.

[*Concerning cutting down vines.*]

294. On cutting down vines. He who deliberately destroys a vine by digging [and thus cutting the root of the vine], shall pay one solidus as composition.

[*On vine shoots.*]

295. On vine shoots. He who cuts a vine shoot shall pay half a solidus as composition.

[*Concerning stealing grapes.*]

296. On stealing grapes. He who takes more than three grapes from another man's vine shall pay six solidi as composition. He who takes less than three shall bear no guilt.

[*On animals at pasture.*]

297. Concerning animals at pasture. He who takes the hobble (*pastoria*) from another man's horse shall pay six solidi as composition.

[*On halters.*]

298. Concerning halters. He who takes the halter of a horse shall pay six solidi as composition.

[*On nets.*]

299. On nets. He who raises another man's nets or wicker baskets or who takes fish from another man's fishing preserve shall pay three solidi as composition.

[*On cutting trees.*]

300. On trees. He who cuts down a neighbor's oak tree (*robora, cerrum, quercum,* or *modola*) or beech tree *(hisclo)* within that man's field or pasture or enclosure shall pay two tremisses as composition for the tree. The traveler who cuts down a tree outside an enclosure for his own use shall not be blamed.

[*On chestnut, hazel-nut, pear, or apple trees.*]

301. He who cuts down a chestnut, hazel-nut, pear, or apple tree shall pay one solidus as composition.

[*On olive trees.*]

302. On olive trees. He who destroys or fells an olive tree shall pay three solidi as composition.

[*Concerning the man or animal that impales himself on another man's fence.*]

303. If a man or animal impales himself on the pole of another man's joined fence and dies or suffers injury therefrom, then the man who made the fence and allowed the head of the pole to extend above the fence shall be liable to pay composition for the homicide or for the injury.

[*Concerning the horse or other domestic animal that impales itself (while jumping) into another man's enclosure.*]

304. If a horse or any other animal impales itself while jumping into another man's enclosure, it shall not be redeemed by him whose fence it is. But if the animal impales itself while jumping from inside to the outside, then he whose fence it is shall pay composition. If the animal causes damage while within the enclosure, the owner of the animal shall pay composition to him whose enclosure it is.

[*Concerning the man who makes a ditch around his field.*]

305. If anyone digs a ditch around his field and a horse or other animal falls in or a man is injured, nothing shall be required from him who dug the ditch because he did it for the protection of his field and not with treacherous purpose. But if he covered the ditch secretly and any damage is done, he shall pay composition for that damage.

[*On wells.*]

306. Concerning wells. If an animal falls into another man's well and dies or is crippled as a result, nothing shall be required from him whose well it is because the waters of a well should be for the common usefulness of all.

[*On weapons.*]

307. Concerning arms. If a man lends his weapons to someone else and that man commits some evil deed with them, [the owner of the weapons] shall not be held liable but rather he who did the evil deed shall be liable. However, if he who lent the weapons consented to the act, he shall be regarded as an accessory to that one who is paying composition for the deed.

[*On taking weapons without consent.*]

308. If anyone on his own authority presumes to take another man's weapons and does some evil deed with them, no blame shall be imputed to him whose weapons they are but to him who committed the evil with them.

[*On wild animals.*]

309. On wild animals. If a wild animal has been hit by one man and in its agony it kills another man or does other damage, then he who struck it shall pay composition for the death or for the damage according to this provision, namely, that the liability of the hunter shall be recognized to last so long as he or his dogs follow the animal. But if he has abandoned the animal and has turned away from it, and afterwards the animal causes some damage, nothing shall be required from him who struck or incited the beast.

[*On animal traps.*]

310. On traps. If a wild animal caught in a trap or in a cage causes damage to some man or domestic animal, he who set the trap shall pay the composition.

[*Concerning men killed by trapped animals.*]

311. If a man interrupts his journey in order to pick up an animal struck by another man or held in a cage trap or surrounded by dogs and the man is struck or killed by that animal, nothing shall be required from him who had hit or trapped it, but rather the blame shall be imputed to him who had the audacity to attempt to take it for his own.

[*On finding wounded animals.*]

312. On finding wounded animals. He who finds an animal which has been wounded by another man or which is held in a trap or surrounded by dogs, or which is dead, and he kills the animal himself and leaves it, may take the right foreleg of the animal together with seven ribs if he makes it clear that he has done it with good intent.

[*On hiding found animals.*]

313. On hiding animals that have been found. He who finds and hides an animal wounded or killed by someone else shall pay six solidi as composition to him who wounded it.

[How long animals belong to the hunter.]

314. On how long animals belong to a hunter. If a stag or other animal is shot [and killed] with an arrow by any man, it belongs to that one who shot it up until the next same hour of the day or night, that is, for twenty-four hours after he set it aside and went away. Anyone who finds the animal after the prescribed number of hours has passed shall not be liable but may have the animal for himself.

[On domesticated stags.]

315. On domesticated stags. He who strikes a domesticated stag which has reached maturity (is "able to roar in its season") shall pay twelve solidi as composition to its owner. He who steals it shall return it eightfold.

[Concerning the trapping of someone else's stag.]

316. He who ensnares another's domesticated stag which is not yet mature shall pay six solidi as composition to its owner. He who steals it shall return it eightfold.

[On domesticated birds.]

317. On domesticated birds. He who ensnares another man's falcon, crane, or domesticated swan shall pay six solidi as composition.

[On bees.]

318. On bees. He who steals one or more hives with bees shall pay twelve solidi as composition.

[On taking bees from a marked tree.]

319. He who takes bees from a marked tree in someone else's wood shall pay six solidi as composition. If the tree is not marked, whoever finds the bees may have them, according to the law of nature, except in the king's preserve. If the lord whose wood it is comes along, he may take the honey but no further blame will follow.

[On falcons.]

320. On falcons. He who takes a falcon from someone else's wood may have it, except in the king's preserve. But if the lord of the forest comes along, he may take the falcon and no further blame will be imputed to him [who found the falcon]. We order, however, that

he who takes a falcon from the king's preserve shall pay twelve solidi as composition.

[*On taking falcons from a marked tree.*]
321. He who takes falcons from a nest in a marked tree in someone else's wood shall pay six solidi as composition.

[*On inciting dogs.*]
322. On inciting dogs. If anyone calls out to or incites another man's dogs and the dogs do damage to man or beast, no blame shall be imputed to him whose dogs they are but to him who incited them.

[*On madmen.*]
323. On madmen. If a man, because of his weighty sins, goes mad or becomes possessed and does damage to man or beast, nothing shall be required from his heirs. If the madman is killed, likewise nothing shall be required, provided, however, that he not be killed without cause.

[*On mad dogs or other animals.*]
324. If a dog or horse or any other animal goes mad and does damage to man or beast, nothing shall be required from its owner. And from him who kills such an animal, likewise nothing shall be required, as above.

[*On four-footed animals.*]
325. If a four-legged beast does damage to a man or to another animal, he whose animal it is shall pay the composition for such damage.

[*Concerning injuries caused by animals.*]
326. If a horse injures a man with its hoof, or an ox injures a man with its horn, or a pig injures a man with its tusks, or if a dog bites a man—except in the case where the animal is mad as above— he whose animal it is shall pay the composition for the killing or damage, but the feud, that is the enmity, shall cease since the thing was done by a dumb animal without any intent on the part of its owner.

[*On borrowed horses.*]
327. Concerning borrowed horses. In the case where a man

borrows or hires a horse, ox, dog, or other animal, and while the
animal is in his service or under his charge it does some damage,
nothing shall be required from the animal's owner, but the man who
borrowed it for himself shall pay the composition for the killing or
other damage.

[*On killing another man's animals.*]
328. In the case where an animal kills or injures someone else's
animal—that is, if an ox injures or kills an ox or any other animal—
we order that the man whose animal was injured or incapacitated or
otherwise weakened turn the injured animal over to him whose
animal injured it. And he shall receive in return from that one whose
animal caused the injury another animal of the same kind and value
as the injured one was at the time it was hurt.

[*On stolen dogs.*]
329. On stolen dogs. He who steals a dog shall return it ninefold.

[*Concerning the man who kills another man's dog in revenge.*]
330. If a man in defending himself kills another man's dog with
a broad sword or with a staff or with any other weapon which is held
in the hand, nothing shall be required of him so long as the weapon is
simply a staff or medium-sized sword. But the man who throws a
weapon at a dog and kills it shall return it singlefold, that is, he shall
return a dog of similar sort.

[*Concerning the man who finds another man's dog causing damage.*]
331. If a man finds another man's dog causing damage in his
house by day or night and kills it, nothing shall be required from him.
If it is not killed, its master shall restore the damage which it caused.

[*On cows in calf.*]
332. On cows in calf. He who strikes a cow in calf and causes a
miscarriage shall pay one tremissus as composition. If the cow dies,
he shall pay for it the price at which it is valued, and in addition he
shall pay for the calf.

[*On mares in foal.*]
333. On mares in foal. He who strikes a mare in foal and

causes a miscarriage shall pay one solidus as composition. If the mare dies, he shall pay as above for it and its young.

[*On pregnant female slaves.*]

334. On pregnant woman slaves. He who strikes a woman slave large with child and causes a miscarriage shall pay three solidi as composition. If, moreover, she dies from the blow, he shall pay composition for her and likewise for the child who died in her womb.

[*On animals which have been skinned.*]

335. On the skinning of animals. If a wolf kills an animal belonging to one man and another man skins it and hides it without its owner knowing it and the deed is discovered through an informer (*proditor*) [see note 70], he [who skinned the animal] shall pay twelve solidi as composition.

[*On dead animals found in a river.*]

336. If an animal which has died in a river or in any other place has been skinned by a man to whom it did not belong, he who skinned it shall pay twelve solidi as composition.

[*On injuries to horses.*]

337. On injuries to horses. He who cuts off the ear or strikes out the eye of another man's horse or causes any other injury to it shall keep the animal which was injured and restore it singlefold to its owner, that is, he shall restore a horse similar to the one injured.

[*Concerning the tails of horses.*]

338. About horse tails. He who cuts off the tail of another man's horse to the very bristle shall pay six solidi as composiiton.

[*Concerning the man who strikes another man's horse.*]

339. In the case where someone strikes or causes injury to another man's horse, the owner of the horse shall hand the horse over to that man who injured it in order that he may heal it. And while the latter is healing it, he should give his own horse [to the owner of the injured horse] that the latter may put it to his own use. If the horse which was injured is returned in the same state of health as originally, then its owner shall return the substitute to its own master. If, however, the horse dies from the injury, he who struck it shall restore

another like it. And if the horse which was received as a pledge dies while being held, then that one who held it as a pledge shall, if he is accused, offer oath to the effect that the horse held in pledge did not die through his neglect; and afterwards there shall be no further controversy.

[*Concerning the man who rides another man's horse.*]

340. He who mounts another man's horse and rides it around within the neighborhood near the village shall pay two solidi as composition. He who presumes to ride it around at a greater distance without asking its owner shall return it eightfold.

[*Concerning the mutilation of horses.*]

341. On the mutilation of horses. He who borrows another man's horse and mutilates it or breaks its spirit shall be liable to the punishment for theft, that is, he shall pay eightfold [plus the value of the animal itself] or nine times the value of the horse.

[*Concerning the man who takes another man's animal thinking it to be his own.*]

342. If a man takes someone else's horse or other animal believing it to be his own, and its owner recognizes it and wants to make an accusation, we decree as follows. The man who took the animal shall offer oath that he did not take it with evil intent or with the purpose of causing contention, but because he believed it to be his own. He shall then be absolved from blame for theft and shall return the horse uninjured to its proper owner. If, however, he does not dare so to swear, he shall return the horse eightfold; for after he recognized that the horse was not his own, he ought immediately to have made it known to its owner. But if, after he has announced that it is not his own, he mounts it, he shall be liable to pay two solidi as above.

[*On finding animals that are causing damage.*]

343. On the finding of animals causing damage. In the case where a man finds someone else's horse or other animal causing damage and shuts it up in his courtyard and its owner does not come, then he who found it causing damage should lead it before a judge established in that district, or he should bring it before a gathering in front of the church four or five times. And it should be made known

to all by public proclamation that he has found the horse. If the owner of the horse does not come, we decree that he who found it may ride it and keep it for his own. When it dies, he should keep the hide with its marks so that if the owner comes later, he may show him what he has. If he neglects this and it is discovered, he shall return the horse ninefold; but if this precaution has been observed, he shall be absolved from blame.

[Concerning the man who causes his animals to do damage.]

344. On deliberately causing animals to do damage. If anyone with evil intent sets his horse or oxen to do damage to another man's field or meadow, he shall pay one solidus per head as composition in addition to composition for the damage as is appraised according to the custom of the place. It shall be done thus only if the animal herder does not dare to swear that he did not send them in with evil intent. If he does so swear, he shall be absolved from blame; but he must pay the composition for any damage.

[Concerning the man who causes his pigs or cattle to do damage.]

345. He who deliberately sets his pigs or cattle to do damage to someone else and does not dare to clear himself [by oath], shall pay one solidus as composition in addition to paying the composition for any damage caused.

[Concerning the man who seizes an animal causing damage.]

346. If a man pens an animal found causing damage and brings an accusation against him whose animal it is, then the owner shall pay one solidus as composition in addition to the composition for any assessed damage. And if he [the first man] keeps it in his courtyard, then he to whom the animal belongs shall ask that it be returned to him [and it shall be returned] provided that the owner gives three soliquae as a pledge for the ultimate redemption [of the damage done] or that he provides a surety to guarantee that he will pay compensation for the damage which shall be assessed in accordance with the amount which is agreed upon by his neighbors. If the first man does not want to accept the pledge and holds the animal more than one night, he shall pay one solidus as composition. And if the owner of the animal, being hard of heart, does not bother to free it, then the man who found it doing damage shall keep it nine nights, and he shall

give it water only; let him then be content concerning the damage done to him on account of the fact that he held the animal for nine nights. And if anything is killed by that animal, it shall be imputed to the negligence of him who neglected to disengage his pledge.

[*Concerning animals that follow a man.*]

347. If a horse or any other animal follows after a man who is traveling, the man whom it follows should place it in bonds or in an enclosure and so secure it that it may be found by its owner following after, just as it is provided above [Rothair 343]. But if the animal begins to follow a man and then turns away from the road, then no blame shall be imputed to him whom it began to follow.

[*Concerning the man who is seeking his lost animals.*]

348. In the case where someone is asked by another man to search for his horse or other animal and the [animal's] marks are described to him and if that one who was asked takes someone else's horse or animal by mistake, then if the real owner comes along and seeks to bring charges against him, we decree that he who holds the animal through error shall offer oath that he believed the animal to be the one about which he had been asked. He shall then return the horse and not be blamed further. If the true owner does not come, then he shall return the animal to that one from whom he took it that he may keep it again according to law, just as provided above [Rothair 343].

[*On pigs which feed in another man's mast.*]

349. If fewer than ten pigs feed in someone else's mast and are discovered, none of them may be killed; but he who discovered them shall take one of them and keep it safe, and three siliquae shall be paid to him as composition for the pig. If there are more than ten pigs, or even ten, an average one of them may be killed and nothing shall be required for it. But if there are less than ten pigs and he kills one of them, he shall return it singlefold, that is, he shall return a similar pig.

[*Concerning the man who finds pigs making holes in his meadow.*]

350. He who finds one or more pigs making holes in his meadow may kill one of them and nothing shall be required for it.

[*On stealing boars.*]

351. On boars. He who steals another man's boar shall pay twelve solidi as composition in the case of that boar called the leader of the herd (*sonorpair*) which has fought and conquered all the other boars in the herd. In any one herd, however many pigs there may be, only one is regarded as the sonorpair. Moreover, if the herd is smaller than thirty head, there is no sonorpair. If the sonorpair is killed while doing damage, he who killed it shall return a similar sonorpair or a better one, and composition for the damage shall be paid to him. But if other boars or pigs are stolen, they shall be returned eightfold.

[*On beating swineherds.*]

352. On beating swineherds. He who beats a freeman's swineherd—one who goes out from his own house and not from the house of a tenant field slave (massarius)—shall pay twenty solidi as composition, provided the swineherd who was struck did not first create some violent disturbance. But if the swineherd inflicted any blows, they shall be appraised and composition paid for them.

[*Concerning swineherds who fight among themselves.*]

353. If two swineherds fight between themselves or raise a violent disturbance, composition shall be paid for their strikes and blows, but other penalty shall not be required.

[*On plowing someone else's field.*]

354. On plowing someone else's field. He who plows another man's field knowing it not his own or presumes to scatter seed on it, shall lose his work and its fruit, and he who proves the field to be his own shall have that fruit.

[*On plowing over someone else's seeded field.*]

355. On plowing over someone else's field. He who plows over another man's seeded field and cannot prove it to be his own shall return such fruits as he destroyed to the proper owner and shall pay six solidi as composition for his heedless presumption.

[*On reaping someone else's meadow.*]

356. On reaping someone else's meadow. He who reaps or plows over another man's meadow shall return the hay and pay six solidi as composition.

[*Concerning the man who fetters his animal in someone else's field.*]

357. He who deliberately destroys another man's field with his animal, or pulls out stalks with his hands, shall pay six solidi as composition.

[*No one shall deny fodder to those who are traveling.*]

358. No one shall deny fodder to those who are traveling, except in the case of a meadow or field which is unreaped at the time. Before the hay or fruits have been collected, he whose land it is may protect as much as he can defend with his enclosure. But he who presumes to remove horses being used on a journey from the stubble or from a [mowed] pasture shall render an eightfold composition for those horses on account of the fact that he presumed to move them from an arable field which had already yielded its crops.

[*On oaths.*]

359. On oaths. In a case between freemen involving twenty or more solidi where an oath is to be given, the parties shall swear on the sacred gospels with twelve oathhelpers (*aidos*) or oathtakers (sacramentales) selected in such a way that six of them are named by that one who brings the case, he against whom the case is brought is the seventh, and the accused shall choose five additional freemen to make twelve. If the case involves from twelve to twenty solidi, six men shall take oath on consecrated arms: three shall be named by him who brings the case, two freemen shall be chosen by him against whom the case is brought, and he himself [the accused] shall be the sixth. And if it is a case involving less than twelve solidi, then three shall swear on their arms: one named by him who brings the case, one by the other, and the accused himself shall be the third.

[*On pledges and sureties.*]

360. On pledges and sureties. He who gives pledges to another man or gives a surety for his oath shall perform all those things to which he obligated himself through the pledges. He who brings the case and receives the pledges ought to name oathhelpers who are most nearly related to him. This should be done except in the case of those who have committed some grave injustice against that one who brings the case—such as striking him, consenting to his death, or transferring his property to someone else—such persons cannot be

oathhelpers even though they are near relatives on account of the fact that they are enemies to or estranged from [the accuser].

[*Concerning the man who gives pledges.*]

361. He who gives pledges or a surety that he will take oath to someone else in a certain cause should be given a period up to twelve days to offer his oath. If perchance illness or some other cause prevents and he is unable to take oath within this prescribed time, then the time should be extended another twelve days. If the oath has not been completed then, and if he deliberately delays and does not give the oath for a whole year, he shall lose that property which is under consideration and the man who received the pledges shall acquire ownership of them. And in the contrary case: if the man who received the pledges delays to hear the oath and drags out the case for a whole year, after the year has passed he shall have no right to claim that property; but that one who was prepared to give the oath shall possess it incontestably.

[*Concerning the man who dies after naming oathhelpers and surety.*]

362. Concerning the man who dies after an oath has been allowed by judgment. If a man dies after giving surety for his oath and the oathhelpers have been named, and the dead man leaves sons, and if afterwards he who brought the case brings charges against the sons saying that whatever the father had obligated through pledges and a surety the sons ought to complete; then the sons, even though they may have less wealth than their father, either ought to deny by oath that their father promised these things, or they must fulfill that which their father promised. If any one of the oathhelpers dies, the man who brought the case shall have the right to name a person of like condition in place of the dead man from among his near relatives, either from his own relatives or from the relatives who are related by the marriage contract. If he who brought the case claims that the oath has been broken, that one who would deny it shall offer oath, if he dares, that neither he nor his father broke their oath with him; afterwards he shall take the oath just as it is provided.

[*On broken oaths.*]

363. On broken oaths. An oath is known to be broken when he who is accused, joined by his oathhelpers, does not dare to swear on

the holy gospels or consecrated weapons, i.e., if he or one of his oathhelpers withdraws from the oath: then the oath is known to be broken.

[*Concerning the man who confesses a crime.*]

364. Concerning him who first confesses and offers oath. That man who is accused by someone else and he denies it may clear himself according to the law and the nature of the case. If, however, he confesses that he did it, he shall pay composition according to the provisions of this lawbook. But no one, after first confessing, may deny it later by oath, because a man may not be blameless after he himself has indicated his guilt. We have become aware that many in our realm raise controversies with evil purpose and we have therefore been moved to correct the present law and to establish a more equitable provision.

[*Concerning the debts of a dead father.*]

365. Concerning the debts of a dead father. If a man attempts to collect a debt from a son after the death of that one's father and the son denies the existence of the debt, the case shall be handled thus: the son may offer oath, the strength of which will vary according to the amount of money sought [Rothair 359], that his father was not a debtor, or he may defend himself by combat if he can.

[*On disputes between creditors and debtors.*]

366. If any controversy arises between a creditor on the one hand and a debtor and his surety on the other, and the creditor says that pledges have been designated in a certain cause, and if the surety denies this fact, it is not the place of the surety to offer oath, but the debtor alone should offer satisfaction by taking oath either on the gospels or on his arms and swearing that he has neither given pledges in such a case nor offered a surety.

[*On foreigners* (waregang).]

367. On foreigners (waregang). All foreigners who come from outside our frontiers into the boundaries of our kingdom and yield to the jurisdiction of our power ought to live according to the Lombard laws, unless through our grace they have merited another law.[75] If they have legitimate children, these heirs shall live just as do the children of Lombards. If they do not have legitimate children, it shall not

be in their power to give away any of their property or to alienate it by any means without the king's consent.

[*On duelling.*]

368. Concerning duellers. When a man participates in a duel, he may not have upon himself witch's herbs or other like things. He may have nothing except those arms which are agreed upon. If it is suspected that a man carries such prohibited things secretly, they shall be searched for by the judge and if they are found on him, they shall be torn out and cast aside. After this search, the one engaging in the combat shall place his hand in the hand of his relatives or fellow freemen and say before the judge to whom he is making satisfaction that he does not have on himself anything that belongs to witches. Then he may proceed to the contest.

[*On royal cases.*]

369. On royal cases. In royal suits which belong to the crown and in which compensation is expected or guilt sought a double composition shall be paid according to ancient custom. However, in cases involving the guardianship (mundium) of free women, or murder, or like causes for which a composition of 900 solidi has been established, we order a singlefold payment remain in force [even in royal cases]. All other compositions, as we have said above, shall be exacted twofold.

[*Concerning slaves of the king who commit murder.*]

370. If a slave of the king commits murder, we decree that composition be paid according to the value at which the dead man is assessed, and the slave shall be hung over the grave of the dead man that vengeance may be inflicted upon him. There the case shall cease.

[*Concerning other cases involving the king's slaves.*]

371. In other cases where freemen and the slaves of other men are liable to pay 900 solidi—that is, in the case where someone blocks the road to a free woman or causes her some injury, or takes pledges from a herd of mares or pigs, or does other such things for which we have decreed that 900 solidi are to be paid as provided above in this code [Rothair 5, 8, 13–15, 18, 19, 26, 186, 187, 191, 249, 279, 378]—if a slave of the king does this, he shall be killed and the 900 solidi shall not be required from the king's court.

[*Concerning slaves of the king who steal.*]

372. If a slave of the king commits a theft, it shall be returned eightfold but he shall not be held as one taken in the act of theft.

[*Concerning slaves of the king who violate a courtyard.*]

373. If a slave breaks into a courtyard or blocks the road or throws a man from his horse, or commits any other minor crime, composition shall be paid just as in the case of the slaves of other freemen, the amount of the composition being as provided above [Rothair 27, 30, 254, 277, 380; Grimwald 9].

[*On the killing of a schultheis (sculdahis).*]

374. On the schultheis. If a schultheis or other official of the king is killed while in the king's service, he shall be valued at the price of a freeman as noted in this edict, and composition shall be made to his legitimate relatives. In addition, the man who killed him shall pay eighty solidi as composition to the king's fisc. If a schultheis or other official is struck or beaten composition shall be paid in like manner as for a freeman or according to his birth as is provided in this code. In addition, the offender shall pay eighty solidi as composition to the king's fisc for his guilt.

[*Concerning property acquired by the gastald (gastaldius).*]

375. If the gastald or other official of the king, after he has received his office and carried out the royal will in connection with administering the court of the king, acquires anything by formal gift (gairethinx), that is, by a gift made by anyone, it shall remain his if it is confirmed to him by order of an indulgent king. Otherwise anything which he acquires by gift after his work of administration has been undertaken, as mentioned above, all this shall belong to the king and neither [the royal agent] nor his heirs may claim it in their own name.

[*Concerning him who tries to kill another's aldia or woman slave because she is a witch.*]

376. No one may presume to kill another man's aldia or woman slave as if she were a vampire (striga), which the people call witch (masca), because it is in no wise to be believed by Christian minds that it is possible that a woman can eat a living man from

within. If anyone presumes to perpetrate such an illegal and impious act, that is, if he kills an aldia [for such a reason], he shall pay sixty solidi as composition according to her status and, in addition, he shall add 100 solidi for the guilt, half to the king and half to him whose aldia she was. If, moreover, she is a woman slave, he shall pay composition for her status as is provided above according to whether she is a household slave or a field slave [Rothair 130–36]. In addition, he shall pay sixty solidi as composition for the guilt, half to the king and half to him whose slave she was. If indeed a judge has ordered him to perpetrate this evil act, then the judge shall pay composition according to the above written penalty from his own property.

[*On striking out a freeman's one eye.*]

377. If anyone strikes out the eye of a one-eyed freeman, he shall pay as composition two parts [i.e., two-thirds] of the price at which that one would have been valued if he had killed him. If, moreover, anyone strikes out [the eye of] a one-eyed aldius or slave belonging to someone else, he shall pay composition for him as for a dead man.

[*On free women who are involved in a breach of the peace (scandalum).*]

378. If a free woman participates in a brawl (scandalum) where men are struggling, and if she inflicts some blow or injury and perhaps in turn is struck or killed, she shall be valued according to her rank and composition shall be paid for her as if the deed had been done to a brother of that woman. But the penalty for such injury, for which 900 solidi have been adjudged, shall not be required since she had participated in a struggle in a manner dishonorable for women.

[*On destroying a hut on another man's land.*]

379. If, while there is a controversy over the land, anyone disturbs or tears down another man's hut (*cassina*) or building (*tectum*) which is outside the courtyard and where men do not live, and if he is not able to prove that the land is his own in the manner provided by law, he shall restore the hut and pay as composition another like it as its value is appraised. If he disturbs a house which is inhabited, he shall pay composition as if it were an attack by an

armed band ([h]aratraibus), just as is read in this lawbook [Rothair 19, 279].

[Concerning taking one's animals secretly from another man's enclosure.]
380. If anyone secretly removes his animal from another man's enclosure and has not asked for it, he shall pay twenty solidi as composition for breach of the courtyard, which is hoberos [Rothair 278, 373].

[Concerning the charge of cowardice.]
381. If anyone in anger calls another man a coward and cannot deny it, and if he claims that he said it in anger, he may offer oath that [it was said in anger and] he does not know him to be a coward. Afterwards he shall pay twelve solidi as composition for this insulting word. But if he perseveres in the charge, he must prove it by combat, if he can, or he shall pay composition as above.

[On him who knocks down a freeman.]
382. If anyone strikes a freeman so that he falls, he shall pay six solidi as composition provided that he has not caused other injury. If, moreover, he strikes the man in a way that he does not fall, he shall pay three solidi as composition.

[On him who drags a freeman by his beard or hair.]
383. If anyone in a quarrel with a freeman drags him by the beard or hair, he shall pay six solidi as composition. If he drags an aldius or household slave or a field slave by the beard or hair, he shall pay the composition for one blow.

[Concerning broken arms, thighs, or legs.]
384. On broken arms, thighs, or legs. If anyone breaks a freeman's arm above the elbow, which bone is the murioth, he shall pay twenty solidi as composition. If, moreover, the break is below the elbow, which bone is trene, he shall pay sixteen solidi as composition. If he breaks the leg above the knee, which bone is lage, he shall pay twenty solidi as composition. If below the knee, which is the tibia, he shall pay sixteen solidi as composition. If indeed the limb was muti-

lated or crippled, he shall pay a fourth part of the wergeld, as is read in this edict, as composition [Rothair 112].

[*Concerning the guardianship (mundium) and debts of a girl.*]

385. On the mundium or debts of a girl. If the mundium of a free girl, her relatives being dead, has fallen to the king's court and her father or brother has left a debt, in such proportion as the heirs of the father or brother succeed the debt shall be resolved. In like manner it shall be resolved if there were natural sons.

[*Concerning the present laws.*]

386. With the favor of God and with the greatest care and most careful scrutiny, obtained by heavenly favor, after seeking out and finding the old laws of our fathers which were not written down, and with the equal counsel and consent of our most important judges and with the rest of our most happy nation (exercitus) assisting, we have established the present lawbook containing those provisions which are useful for the common good of all our people. We have ordered these laws to be written down on this parchment, thus preserving them in this edict so that those things which, with divine aid, we have been able to recapture through careful investigation of the old laws of the Lombards known either to ourself or to the old men of the nation, we have put down in this lawbook. Issued and confirmed by the formal procedure (gairethinx) according to the usage of our nation, let this be strong and stable law: let it be observed firmly and inviolably by all our subjects in our own most happy and in future times.

[*On him who accidentally kills a freeman.*]

387. If anyone unintentionally kills a freeman, he shall pay composition according to the price at which the dead man is valued, and the feud shall not be required since it was done unintentionally.

[*We decree these things.*]

388. We add and decree that those cases which have been concluded shall not be renewed. But those cases which have not been settled by the present twenty-second day of this month of November (643) in the second indiction and which have been begun or instigated, shall be affected and settled in accordance with this edict.

We add this general order lest any fraud be applied to this edict through the fault of the scribes: if any contention arises, no other copies of this code shall be accredited or received except those which have been written or recognized or sealed by the hand of our notary Answald who has written this in accordance with our command.

HERE ENDS ROTHAIR'S EDICT

II. The Laws of King Grimwald (A.D. 668)

These are the laws added by our most glorious King Grimwald:

In an earlier portion of this work, our predecessor urged that, with the help of God, we should add to our lawbook those provisions which we are able to recover of particular causes which up to the present have not been recorded. Those cases which have already been judged and concluded may nonetheless not be renewed. Therefore I, the most noble Grimwald, king of the Lombard nation, with the help of God in the sixth year of my reign, in the month of July, in the eleventh indiction, with the advice and consent of our judges and of all the people have undertaken to amend those provisions of this code that seem harsh and unjust, and to bring them to a better state of justice.

TITLES

1. On the man or woman slave who serves his or her lord for thirty years.
2. Concerning the freeman who remains at liberty for thirty years.

3. Concerning the slave who commits an offense for which payment of 900 solidi has been prescribed.

4. On the possession of property for thirty years.

5. Concerning the succession of grandsons who, after the death of their father, remain in the home of the grandfather.

6. On abandoned wives.

7. Concerning a wife's offenses.

8. On women who knowingly go to a man who already has a wife.

9. On female slaves who steal.

LAWS

[*On the man or woman slave who serves his or her lord for thirty years.*]

1. On prescriptive title [acquired by possession] for thirty years. If a man or woman slave serves his or her lord for thirty years and in such wise the truth of the matter is recognized, then if through pride or an illegal claim to be in the *patrocinium* of another the slave tries to claim himself [i.e., his freedom] from his true lord by combat, we shall not allow it to him by any means, but he shall serve his own lord as befits a man or woman slave. Likewise, if he is an aldius, he shall continue to render obedience to his patron just as he has done for thirty years, although further new duties should not be imposed upon him by his lord. A man should indeed keep that property which he has possessed without opposition for as much as thirty years.

[*Concerning the freeman who remains at liberty for thirty years.*]

2. If freemen have remained at liberty for as long as thirty years, they shall thereafter suffer no molestation through combat, but they shall remain in their state of freedom. And if anyone accuses them of some offense, they may clear themselves with their legitimate oathhelpers.

[*Concerning the slave who commits an offense for which payment of 900 solidi has been prescribed.*]

3. On the guilt of slaves. If a slave commits an offense for which [the payment of] 900 solidi has been prescribed in this edict and it has been adjudged that the lord should pay composition for his slave, we order this to be modified. If the slave commits such a crime,

his lord shall not pay composition, but he should hand over that person [the slave] to be killed; and the lord shall pay sixty solidi as composition for the illegal act which the slave committed, but more shall not be required.

If the slave flees and his lord is not able to find him, his lord shall pay twenty solidi for each slave who has sought flight or hid himself and the lord should offer oath that he was not able to find his slave. And if he finds him at any time whatever thereafter, he shall hand the slave over, as above, to be killed, and the lord shall receive back the twenty solidi which he gave for the flight of that one; in addition he must pay sixty solidi as composition for any offense that the slave may have committed.

If the slave takes spoils from the crypt of a man's grave, the lord shall return whatever the slave took and shall pay sixty solidi as composition, as noted above, and the person of the slave shall be handed over to be killed.

[On the possession of property for thirty years.]

4. On the possession of property for thirty years. If anyone possesses houses, families, or lands for thirty years or more and this is recognized, his possession may not be challenged by combat after this time. He who possesses [for such a period of time] may defend himself by oath according to the value of his property and, as has been said, he shall not be harassed by the threat of combat.

[Concerning the succession of grandsons who, after the death of their father, remain in the home of the grandfather.]

5. On the succession of grandsons who, after the death of their father, remain in the home of their grandfather. If anyone has one or more legitimate sons and one of the sons dies while the father is still living, and the son who dies leaves one or more legitimate sons, and if the grandfather then dies, they [the grandson or grandsons] together shall receive such a portion of the property of their grandfather as their father would have received had he lived (a portion equal to that of his brothers, the uncles of his sons).

Likewise, if there are one or more legitimate daughters, or one or more natural sons, they shall have such rights as are provided in this lawbook. For it seems inhuman and unjust to us that sons should be disinherited from succession to their father for such a cause—

namely, the fact that their father died in the home of their grandfather—but after the death of the grandfather, they, in place of
their father, shall receive a portion of all the property, [their collective share] being equal to that of each of the uncles.

Likewise, if there are no legitimate children and one or several
natural sons are found, they shall have their right; that is, they shall
have a third part of all the property [which their father would have
received] [Rothair 154].

[On abandoned wives.]

6. On abandoned wives. If anyone puts aside his wife without
legal cause and receives over her another woman into his house, he
shall pay 500 solidi as composition, half to the king and half to the
relatives of the wife; and moreover, he shall lose the mundium of the
woman whom he put aside. If the wife does not wish to return to her
husband, she may return to her relatives together with her property
and her mundium [cf. Rothair 188–90, 214].

[Concerning a wife's offenses.]

7. On a wife's offenses. If anyone maliciously and without legal
cause accuses his wife of having committed adultery or of having
conspired against the life of her husband, that woman may clear herself by the oath of her relatives or by combat. If she clears herself,
then the husband shall offer oath together with his legal relatives,
twelve with himself, [to the effect] that he accused her of the offense
neither with evil intent nor maliciously, and that he ought to leave her
only if he has had his suspicions confirmed. If he does this, he shall be
absolved from blame. But if he does not dare so to swear, he shall pay
the wergeld of that woman in composition, such an amount as if he
had killed her brother, half to the king and half to the relatives of the
woman.

[On women who knowingly go to a man who already has a wife.]

8. If a woman or girl knows that a man has a wife and enters
[his house] in spite of her and so takes a husband not her own, we
order that that woman lose all her property who knowingly and willingly consented to the husband of another woman, and the court of
the king will receive half of her property and the relatives [of the
injured wife] half. And the husband shall take back that first woman

and live with her, his legal wife, as is proper. The blame shall be imputed to her who presumed to enter in spite of the other wife, and no composition shall be paid by the husband and the feud shall not be required.

[On female slaves who steal.]

9. If a woman slave commits a theft, her lord shall pay a ninefold composition for that theft. But the forty-solidi payment for guilt which is provided in this edict(which is for one taken in theft [fegang]),[1] is not required nor should it be exacted from the slave's lord.

III. The Laws of King Liutprand

TITLES

Eighth Year

15. On the giving of sureties and the offering of pledges in the presence of witnesses.
16. On the borrowing of money and the giving of notes.
17. Concerning the man who kills his brother with evil intent.
18. Concerning those merchants and artisans who travel within or without the country.

Ninth Year

19. Concerning legal age.
20. Concerning homicide in self defense.
21. Concerning the slave who kills a freeman, his lord consenting.
22. On the means whereby a woman may sell her property with the consent of her husband.
23. On the freeing of slaves in church.
24. Concerning free women who marry slaves.
25. Concerning the man who has taken his case to the schultheis.
26. On the method whereby two men who live in the same judicial district but in territories presided over by different schultheis may settle their suit.
27. On the means whereby a man may bring suit against someone living in another judicial district.
28. Concerning the man who feels that he has not received justice from his judge.

Tenth (Eleventh?) Year

29. Concerning women who wish to sell their property.

Eleventh Year

30. Concerning women who take the veil.
31. On the abduction of free women who have not taken vows.
32. Concerning the offspring of an illegal marriage.
33. No man shall marry the widow of his cousin on either his mother's or his father's side.
34. No man shall marry his godmother or his goddaughter.
35. Concerning the man who engages in sedition against his judge.
36. Concerning pledges which have been given but not returned.
37. Concerning pledges which have been given and then reclaimed by force.

38. Concerning the man who has given a pledge and wishes to reclaim it by offering a surety.
39. Concerning the man who gives a pledge and then offers a surety.
40. Concerning the man who gives pledges and names a surety.
41. Concerning him who retakes pledges before the prescribed time.
42. Concerning the judge or public official who exacts a written agreement from the parties to a suit.
43. On gifts of property.
44. Concerning fugitive slaves and strangers.
45. Concerning him who destroys another man's fence.
46. Concerning him who digs a ditch on someone else's land.
47. Concerning him who puts a fence on someone else's land.
48. Concerning him who sells a freeman outside the country.
49. Concerning him who sells someone else's slave outside the country.
50. On putting slaves to the oath.
51. On handing someone else's slave over to the king.
52. Concerning him who frees someone else's slave.
53. Concerning him who makes a cleric of another man's slave without the consent of his lord.

Twelfth Year
54. On the gift made in formal manner and confirmed by a charter.
55. Concerning him who allows his slave to become folkfree and legally independent (amundius).
56. Concerning him who accuses another man of theft.
57. Concerning the man who incurs a debt and sells his property.
58. Concerning the child who sells his property while he is under age.
59. Concerning the gastald or agent of the king who gives anything from the property of the fisc.
60. Concerning the aldius who has intercourse with a free woman or girl.
61. On the giving of pledges for an oath.
62. Concerning him who kills a freeman while defending himself.
63. On false testimony.
64. Concerning the slave who is taken in theft.

Thirteenth Year

65. On the disposition of a man's property if he leaves unmarried daughters and no sons.
66. Concerning the freeman who takes the wife of a slave or of an aldius while her husband is still living.
67. On the agreement which has been made without mortgaging itemized property to guarantee it.
68. Concerning aldii.
69. Concerning the aldius who has been in another man's house without his lord's knowing it.

Fourteenth Year

70. Concerning brothers who share their property for forty years.
71. On the malicious challenge to combat.
72. Concerning the freeman who advises another to perjure himself.
73. On gifts which are made without receiving a return gift or going through a formal ceremony.
74. Concerning the child who, while under age, wishes to divide his property with his brothers or relatives.
75. Concerning the child who, while under age, is involved in a lawsuit.
76. On adultery committed by women who have taken vows.
77. On the succession of two brothers, or of a father and his son, who have been freed by formal ceremony.
78. On the possession of property acquired from the public lands.
79. How a man shall buy a horse in the market.
80. Concerning thieves.
81. How a man shall recover a lost horse or other property.
82. On the finding of someone else's wagon and oxen in one's own wood.
83. Concerning judges and how many men they may leave behind from the army.

Fifteenth Year

84. Concerning him who seeks the advice of a sorcerer.
85. What is to be done if the judge or other public officials of a place fail to seek out sorcerers or witches.
86. What a man shall do if he finds someone else's horse doing damage to his property.

148. On those who claim another man's land.
149. On minor children who are found to be in need.
150. On him who digs a ditch along the road.
151. On him who sends his pigs into another man's defended forest.
152. Concerning the prodigal man who has sold or dissipated his substance so that he is unable to pay composition.
153. Concerning the children of a man who becomes a priest.

LAWS

From the First Year (a.d. 713)

PROLOGUE

This Catholic Christian prince has been influenced to promulgate these laws and to judge wisely not by his own foresight but through the wisdom and inspiration of God: he has conceived [these laws] in his heart, studied them in his mind, and happily fulfilled them in his word. For the heart of the king is in the hand of God, as the most wise Solomon attests, who has said: "Just as the flow of the waters, so the heart of the king is in the hand of God; if he holds them back, all things should be dried up; if, moreover, out of mercy he releases them, all things will be watered and their sweetness will be restored." A certain James, an apostle of the Lord, has put it thus in his epistle, saying: "Every good and every perfect gift is from above, coming down from the father of light."

Therefore these things having been fulfilled, we recall that our most powerful predecessor, the most eminent King Rothair, just as is set forth in the preceding writing, renewed and established an edict for the Lombards. There he wisely took care to add that should a prince of the Lombards, one of his successors, discover anything superfluous there, he should remove it, and that which he finds to be lacking, he should add, under inspiration from God. And later the most glorious King Grimwald, with the help of God, removed or expanded those laws which seemed fitting to him. Following this precept and believing ourself inspired by divine providence, we shall delete and add those things in a like manner which seem fitting to us according to the law of God, and such we have ordered to be written on the present page.

Thus I, Liutprand, most excellent king of the Lombards, in the name of the Lord and with the protection of God in the first year of my reign; and on the day before the first of March, in the eleventh indiction, together with all my judges from the regions of Austria as well as of Neustria, and even from the area of Tuscany,[1] as well as with the remainder of my sworn Lombard followers (fideles),[2] and with the rest of the people attending, with the common counsel of these people and with the fear and love and holiness of God, [I decree] these laws as suitable.

First of all [is the law] concerning the succession of daughters.

[*On the succession of daughters.*]

1.I. If a Lombard dies without legitimate sons but leaves daughters, the daughters shall succeed as heirs to all the inheritance of the father or mother as if they were legitimate sons.

[*On the succession of married and unmarried daughters.*]

2.II. If a Lombard while living has handed over some of his daughters in marriage and other daughters remain at home unmarried (*in capillo*),[3] then all of the daughters shall equally succeed as heirs to his substance as if they were sons.

[*On the succession of sisters.*]

3.III. If a Lombard leaves sisters, and while he was still alive they had gone to husbands, and if this man also leaves daughters, then the sisters shall have from the property of their brother [only] such an amount as they received on the day of their vows when they went to their husbands [and the daughters shall have the rest of the inheritance]. If the brother leaves neither sons nor daughters, or if the sons and/or daughters die before him without leaving sons or daughters of their own, then the sisters—those who remained unmarried as well as those who have gone to husbands—shall succeed as heirs to all his property.

[*On the succession of unmarried sisters and daughters.*]

4.IIII. If a Lombard leaves sisters or daughters at home unmarried, then they ought to succeed to his inheritance in the same

manner and equally, however many there are, as if he had left legitimate sons.

[*Concerning daughters or sisters who have acted against the wish
of their father or brother.*]

5.V. If daughters or sisters act contrary to the wish of their
father or brother, then the father or brother has the right to judge
concerning their property in whatever manner and to whatever extent
is pleasing to him.

[*On the disposal of property by the ill on behalf of their souls.*]

6.VI. If a Lombard, suffering from human infirmity, is ill, even
though he is confined to his bed he has the right, while he lives and is
able to speak rationally, to make decisions on behalf of his soul or to
dispose of his property in whatever manner and to whatever extent is
pleasing to him. And that which he decides shall remain firmly in
effect.

If any case, which involved the subject matter dealt with in the
titles recently added to the lawbook, was completed before this time
by negotiation or compromise, the decision shall remain in effect as
decided before. Those suits which have not been determined by decision or compromise shall be decided according to these provisions
and shall remain in effect in the manner now decreed which is set
forth in these laws.

[HERE END THE LAWS FROM THE FIRST YEAR]

FROM THE FIFTH YEAR (A.D. 717)

In the name of God Almighty, I, Liutprand, most excellent
king of the most happy and Catholic, favored by God, nation of the
Lombards, take occasion to remember that those laws issued earlier
by us can now be found in the lawbook of the Lombards—laws
issued in an [earlier] page [of this edict]—in the first year of our
reign in the eleventh indiction which, through our fear and love of
God, seemed proper to us and to our judges and to the other Lombard fideles and which we, with due consideration, took care to add

to the body of the ancient law. Now, therefore, with the compassion of an Almighty God favoring us, on the first day of March in the fifth year of our reign, in the fifteenth indiction, in a like manner with God willing and together with all our judges from the regions of Austria and Neustria as well as from the bounds of Tuscany, and together with the rest of our Lombards, we with foresight add these provisions which we believe to be pleasing to God so that false oaths can be avoided in many circumstances and suits can be disposed of compassionately by certain men without the charge of corruption arising, and that which seemed obscure before may now be clear.

First of all is a provision about the morning gift of women.

[Concerning a woman's morning gift.]

7.I. If a Lombard wishes to give his wife a morning gift (morgincap) at the time he marries her, we decree that before the marriage in the presence of friends and relatives he announce the gift by means of a written instrument confirmed by witnesses which states, "Observe that which I give as a morning gift to my wife," so that in the future she may not lose the gift by any perjury. The morning gift may not be more than a fourth part of the property of him who makes the gift. If a man prefers to give his wife less than this fourth part, he may give whatever amount pleases him; but more than a fourth part he may not give.[4]

[Concerning cases which arise between fellow freemen or relatives.]

8.II. Concerning witnesses. If any agreement is reached between fellow freemen or relatives, and three or four good men are present as witnesses, the agreement may not be denied later, provided that both parties believe the testimony of those who were present. That man in whose favor the witnesses render evidence shall offer satisfaction by oath to his accuser. Suitable witnesses are those whose reputation excels in good works and whose trustworthiness is recognized—such witnesses are the kind whose testimony the prince or his judges can believe. If it is thought that informed witnesses have attempted to conceal the truth, they shall offer satisfaction by oath to the prince or to his representative that they have not obscured the truth. If indeed an obligation has been made and pledges given and controversy has arisen on account of this, it shall be adjudicated afterwards as is read in an earlier law established by the most glorious King Rothair [Rothair 360–62, 366].

[Concerning the male or female slave handed over to the king.]
9.III. On freedmen. If anyone hands over his man or woman slave to the king and the prince himself sets him or her free by handing him or her over to the hands of a priest in front of the holy altar, he or she shall remain free just as those who become folkfree. He who obtains the mundium of such a woman freed by the prince shall have it as for a woman who is folkfree; and there shall be no further [servile] condition either for her or for her children. We decree that male children who are born of such a free woman are without mundium [i.e., they are legally independent][5]; moreover, female children shall have a mundium just the same as their mother, and that mundium shall not be more than three solidi.

[On the manumission of slaves.]
10.IIII. Also on freedmen. If anyone sets free his man or woman slave and retains the mundium for him or her of one, two, three, or six solidi—whatever the value of the mundium, this amount should be confirmed in a charter for him or her. Those children who afterwards are born of such a freed woman, whether they are male or female, shall not have a greater mundium than the amount of that of their mother.

[Concerning thefts committed by fugitive slaves.]
11.V. On fugitive slaves. If a slave commits a theft while he is in flight and in his flight he goes outside the country, the judge shall proceed just as King Rothair of glorious memory decreed [Rothair 256]. But if the slave dallies within the country, then his lord shall have a period of three months to seek him out. If his lord finds him, or if he does not find him, and the fact is clear that the slave did commit that theft, then his lord shall pay composition for the theft, just as is the law. If, however, it is not clear and the slave's lord denies that his slave committed the theft, he shall defend himself by combat or by oath, if he can.

[Concerning him who betroths or marries a girl who is less than twelve years old.]
12.VI. On [the marriage of] girls who are under age. If a girl

is betrothed or married before she is twelve years old, he who took or betrothed her shall pay the composition for abduction, as is provided in this lawbook; that is, he shall pay 900 solidi, half to the king and half to the child herself [cf. Rothair 191] and she shall return to her home and to her property. She shall remain there up to the above-mentioned time [i.e., until she is twelve years old]; afterwards, moreover, she may choose for herself and marry him whom she chooses.

If, moreover, her mundwald had given his consent or had handed her over before the girl was twelve years old, he shall pay 300 solidi as composition to the royal fisc and he shall lose her mundium and the girl with her property shall be in the mundium of the palace. However, a father or brother has the right to give or betroth his daughter or sister to whomever or at whatever age he pleases. We have conceded this privilege because we believe that a father ought not [and will not] give his daughter or a brother [give] his sister to any man with evil intent contrary to reason.

[*On the killing of freemen.*]

13.VII. On the killing of freemen. If a Lombard is killed by another man (which God forbid), and according to law it is a case where composition should be paid and if he who is killed does not leave a son: although we have [earlier] established that daughters could be heirs, just as if they were boys, to all the property of their father or mother [Liutprand 1], nevertheless we decree here [in this case] that the nearest [male] relatives of him who was killed— those who can succeed him within the proper degree of relationship —shall receive that composition. For daughters, since they are of the feminine sex, are unable to raise the feud. Therefore we provide that the daughters not receive that composition, but, as we have said, the abovementioned [male] relatives [ought to have it]. If there are no near [male] relatives, then the daughters themselves shall receive half of that composition, whether there is one or more of them, and half [shall be received] by the king's treasury.

[*Concerning sisters and in what manner they shall succeed one another.*]

14.VIII. On sisters and how they may succeed one another. Whether sisters remain in the house of their father or go out of it to a husband, they may succeed to all of the property of their father and mother, just as we have established before [Liutprand 1]. If it happens that one of the sisters dies, then those who have remained unmarried and those who have gone to husbands shall succeed to the portion of their dead sister. The near [male] relatives of her mundwald may receive as much as her mundium was worth; but they shall receive nothing from her property. If, however, she who died had already been given in marriage, then he who had acquired her and her mundium shall succeed to her property.

Any case that arises concerning matters covered in the laws which our excellency has now issued in the name of God on the present first day of March in the fifteenth indiction and in the fifth year of our reign, shall be completed in the way we, with our judges and the rest of the Lombards, have decreed and as is read above. But those matters which have arisen heretofore concerning such things which have already been concluded or determined, shall remain as the decisions were first announced.

HERE END THE LAWS FROM THE FIFTH YEAR

FROM THE EIGHTH YEAR (A.D. 720)

In the name of Almighty God, I, the most excellent Liutprand, king of the most happy nation, the Lombards, in the eighth year of my reign, God favoring, on the first day of March, in the third indiction, together with my most illustrious nobles (*obtimates*) from the bounds of Neustria, Austria, and Tuscany, and with the rest of the noble (*nobiles*) Lombards [issue these laws]. We have investigated earnestly and carefully those particular matters which were covered in the earlier issues of our lawbook; now with all the people assisting, we have taken care to add, to clarify, or to establish the present rules contained in the following passages.

[*On the giving of sureties and the offering of pledges in the presence of witnesses.*]
    15.I. That man living under the jurisdiction of our realm who

gives pledges to anyone in any manner or offers a surety in the presence of two or three witnesses whose trustworthiness is accepted, ought to fulfill [his obligation] in every respect. If he delays and a pledge is taken from his property from among those things which it is lawful to pledge, no guilt shall be incurred by him who took the pledge. But he who presumes to take a pledge without such witnesses shall restore the pledge twofold. If a controversy arises between the creditor [on the one hand] and his debtor and the surety [on the other], the case shall be settled by oath just as is read in an earlier edict and as has been established by King Rothair of glorious memory [Rothair 366]. If the agreement was made in the presence of two or three witnesses, the testimony of these shall be credited in order that an oath may not occur between those giving and receiving the pledges. If these witnesses confirm [the agreement] with their testimony, they should confirm it to us or to him who is prince at the time or to the judge. If witnesses were not present when the pledge [agreement] was made, whoever takes a pledge as if from a surety shall pay composition as is provided above.

[*On the borrowing of money and the giving of notes.*]

16.II. If anyone borrows money from another man on agreement, and if within five years the creditor demands his money and the debtor does not have that with which to pay, then the agreement shall be renewed up to ten years. If within ten years the debt is demanded and not repaid, and he [the debtor] delays up to twenty years, then if the debt has been demanded either by the prince or by the judge of the district and the agreement is proved, the debtor or his heirs shall pay. But if the agreement was not renewed twice in the ten years and the prince or the judge had not made the demand clearly within the twenty years, we order that the creditor be silent afterwards and he shall have no right of bringing charges against his debtors, unless he was in captivity. With regard to those agreements which have been made up to this time in the present third indiction, we order that those coming due within five years be renewed or repayment exacted. If they [the creditors] delay for the five years to demand that their debtors either renew their agreements or repay their debts, if they are guilty of this negligence, they shall afterwards have no right of seeking back this debt. Morever, concerning those agreements made in the future, they shall be concluded just as we have set out above.

[*Concerning the man who kills his brother with evil intent.*]

17.III. In that case where a brother sinfully kills his brother, although an earlier law stated that the nearest relatives shall succeed, we shall now name who are the nearest relatives of the brother. If [another] brother is left, that brother of the man who committed the homicide shall succeed to his property on condition that he make a composition payment from the property of the man who committed the homicide according to the quality of the person if the man who was killed left children. That which remains [above this amount] he shall have for himself. If the property of the man who committed the homicide is adjudged to be only as much as is the amount of the composition, or perhaps less, then the children of him who was killed shall succeed to it. If he [the man killed] does not have children, then the nearest relatives shall succeed him according to degree, and if there are no relatives who can legally succeed him, the king's treasury shall succeed. The life of the man who committed the homicide shall be in the power of the king, as is read in an earlier law.

[*Concerning those merchants and artisans who travel within or without the country.*]

18.IIII. On merchants (*negotiatores*) and master craftsmen (magistri). If anyone travels within the country or outside the country for the purpose of carrying on any business or any craft whatever, if he does not return within three years because some illness has befallen him, he should make it known to his judge or his agent. If he neglects to do this [i.e., to inform his judge] and he leaves children behind him, they [the children] shall have his property in their legal possession. Whatever sales or other obligations the children undertake from their father's property after the expiration of the time period set [three years], shall remain permanent and they [the children] shall pay their own or the debts of their father.

If the father returns after this we order that he may receive nothing from his children nor may he have his property back in his possession. And if his children presume to take him back without the king's consent or order, all of their property and the substance of the father shall pass to the king's treasury.

If the man has a wife and he does not return within the established three-year period, she shall come to the king's palace, whoever is king at the time, and it shall be done thus: according as the king gives her the privilege of remarrying or as he orders or establishes concerning her affairs, it shall be done. But she shall not presume to take another husband without the king's permission. If such things occur after the expiration of this time period, the king shall have the power to judge concerning them in whatever manner is pleasing to him.

HERE END THE LAWS FROM THE EIGHTH YEAR

FROM THE NINTH YEAR (A.D. 721)

I, Liutprand, in the name of God the almighty, most excellent king of the divinely chosen Catholic nation of the Lombards, recall that it is now some time since we provided an addition to the body of earlier laws. In some small fashion, it is true, but nevertheless in three issues, in the first, in the fifth, and in the eighth years of my reign, in the eleventh, fifteenth, and third indictions, we have added those regulations which seemed right and proper and according to God. Now, moreover, in the ninth year of our reign, with God protecting, on the first day of March, in the fourth indiction, after going over and reviewing all the titles of the earlier edicts with the judges and the rest of our Lombard fideles, repeating the process followed before, we take care to supplement and expand in a fourth issue those provisions which seem right to us according to God.

[*Concerning legal age.*]

19.I. On legal age. We decree that it is not legal for a man under eighteen to alienate his property, except in that case where his father has left a debt. In that case he [the minor] may have the right, with the approval of the prince of the land, to alienate so much from his property as is the amount of the debt in order that greater damage may not accrue to him because of the accumulation of interest on the debt. Whoever is ruler at the time, fearing God and mindful of his soul, shall appoint a God-fearing person from among those around him, and that one shall supervise the matter so that no unreasonable or negligent loss shall in any wise befall the minor. Nineteen shall be the legal age for a Lombard man; whatever he does or judges concerning his property then ought to remain permanently valid. We also decree and establish this: if any illness befalls him [the minor] before he is eighteen and he realizes that he is in danger of dying, then, acting in piety with concern for his soul, he shall have the right to provide as he wishes concerning his property to the benefit of some sacred place or hospital. That which he disposes for the sake of his soul ought to remain valid.

[*Concerning homicide in self defense.*]

20.II. On homicide. If any freeman in self-defense kills another freeman and it is proved that he killed the man while defending himself, he shall pay composition for him [the man killed] just as is provided in an earlier law established by King Rothair of glorious memory. But whoever falls upon another man and kills him for any other reason whatsoever shall lose all his property and the heirs of the one killed shall have it in the following manner. If the property of the man who committed the homicide is less than the amount of the composition established earlier or of the same value, then the man who committed the homicide shall lose his property and his person shall be handed over to the nearest relatives of the dead man. But if the property of the man who committed the homicide is more than the amount of the earlier composition, then he shall lose all his property and the heirs of the man killed shall receive as much of it as is equal to the amount of the earlier composition. Concerning that which remains over and above this amount, the king's treasury shall have half and the heirs of the dead man half; in this way the man who committed the homicide may redeem his life.

[*Concerning the slave who kills a freeman, his lord consenting.*]

21.III. If a slave kills a freeman with the consent of his lord, and it is proved to be so, the slave's lord himself shall lose all his property in the manner indicated above. If the lord denies that the crime was committed with his consent, he may clear himself according to the law of God and he shall pay composition for the dead man as has been established before; in addition he shall turn the slave over to the relatives of the dead man.

[*On the means whereby a woman may sell her property with the consent of her husband.*]

22.IIII. If a woman wishes to sell her property with the consent of her husband or in community with him, the man who wishes to buy [from her] or those who wish to sell to her shall notify two or three relatives of the woman who are nearest in relationship to her. If in the presence of these relatives the woman says that she has acted under compulsion, then that which she sold shall not be valid. But if in the presence of her relatives or of the judge who presides in that place she claims that she did not act under compulsion but voluntarily sold her property, then that which she sold ought to remain valid from that day forth, provided nevertheless that the relatives who were present or the judge set their hand to the charter [detailing the sale]. If it happens that the woman's husband dies [thereafter] and she goes to another husband, the sale shall still remain valid. Moreover, the scribe who prepares the charter shall write it only with the approval of the relatives or of the judge, as is said above. If it is done otherwise, the sale shall be invalid and the above noted scribe shall be as guilty as the man who forges a charter [Rothair 243].

[On the freeing of slaves in church.]
23.V. If anyone sets free his man or woman slave in church before the altar, that one shall be as free as the slave who is handed over into four hands and been made folkfree and legally independent (amundius). But if he wishes only to raise the slave to the status of an aldius, the lord shall not lead the slave into a church, but he may accomplish this in any other manner he wishes—by means of a charter or by any other means which pleases him [Rothair 224].

[Concerning free women who marry slaves.]
24.VI. If a free woman takes a slave [as husband], and her relatives neglect to take vengeance on her within a year, as is provided in an earlier law [Rothair 221], then whenever she is found after the expiration of a year she shall become a palace slave. And the slave [her husband] shall be turned over to a public official and their children shall serve the king's court in all things. But if the relatives of that woman, or the slave's lord, have carried out within a period of one year that which the earlier edict commands, it shall remain permanently in effect.

[Concerning the man who has taken his case to the schultheis.]
25.VII. If anyone has a case and states his case to the schultheis, and if his schultheis neglects to do justice for him within four

days, then if both parties to the case live in an area under the same
schultheis, that official shall pay six solidi as composition to him
who announced his claim, and he [the schultheis] shall likewise pay
six solidi to his judge.

If the schultheis before whom the case is brought is ill or is
known to be in another district on his own business, he shall be
awaited until he returns or until he convalesces from his illness. And
when he has returned or recovered from his illness, if he delays to do
justice within the established four days, the schultheis himself, as has
just been said, shall pay six solidi as composition to him who brought
the case and a like six solidi to his judge.

If the judge delays this case and does not adjudicate between the
parties according to law within six days, then the judge shall pay
twelve solidi as composition to him who announced the case. If the
judge is not able to settle the suit within twelve days he shall direct
both parties to the presence of the king. If the judge does otherwise
and he who brought suit does not obtain justice within the stated
twelve days, the judge himself shall pay twelve solidi as composition
and he shall pay twenty solidi to the king.

[*On the method whereby two men who live in the same judicial
district but in territories presided over by different schultheis may
settle their suit.*]

26.VIII. If men who reside in a district under the same judge
but under two different schultheis are involved in a suit, then that one
who is the complainant should go with a representative or letter from
his own schultheis to that one under whose jurisdiction the person
lives against whom he is bringing suit. If he [the latter schultheis]
does not render justice within four days, that schultheis who neglects
to take action shall pay six solidi as composition to him who brings
the suit, and he shall also pay six solidi to his judge.

If it is such a case that the schultheis cannot render decision, he
shall direct the parties to his judge [for a decision] within six days,
according to the earlier law. It is thus established as in the above law
where either the schultheis or judge does not fulfill all his duties:
[the schultheis] shall pay six solidi as composition to him who
brought the suit, as noted above, and six solidi to his judge; and the
judge shall pay twelve solidi as composition to him whose case it is
and twenty solidi to the king.

[*On the means whereby a man may bring suit against someone living in another judicial district.*]

27.VIIII. If anyone has a case [with a man who lives] in another judicial district, he shall go with a letter from his own judge to that judge who presides in the other place. If that judge delays to do justice for him and has not settled the suit within eight days, he shall pay twenty solidi as composition to him who brought he suit and another twenty solidi to the king.

If it is such a case that the judge cannot render a decision, let him make this known and within twelve days he shall require the man who lives under his jurisdiction to come into the king's presence. If he acts otherwise and neglects so to constrain him [the man against whom the suit is brought], the judge shall pay forty solidi as composition, as provided above, half to the king and half to him who brought the case.

[*Concerning the man who feels that he has not received justice from his judge.*]

28.X. If anyone brings suit against another man and the schultheis or judge renders a decision for him according to law and the tenor of the edict, and if he does not abide by this judgment, he shall pay twenty solidi as composition to that one who adjudicated the case. In those cases which have been settled by a decision and he [against whom the case was brought] does not believe that it was judged according to law and therefore he appeals to the king, he shall not be liable to blame. And if the judge had judged contrary to law, he shall pay forty solidi as composition, half to the king and half to him whose case it is. If the judge heard the case and made his decision and his judgment did not appear to be right, he shall not be guilty if he can offer an oath to the king that he did not judge that case with evil intent nor had he been corrupted by a bribe but [he judged] as the law appeared to him; and he shall then be cleared. If he does not dare to offer such an oath, he shall pay composition as stated above.

We decree that those suits involving subjects covered in the above laws that have arisen or been settled before this time, shall be settled and remain as were provided earlier or as was contained in the ancient lawbook. Those things which come up or occur in the future, that is, from the first day of March, in the fourth indiction, shall be settled and brought to an end according to the provisions established here. Except, however, in the case of a free woman who marries a slave and who has not been condemned as is provided in the older law: wherever she may be found, she shall become a slave of the palace and her children shall be slaves of the king.

[HERE END THE LAWS FROM THE NINTH YEAR]

[FROM THE TENTH (ELEVENTH?) YEAR]

[Concerning women who wish to sell their property.]

29. If a woman wishes to sell any of her property, she should not do it secretly but it should be done in the presence of the king or of the judge or of the schultheis, and she should have two or three of her relatives with her. She should say to the judge: "I wish to sell my property." The relatives shall set their hands to the charter of sale and she may then make the sale; if her mundwald thus consents to it, that which she has sold shall be valid. Moreover, the scribe who prepares the charter shall not presume to write it except with the approval of the relatives and the judge who presides in that place. If he does otherwise, the sale shall be invalid and the abovementioned scribe shall be as guilty as he who forges a charter, as set forth above [Rothair 243].

FROM THE ELEVENTH YEAR (A.D. 723)

We have established in four additions to the lawbook those laws which seemed fitting to us and to our judges and to the rest of the Lombards. Now we add additional titles designed for the salvation of our nation; we believe that the approval of God will be obtained for these provisions and that we will be deserving in no wise of eternal punishment from our Lord Jesus Christ. Therefore, in the name of Almighty God, I, Liutprand, most excellent king of the Lombard nation, in the eleventh year of my reign with God protecting, on the first day of March in the sixth indiction, issue this fifth addition to the code. The first law follows.

[*Concerning women who take the veil.*]

30.I. Concerning those women who take the veil or who are dedicated to God by their relatives or who choose for themselves to adopt the religious habit of monastic garb: even though these women have not been consecrated by a priest, it seems just to us, on account of the love of God, that they continue in that habit in every way. Nor may men say, "Since they have not been consecrated, if they fornicate, they have no guilt." But, as we have ordered above, those who have accepted such a habit by taking the veil and assuming the holy garb of Mary the Mother of God shall not presume in any wise to return thereafter to a secular life or habit. For every Christian ought to consider that if a nonconsecrated man betroths a nonconsecrated woman and pledges her with a single ring and acquires her mundium and if afterwards that man takes another wife, he is liable [to pay a composition of] 600 solidi: the cause of God and of the blessed Mary is so much greater that those who receive the veil or take the habit upon themselves ought to persevere in it.

Therefore, if any woman contrary to this provision which our excellency has established goes out or takes a husband for herself, she shall lose all her property and that property shall fall into the possession of our treasury. Moreover, concerning the person of that woman who committed such an evil deed, whoever is king shall judge as is pleasing to him whether it is better to send her to a convent or [to provide for her] in some other manner according to God. Likewise the prince may ordain as it pleases him concerning her habit of life or vestment.

If, moreover, that one in whose guardianship (mundium) such a woman is had consented to the abovementioned evil and this is proved, he shall pay his wergeld as composition to the royal treasury and that one who presumed to take her shall pay 600 solidi as composition. If, however, the mundwald did not consent to such an evil deed, he shall receive half of the 600 solidi composition and the king half.

He who abducts such a woman shall pay 1,000 solidi as composition in order that a case involving someone dedicated to God may exceed [the usual payment] to the amount of 100 solidi; for a composition of 900 solidi has been established in the edict for the abduction of an unconsecrated woman [Rothair 191]. The woman who does not observe the regulation set out above and who has consented to such evil shall be subjected to the abovewritten punishment.

[*On the abduction of free women who have not taken vows.*]

31.II. In the case where someone abducts a free unconsecrated woman, for which offense an earlier edict set a composition of 900 solidi, we decree that of the 450 solidi designated to go to the relatives or to the mundwald, whoever the mundwald is shall receive 150 solidi for his trouble in collecting the penalty. The woman herself who endured the shame or injury shall have the remaining 300. If, however, the woman has father or brother and she is in his mundium, then the father or brother may share the 450 solidi composition with the daughter or sister as pleases him. But any other mundwald or relative shall divide that composition as set forth above.

[*Concerning the offspring of an illegal marriage.*]

32.III. This law concerns those who have been or who shall be born of an illegal marriage, that is, of a marriage with stepmother, or step-daughter, or with the woman who was the wife of a brother or the sister of a wife (because the canons have established it thus concerning two sisters as also concerning two brothers). Those who are born of such a marriage cannot be the legitimate heirs of their father but the nearest relatives shall have his property. If there are no near relatives, the king's treasury shall succeed.

[*No man shall marry the widow of his cousin on either his mother's or his father's side.*]

33.IIII. It is the wish of God that we decree that no man may presume in the future to take to wife the widow of the cousin on his mother's side (*consubrino*) or the widow of the cousin on his father's side (*insubrino*). If anyone presumes to do this illegal act, he shall lose his property, and the children who are begotten of such a union cannot be legitimate heirs, but the nearest relatives shall succeed. If there are no near relatives, the king's treasury shall succeed.

We have added this measure because, as God is our witness,

the Pope at Rome, who is the head of the church of God and of priests thoughout all the world, has exhorted us through a letter that we not permit such unions to be contracted in any way.

[*No man shall marry his godmother or his goddaughter.*]
34.V. We likewise decree that no one may presume to take to wife his godmother, nor that goddaughter whom he raised from the baptismal font; nor may he presume to take to wife the daughter of that one who received him from the font, because such are known to be spiritual brothers and sisters. He who attempts to do this evil thing shall lose all his property and the children who are born of the illegal marriage may not be his heirs, but the nearest relatives shall be. If there are no near relatives, then the king's treasury shall succeed. Moreover, wherever are found those who have contracted such an illegal union as mentioned above they shall be separated immediately and subjected to the above punishment.

[*Concerning the man who engages in sedition against his judge.*]
35.VI. If anyone raises sedition against the judge of his own district without the king's consent, or commits any evil, or seeks to expel the judge except on command of the king, or if men from one district raise sedition against another district or another judge, or seek to expel him except with the consent of the king: then that man who is at their head shall lose his life and all his property shall revert to the public treasury; moreover, the others who are accomplices with him in that evil shall each pay his wergeld as composition to the royal fisc.

If they plunder anyone's house or take property from those men who hold from the fisc or from the king (*qui cum palatio aut cum rege tenent*) and keep (*conservant*) faith with the fisc and with their judges, those who commit such a deed shall pay as a composition eightfold the value of all those properties to him from whom they took them, and they shall pay their wergeld as composition to the fisc, as we have said above. We have taken care to include this provision in the present addition to the edict in order that such evil deeds may not increase but will be cut off and all men will be worthy to live in peace in the grace of God and of the king.

[*Concerning pledges which have been given but not returned.*]
36.VII. If anyone gives a pledge and [that one to whom it was given] delays in giving it back [at the proper time], he [the latter] shall pay composition as is read in an earlier edict. If that one who received the pledge refuses to return it when sureties are offered and he keeps it with him, he shall pay composition in the same manner as that one who refuses to release a pledge.

[*Concerning pledges which have been given and then reclaimed by force.*]
37.VIII. He who gives a pledge to another man and, before he has [properly] freed it by providing a surety, snatches it violently from the hand of the man to whom he gave it, shall pay twenty-four solidi as composition to him from whom he snatched the pledge. We have ordered this provision to be added to the edict in order that no breach of the peace (scandalum) may occur or any life be lost on account of such a case.

[*Concerning the man who has given a pledge and wishes to reclaim it by offering a surety.*]
38.VIIII. If anyone gives a pledge to another man and wishes to recover it through [the offer of] sureties and for that purpose he offers one, two, or three sureties to him who received the pledge, and if that one [refuses to accept them] saying, "I do not know who these men are," and this fact could cause him damage: the man who is offering the surety ought to provide a surety either from his own district or from the district from which he who received the pledge comes. If such a surety cannot be found, then he who received the pledge ought to accept that freeman as surety whom his fellow freemen know and about whom they will say, "I know that he can be trusted." In this case the man who gave the pledge shall not suffer damage.

[*Concerning the man who gives a pledge and then offers a surety.*]
39.X. If anyone gives a pledge to another man for any reason and then offers a surety [to obtain release of the pledge], and if he [who received the surety and then released the pledge] afterwards objects to the surety or takes back the pledge from his hand and it

is proved, then he [who received the surety] shall pay twenty solidi as composition.

[*Concerning the man who gives pledges and names a surety.*]

40.XI. If anyone gives pledges to another man and then names a surety, and if the surety provides [new] pledges for him and gives these pledges to the creditor, and if afterwards [the creditor] takes [the original pledges] by force from the debtor who had reclaimed his pledges [by naming a surety], then [the creditor] shall pay an eightfold composition for those pledges.

[*Concerning him who retakes pledges before the prescribed time.*]

41.XII. If anyone retakes his pledges from another man before the established time [i.e., before he provides a surety], and if it is proved, he shall pay an eightfold composition for those pledges.

[*Concerning the judge or public official who exacts a written agreement from the parties to a suit.*]

42.XIII. If the judge or other public official of a district exacts an agreement (*treuvas*) [setting forth a penalty for breach] from two men who have some quarrel, and if one of the men between whom the agreement was made breaks it, he who broke the agreement shall pay half of the amount stated in the agreement into the public treasury as composition, and half to him whose case it is. The amount set in the agreement shall not be less than 200 solidi; however, those who wish to set the amount higher in more important cases may do so.

[*On gifts of property.*]

43.XIIII. On gifts. If anyone gives any property whatever to another man and receives a return gift (launigild) [Rothair's Edict, note 46] in exchange, and if afterwards he is not able to defend himself [i.e., his title to the property he gave] at all, then he shall return to him to whom he gave the gift another property of the same value the first was on that day when he gave it; and he shall not then suffer further blame. If he is accused of collusion, he shall offer oath on the gospels that he had entered into collusion with no one in this case; and he shall be absolved of blame. Nonetheless he shall return a property equal to the abovementioned property to him to whom he originally gave it.

[*Concerning fugitive slaves and strangers.*]

44.XV. If a fugitive or a stranger has been found in another judicial district, then the deganus or the forester (saltarius) in that region ought to take him and lead him to his own schultheis [i.e., the schultheis of the deganus or saltarius], and the schultheis shall consign the fugitive to his judge. The judge shall have the power to inquire of him from what place he comes. If it is found that he is a slave or a thief, then the judge should send immediately to the judge or the lord under whom the thief or slave lives, and he shall have two solidi each for the detention of slaves. If, however, after the case has been inquired into it appears that the man who was seized or investigated is free, then no blame shall be imputed to him who took or investigated him.

If, indeed, the deganus or the forester delays in doing this, he shall pay four solidi as composition, half to his schultheis and half to him whose case it is [i.e., to him whose slave was taken in flight or to him who suffered a theft by the fugitive]. If the schultheis is guilty of neglect, he shall pay eight solidi as composition, half to his judge and half to him whose case it is. If, indeed, the judge delays in investigating him or demanding whose man he is, he shall pay twelve solidi as composition to the royal fisc. And if that judge to whom the notice came is guilty of neglect in retaking the man or in making it known to his lord (*arimannus*)[6] that his man had been seized in such a place—if the judge neglects this, he shall pay twelve solidi composition to the fisc. There shall be a time limit of one month in making such a demand in these parts; across the mountains,[7] that is, in parts of Tuscany, it shall be two months.

[*Concerning him who destroys another man's fence.*]

45.XVI. He who destroys (*capelaverit*) another man's enclosure fence (*astalaria*) shall pay six solidi as composition to him whose enclosure it is.

[*Concerning him who digs a ditch on someone else's land.*]

46.XVII. He who digs a ditch on another man's land and is not able to prove [the land] his own shall pay six solidi as composition to him whose land it is.

[*Concerning him who puts a fence on someone else's land.*]

47.XVIII. He who places a fence on another man's land and is not able to prove [the land] his own shall pay six solidi as composition to him whose land it is.

[*Concerning him who sells a freeman outside the country.*]

48.XVIIII. He who sells a freeman outside the country shall pay as composition the same wergeld as if he had killed him.

[*Concerning him who sells someone else's slave outside the country.*]

49.XX. He who sells another man's slave outside the country and it is proved shall pay fourfold the value of that person as composition.

[*On putting slaves to the oath.*]

50.XXI. Concerning slaves put to the oath. He who puts to the oath another man's slave without his lord's consent, or who forces him to put his hand in the cauldron [i.e., to undergo the ordeal], shall pay twenty solidi as composition to the slave's lord.

[*On handing someone else's slave over to the king.*]

51.XXII. He who gives another man's slave into the hand of the king [to be freed] and it is proved that he did not give his own slave, shall pay 100 solidi as composition to the king. The slave shall then be returned to his rightful lord and he shall be a slave just as before. In addition, he who gave the slave into the hand of the king shall pay twenty solidi as composition to his lord.

[*Concerning him who frees someone else's slave.*]

52.XXIII. If anyone sets free another man's slave without his lord's consent, either by his own act or in some other manner, except by the hand of the king, and if it is proved that he freed another man's slave, then the slave shall be returned to his rightful lord and shall be a slave just as before. He who freed the slave illegally shall pay twenty solidi as composition to the slave's lord.

[*Concerning him who makes a cleric of another man's slave without the consent of his lord.*]

53.XXIIII. He who makes a cleric of another man's slave without the consent of his lord shall pay twenty solidi as composition to his lord on account of this illegal presumption, and the slave shall be returned to his rightful lord.

HERE END THE LAWS FROM THE ELEVENTH YEAR

FROM THE TWELFTH YEAR (A.D. 724)

The goodness and mercy of God works in him and illuminates the way of him who advances in good works step by step and day by day and who is always seen to move toward the better: [it is the goodness and mercy of Him] who wishes all men to be saved and to come to an understanding of His truth. We acted for the salvation of our people and to alleviate the vexations of the poor when we gathered together new laws to add to the body of this lawbook in five previous issues; for this we believe that the mercy of God will reward us for such good works because we have done it for the fear and love of God alone so that all controversies may be ended with reason and justice, that error may cease and that His justice will be more clear to all; whence the name of the Lord will be blessed without end.

Therefore in the name of God, I, Liutprand, the most excellent king of the Catholic Christian Lombard nation, in the twelfth year of my reign, with Christ protecting, on the first day of March in the seventh indiction, take care, with our judges and with the rest of our Lombard fideles, to add to our code in a sixth issue laws covering those matters which have been overlooked heretofore and concerning which many cases have already arisen. The first follows.

[*On the gift made in formal manner and confirmed by a charter.*]

54.I. In the case where a man can produce a charter for a gift made by formal act (gairethinx) or with a return gift (launigild) or if he has a bill of sale, but he does not possess the property detailed therein and claims that he [who presently holds the property] does not have a title deed: if possession [of that property by another person] has been for thirty years or more, he [who has the charter or bill of sale] shall not have the right to make a claim against him who cannot show the title deed. He who has possessed for thirty years shall continue to possess firmly because it was so provided by Grimwald, of glorious memory, concerning possession for thirty years [Grimwald 1].

But if possession has been for less than thirty years, he [who has the charter or bill of sale] shall have the right to bring his claim; and he who possesses the property shall reply according to the edict.

[*Concerning him who allows his slave to become folkfree and legally independent (amundius).*]

55.II. If anyone makes his slave folkfree and legally independent (amundius) or sets him free from himself in any manner by giving him into the hand of the king or by leading him before the altar of a church, and if afterwards that freedman [continues] to serve at the will of his patron, the freedman ought at frequent intervals to make clear his liberty to the judge and to his neighbors and [remind them] of the manner in which he was freed.

Afterward the patron or his heirs may at no time bring complaints against him who was freed by saying that because [he continues to serve] he ought still to obey, for it was only on account of the goodness of his lord that the former slave continued to serve his commands of his own free will. He shall remain permanently free.

[*Concerning him who accuses another man of theft.*]

56.III. If anyone accuses another of theft and defeats him in combat, or if perhaps the theft was revealed through torture (*districtione*) by a public official and composition has been paid, and if afterwards it is found that the theft was committed by another man and it is clear that he who first paid the composition did not steal the property: then he [who paid the composition] shall receive back all that which he paid from him to whom he paid it, and that one who afterwards was found to be the thief shall pay the composition instead. And if he [the thief] had given anything as security for his oath, he to whom he gave it shall have it.

If it does not appear to be certain that another man committed the theft, and the thief has been revealed through torture and composition was paid, he to whom the composition was paid shall have it.

[*Concerning the man who incurs a debt and sells his property.*]

57.IIII. In the case where a man incurs a debt and sells his property and the debt is [still] such that he cannot repay it, and his son has acquired property through his wife or by working in some manner, after the father sells all his property or gives [it] to his creditors for the debt or the property is confiscated by a public official, the creditor may not have the right to seek to acquire by force those things which the son has obtained from his wife or by working, but the son shall have them for himself in legal peace. Nevertheless, if the son is accused by his father's creditors, he shall offer oath that he has commended or hidden nothing from the property of his father or of his mother, if she died in the protection (mundium) of his father; [if he can offer such an oath], he shall be absolved from the charge. If afterwards the son is found to have any of the paternal property, he shall pay an eightfold composition.

[*Concerning the child who sells his property while he is under age.*]

58.V. If a child while under age gives or places in pledge his property to anyone and afterwards when he comes of legal age he wishes to break the agreement as the law allows and to repossess those properties, he who bought or took the property in pledge shall not have the right to retain that which the minor gave him. Because when he came to the agreement or took the pledge he ought to have ascertained that the boy was under age and he did it illegally. Since it has been established that he who is under age cannot in any wise sell or place his property in pledge [Liutprand 19], we say that he who buys or takes [this property] in pledge has such a case as he has who buys or takes pledges from a slave or aldius.

[*Concerning the gastald or agent of the king who gives anything from the property of the fisc.*]

59.VI. If any gastald or agent who has a royal court to administer dares to give a tributary holding (casa tributaria) [cf. Aistulf 2] or land or forest, vineyard or meadow from the royal holdings to anyone without the order of the king, or if he presumes to give more than was ordered, or if he neglects to seek back that which was claimed by fraud, for all those things which he dares to do contrary to the royal command he shall pay a double eightfold composition just as that one who steals royal property [Rothair

369]. If the agent dies before the fraud becomes apparent, his heirs shall pay composition as is read above [Liutprand 57].

But if the fraud was committed by an agent and if, before this comes to our attention, it was discovered by the gastald, the gastald shall have a third part of that composition which the agent is to pay, and two parts shall go to the crown. And if it first comes to our attention through some other man before it is discovered by the gastald, then that composition in its entirety shall belong to us and to our treasury.

But if the judge or the agent or his heirs is accused by us of being guilty of neglect in seeking after our property and if they say that they know of no fraud and are guilty of no neglect, they shall offer oath in this manner and say: "Our father did not know of or consent to any fraud nor was he guilty of neglect in seeking after [your property] and we ought not to be liable at law"; if they can so swear they shall be absolved.

We now issue this law so that this arrangement may be clearly understood in the future; and whatever fraud has occurred before this time we shall reserve to our judgment. We have taken care to establish this because we have found many frauds have been committed by our gastalds or agents from which we have suffered many pertubations. But that which has been rightfully given to anyone by our predecessors, we wish to remain in a firm fashion just as that which we ourselves have given or shall give in the future.

[*Concerning the aldius who has intercourse with a free woman or girl.*]

60.VII. If any man's aldius has intercourse with a free woman or girl, he shall pay fifty solidi as composition to him who holds her mundium, but the guilt shall be imputed to her on account of the fact that she consented to an aldius.

[*On the giving of pledges for an oath.*]

61.VIII. If anyone gives pledges to another that he will take oath and then an oathhelper is appointed, and if then the oathhelper, when he has come to take oath and has placed [his hand] on the gospels, withdraws so that the oath is broken, the case shall be settled as was established earlier [Rothair 363]. That one who is to swear shall offer his oath together with his oathhelpers, and they shall swear cleanly with him. But if the oathhelpers do not wish to do this and any one of them seeks to withdraw himself from the whole thing so that he who is to swear shall lose his case, we order that that oathhelper who wishes to withdraw himself ought to make clear for what reason he does not care to swear. And if he cannot make this at all clear, then he shall offer oath that he entered into no collusion with the man who is to hear the oath but that, fearing for his soul, he does not dare to be an oathhelper [in this case]. He who is to swear shall then have twelve days in the case of those who are near—twenty-four days for those who are at a distance somewhere in Tuscany or Austria—to seek another oathhelper whom he can put in the place of that one [who refused to swear], and he may thus provide the oath for which he had given pledges. But if one of the oathhelpers does not dare to swear and is not able to make it clear why, whatever damage he for whom he was to give the oath has suffered, he shall replace from his own property.

[*Concerning him who kills a freeman while defending himself.*]
62.VIIII. I am mindful of the manner in which we have already established [Liutprand 20] that anyone who [deliberately] kills a freeman shall lose his entire property and that he who kills a man while defending himself shall pay composition according to the quality of the person. Now we set forth the means whereby that quality should be determined. For it is the custom that a lesser person (*minima persona*) who is a freeman (exercitalis) shall have a wergeld of 150 solidi and he who is of the first class (*primus*) shall have a wergeld of 300 solidi.

Concerning our gasinds (gasindii) [see Rothair's Edict, note 62], we decree that anyone who kills even the least of these (*minissimus*) shall pay 200 solidi as composition because he serves us. Indeed, this amount may increase to 300 solidi according to the quality of the person as determined by our opinion or that of our successors.

[*On false testimony.*]
63.X. He who renders false testimony against anyone else, or sets his hand knowingly to a false charter, and this fraud becomes evident, shall pay his wergeld as composition, half to the king and

half to him whose case it is. If the guilty party does not have enough to pay the composition, a public official ought to hand him over as a slave to him who was injured, and he [the offender] shall serve him as a slave. And he who in his own interest asks others to give false testimony or to set their hand to false charters shall pay compositions as we have ordered [false] witnesses to pay composition, even though the evil deed was not actually carried out by him.

[*Concerning the slave who is taken in theft.*]

64.XI. It seems right to us concerning the slave who is taken in theft (for which offense it is provided in an earlier edict that he should either be killed or that his lord should redeem him with forty solidi), that if in the future any slave is taken in such a situation, he ought to die or his lord should redeem him with a payment of forty solidi, as has been said before [Rothair 254]. If his lord does not wish to redeem him, the lord himself shall kill the slave. And if his lord does not wish to kill him, that one who has seized the slave shall kill him; and if that one does not wish to do it, then our court shall receive him and carry out our commands. The slave's lord must pay composition to him who suffered the theft, just as the edict provides.

HERE END THE LAWS FROM THE TWELFTH YEAR

FROM THE THIRTEENTH YEAR (A.D. 725)

In the name of Christ, I, Liutprand, king of the Lombard nation, [take this action] in the thirteenth year of my reign, on the first day of March in the eighth indiction; for I remember that men have come into our presence and have brought cases in controversy among themselves which we have not been certain how to adjudicate according to custom and provisions for which have not been included before in the body of our lawbook: therefore we suspended these matters until the abovementioned first day of March so that we, in association with our judges and together with them, might act to establish a certain end to such affairs that there may be no controversy afterwards. So it has been done and the laws are found here. First of all [is the following]:

[*On the disposition of a man's property if he leaves unmarried daughters and no sons.*]

65.I. In the case of a man who has an unmarried daughter at home and who does not have a legitimate son, he may not alienate more than two parts [two thirds] of his property in any fashion as a gift or for the sake of his soul. The third part [of his property] he must leave to his daughter, as King Rothair of glorious memory has already established [Rothair 158].

If a man does make a gift (thinx) [of his whole property] and afterwards a daughter is born, he shall modify the gift so as to retain a third part, as noted above [Rothair 171], and if he has two or more daughters [after making the gift], he shall break the thinx to retain a half; for it seems fitting to us that our edict should provide concerning the thinx which is a gift, that no gift or return gift (launigild) should disinherit a daughter from a third portion of her father's property; and if there are two or more daughters, from a half of his property.

[*Concerning the freeman who takes the wife of a slave or of an aldius while her husband is still living.*]

66.II. In the case of that freeman who takes the wife of a slave or of an aldius while her husband is still living, if sons or daughters are born as a result of this union, none of them shall succeed him as his heirs, even though they are free, and he shall not be able to give them any of his property. For the case is in doubt whose son or daughter it is when both the lord and the slave, he who had her first and he who took her afterward, are still living.

[*On the agreement which has been made without mortgaging itemized property to guarantee it.*]

67.III. If a man makes an agreement (*cautio*) with another man and does not obligate his property [by specific designation] but says only in the agreement that [this debt is guaranteed] by his properties in general; and if afterwards the one whose property was not specifically pledged sells any of that property to another man, he who bought the property shall keep it. If the obligations were named specifically, however, the owner cannot sell them until he has fulfilled his agreement. He who wishes to make an agreement should not only pledge specified objects from his property, as it is agreed between them [the parties to the agreement], but he should note (*faciat*) in the agreement how much the property was worth on that day.

[*Concerning aldii.*]

68.IIII. If any charge is brought against those who are aldii in their persons, their patron shall defend them either by oath or combat according to the nature of the case.

[*Concerning the aldius who has been in another man's house without his lord's knowing it.*]

69.V. If the aldius of one man is found in someone else's house without his lord knowing it, then when he is found the man who had him ought to give up the aldius and pay the equivalent of the work [done while at his house]. Let it be done likewise concerning slaves.

HERE END THE LAWS FROM THE THIRTEENTH YEAR

FROM THE FOURTEENTH YEAR (A.D. 726)

We have already on seven previous occasions taken care to add to the body of the ancient law code certain laws which seemed right to us and to our judges and to our fideles and according to the will of God. Now since many cases which some believe should be judged according to unwritten custom and others according to judicial discretion are known not to be defined clearly, we shall make provision for them so that in the future there can be no misunderstanding but the law shall be clear to all. Therefore we have ordered the following titles to be added, in the fourteenth year of our reign, God willing, on the first day of March, in the ninth indiction. The judges and our fideles from the bounds of Austria and Neustria have been present with us and have discussed all these things among themselves, reporting to us, and they have established and defined these laws equally with us. Since the following titles were pleasing to all, and since those present offered their consent, we have decreed that these laws shall be written in this manner and in none other.

[*Concerning brothers who share their property for forty years.*]
70.I. If the possession of property which consists of houses or land has not been divided but has been held [in common] by brothers for forty years, or by other relatives who have been in possession for forty years, and they affirm this by oath offered on the holy gospels, and they so state on oath and thereby establish that they have held those properties concerned either from their grandfather or from their father or from their brother, or from some other relative either by gift or by exchange or by a contractual agreement or by purchase, or by some other such means: then they may afterwards continue to hold and to possess that property. With regard to other properties which have been divided among the brothers or nephews and where the shares have been established, the division shall be equitable. But where the shares have not been distributed for forty years and it is proved that they [the brothers or relatives] have held possession in legal peace, as is read above, the case shall be brought to an end by oath. [Let it be so] except in the case where they do not possess the property in common.

[*On the malicious challenge to combat.*]
71.II. If anyone with evil intent challenges another man to combat—a thing often done by evil persons—then he who challenged shall offer oath alone to the effect that he sought to engage his opponent in combat with no evil intent, but on positive suspicion of theft or fire or of some other offense for which a challenge to combat should properly be made. If he swears to this, he shall afterwards proceed to the combat. If, however, he does not dare at all to swear thus, the case shall not be judged or ended by combat.

[*Concerning the freeman who advises another to perjure himself.*]
72.III. If any freeman advises another freeman to perjure himself or to burn another man's house where a man lives with his property, or to take another man's woman or girl, he shall pay 100

solidi as composition for that illegal advice which he offered contrary to reason. In those cases for which we have said that a composition of 900 solidi is to be paid by him who commits such an evil deed, the counsellor [in such a case] shall pay 100 solidi as composition [as stated above]. But [in those cases] where composition should be 300 solidi, the counsellor shall pay fifty solidi as composition; and if it is a case in which the composition should be less than 300 solidi, the counsellor shall pay forty solidi as composition, not less. Half of the above stated amounts [shall go] to the king's treasury and half to him whose case it is.

If the man about whom it is said that he had given advice in the above described evil deed wishes to deny that he has given such advice, he shall offer oath with his legitimate oathhelpers according to the nature of the case; he shall then be absolved [of guilt] and shall not be annoyed by combat. But if the truth of the matter is clear, composition shall be paid as above.

[*On gifts which are made without receiving a return gift or going through a formal ceremony.*]

73.IIII. Gifts which are made without a return gift (launigild) or without the formal alienation procedure (*thingatione*) ought not to stand at all. Although this has not been specifically established in the lawbook heretofore, nevertheless it has thus been judged up to now: therefore to remove the oversight we have ordered this provision to be recorded in the edict. He who is the nearest relative shall succeed, unless he who gave the gift without the return gift (launigild) lives, in which case he may receive it back for himself. [This provision applies] except in the case where anyone has given something to a church or to a holy place or to a hospital for the good of his soul, then it ought to remain valid and neither gift (thinx) nor return gift (launigild) ought to interfere since gifts to holy places or to hospitals are made for the good of one's soul.

[*Concerning the child who, while under age, wishes to divide his property with his brothers or relatives.*]

74.V. If a boy who is under age wishes to divide his property with his brothers or with his relatives, or if they wish to divide something with the boy, the brothers or relatives should give notice to the judge. The judge should then cause the relatives of that one to come together, and with them, either through himself or through his agent, a good God-fearing person, he should divide that property. It should be done thus in order that the division may stand to all time and justice may endure.

[*Concerning the child who, while under age, is involved in a lawsuit.*]

75.VI. If a boy who is under age enters into a legal suit with any man, in a like manner the judge should cause the boy's relatives to come together and in the presence of these relatives he should decide that case with justice. He should make known the names of those in whose presence he decided the suit, and he should announce his judgment in order that he who brought suit shall not lose justice on account of the fact that the boy was under age.

May that judge, in accordance with the manner in which he has ordered or handled the case according to the laws concerning those who are under age, have the retribution of Almighty God, whether for good or for ill. But if that agent whom the judge sent for deciding the case, as we have ordered above, lowered his heart to fraud in any manner or carried out the affair in an unfitting manner to the damage of the boy who was a minor: if he did not establish justice and it is proved that he committed fraud or entered some collusion against that infant, then he shall restore from his own property whatever he fraudulently dispersed. Indeed we have provided it thus in order that a boy who does not yet know how to secure justice on behalf of his own cause may not suffer damage.

[*On adultery committed by women who have taken vows.*]

76.VII. In the case of those women, devoted to religion, who have taken upon themselves the garb and habit of blessed religion, if because of their sinful nature they commit adultery voluntarily, then he who committed adultery with such a consecrated woman shall pay 200 solidi as composition. The edict provides that 100 solidi should be paid in composition for adultery with an unconsecrated woman and we declare it to be just that in causes involving God Almighty and his holy mother Mary, whose garb they had adopted, the composition should be doubled. Moreover, concerning the property of that religious woman who, may God forbid, commits adultery voluntarily, it shall be done just as we have already provided concerning religious women who unite themselves with a man.

[*On the succession of two brothers, or of a father and his son, who have been freed by formal ceremony.*]

77.VIII. If two brothers, or if a father and his son, have been freed by the formal gairethinx procedure, and if one of them dies without sons or daughters, the king's court shall succeed him. We have recorded this provision since, although it has not been written thus in the edict proper, nevertheless all the judges and our fideles have said that the old custom (*cawerfeda*) has been thus up to now.

[*On the possession of property acquired from the public lands.*]

78.VIIII. On possession. He who has received anything from the public land and possesses it without protest for sixty years, may in the future have and possess it without any molestation. We have decreed this since, according to the law of the Lombards, the title of other men is established by possession for thirty years [Grimwald 4], but King Rothair, our predecessor, established that in royal cases composition should be doubled [Rothair 369] when applied: therefore it has seemed right to us and to our judges that in this case of possession [of royal lands] the time period be doubled also, that is, that it be sixty years. If either our judge or agent accuses the man who has such property that he has taken possession of or entered upon it unjustly and that sixty years have not elapsed, then that one in whose possession it is, having taken oath on the gospels, shall say that he possesses that property through [gift of] the king, whom he dares to name, either to himself or to his father or to his grandfather, or that he or his relatives have possessed it for sixty years; then he ought not to lose it by law and he shall be secure afterwards.

If he dares not do this, or if the gastald or agent can prove that the property has not been held for sixty years or more and that the property was truly from the public land, he [who claims possession] shall either produce a charter or else lose that property if he has not been in possession for sixty years. If perchance anyone has made an agreement with a slave or an aldius from the king's household and the case is proved, he shall relinquish that property to the public treasury because possession ought not to be obtained from a sale by a slave or an aldius of the king, just as it ought not to be by the slaves or aldii of other men.

[*How a man shall buy a horse in the market.*]

79.X. In the case of the man who wishes to buy a horse in the market, let him purchase it in the the presence of two or three men and not do it secretly. Then if anyone recognizes that horse afterwards, the buyer shall have the testimony of those in whose presence he bought it and he shall not be guilty of theft. If the man who accuses him of theft does not believe the witnesses, these witnesses shall confirm it by oath unless they are men such that the king or judge can believe them without an oath.

If the buyer does not have men in the presence of whom he bought [the horse] and he can only say, "I bought it from some freeman (*de franco*) or I do not know from what man," he shall pay composition for that horse as if for theft.

[*Concerning thieves.*]

80.XI. In connection with thieves, each judge shall make a prison underground in his district. When a thief has been found, he shall pay composition for his theft, and then the judge shall seize him and put him in prison for two or three years, and afterwards shall set him free.

If the thief is such a person that he does not have enough to pay the composition for theft, the judge ought to hand him over to the man who suffered the theft, and that one may do with him as he pleases.

If afterwards the thief is taken again in theft, he [the judge] shall shave (*decalvit*)[8] and beat him for punishment as befits a thief, and shall put a brand on his forehead and face.[9] If the thief does not correct himself and if after such punishment he has again been taken in theft, then the judge shall sell him outside the province, and the judge shall have his sale price provided, nevertheless, that it be a proved case for the judge ought not to sell the man without certain proof.

[*How a man shall recover a lost horse or other property.*]

81.XII. If a man loses his horse or any other property, he

should go to the judge who presides in the place where the theft has been committed and should tell him everything and how it happened. If the judge is guilty of neglect in investigating the theft, he shall pay composition for the theft from his own property. And if the judge claims that he is guilty of no neglect, he should offer oath that he was guilty of no neglect in the investigation, but that he could not find [the stolen property]; and he shall be absolved. But if he does not dare so to swear, he shall pay composition for the theft from his own property, as above.

[*On the finding of someone else's wagon and oxen in one's own wood.*]

82.XIII. If anyone finds oxen and wagon in his forest, and the wagon is loaded with wood or anything else, and if he seizes the oxen and wagon and takes them for his own, he shall not be blamed since he found them on his own property.

[*Concerning judges and how many men they may leave behind from the army.*]

83.XIIII. When it is necessary for all of our judges to go out with the army, they shall leave behind six men—each of whom has no more than one horse—and then altogether they shall have six horses for their beasts of burden. Of lesser men (minimis hominibus) who have neither houses nor land, each judge shall leave no more than ten men, and these men shall each perform three works [services] weekly for that judge until the judge returns from the army. The schultheis shall leave three men (of the sort who have horses) and they altogether may keep three horses for their beasts of burden. Of lesser men he shall leave five men who shall work for him until he returns and, as we have said concerning the judge, they shall each perform three services per week. The forester (saltarius) shall leave [one man and] one horse, and of lesser men to work for him, he shall leave one, and that one shall work for him as is read above. And if the judge or the schultheis or the forester who is supposed to go out with the army presumes to leave more men without permission or order of the king, he shall pay his wergeld as composition to the royal fisc.

All those cases covered in the above laws which have been completed or adjudicated heretofore, and a conclusion has been set to them, shall remain as determined before. Those affairs which shall arise in the future, however, shall be concluded in accordance with these present provisions.

HERE END THE LAWS FROM THE FOURTEENTH YEAR

FROM THE FIFTEENTH YEAR (A.D. 727)

Among other related matters in the ancient lawbook we have taken care to add those provisions which we believed to be pleasing to God and to good men: now with our judges and our other Lombard fideles, on the first day of March, in the fifteenth year of my reign, with God protecting, in the eleventh indiction, as well for the comfort of paupers as for the peace of mind of all our faithful Lombards, we add laws to the edict covering those matters for which judgment has been uncertain before this time inasmuch as some of our judges wish to conclude them according to [unwritten] custom, others according to their own discretion. But now it is better that an end be set to this controversy so that our subjects may not be wearied; and in such manner as the consent of all was one with us, so it ought to remain permanent now and in the future. First of all in defense of our Christian and Catholic law we make provision that no one may presume to wander from the faith of Christ, that we may have God as a defender and helper firmly and permanently in all things.

[*Concerning him who seeks the advice of a sorcerer.*]
84.I. He who, unmindful of the wrath of God, goes to sorcerers or witches for the purpose of receiving divinations or answers of any kind whatsoever from them, shall pay to the royal fisc as composition half of the price at which he would have been valued if someone had killed him, and in addition, shall do penance according to the established canon. In like manner, he who, like a rustic, prays to a tree as sacred, or adores springs, or who makes any sacrilegious incantation, shall also pay as composition a half of his price to the royal fisc. And he who knows of sorcerers or witches and does not reveal them, or conceals those who go to them and

does not reveal it, shall be subjected to the above punishment. Moreover, he who sends his man or woman slave to such sorcerers or witches for the purpose of seeking responses from them, and it is proved, shall pay composition as abovementioned. If indeed the man or woman slave goes to the soothsayer or witch without the consent of his or her lord and so without his authority, likewise for the purpose of seeking responses, then his or her lord ought to sell him or her outside the province. And if his or her lord neglects to do this, he [the lord] shall be subjected to the punishment noted above.

[*What is to be done if the judge or other public officials of a place fail to seek out sorcerers or witches.*]

85.II. If any judge or schultheis or forester or deganus of the place where there are sorcerers or witches neglects to seek them out and find them within three months and they are found by other men, then each of the named officials from that place shall pay half of his worth as composition, just as is read above. And if it becomes clear that the judge or the schultheis or the forester or the deganus of the place where those sorcerers or witches are found has not condemned them or has taken a bribe or has absolved them as if for piety or any other reason, then he shall pay his entire wergeld as composition to the sacred palace.

If the sorcerers or witches have been sought and found by the judge without the notification of the schultheis, then the judge shall have the right to sell them outside the province and keep their sale price for himself. But if they were found through the schultheis, then the judge shall take half of the sale price and the schultheis half. And if the deganus or forester has found the abovementioned sacrilegious sorcerers or witches and has revealed it to his schultheis, then the forester or the deganus by whom they were found shall have a third part of that price for himself, and the schultheis shall have two parts.

We decree that each judge and schultheis shall undertake to send a warning to those who, whether male or female, have in the past done such unspeakable deeds, that they shall not do them in the future. If they do not do them in the future, they shall not be offered for sale. But if after this warning any are found in such evil works, they shall be subjected to the above-stated penalty.

Furthermore, it is our wish and we decree that each schultheis
and forester and deganus shall offer oath to his judge on the Holy
Gospels that he will not be guilty of neglect in this matter, for it is
just that, while they should not be neglectful in one of our causes
nor hide from us those who act and advise against us, so much the
more ought they not to be guilty of neglect in inquiring into the
cause of God, who is greater.

[*What a man shall do if he finds someone else's horse doing
damage to his property.*]

86.III. If anyone finds another man's horse doing damage
[to his property], and, in accordance with the earlier edict [Ro-
thair 343], shuts it up in an enclosure and announces this reason,
judgment shall proceed according to the earlier edict established by
King Rothair of glorious memory. But if the man presumes to do
anything more to that horse than the earlier edict provides and the
horse does not suffer any injury, then the man who enclosed him
shall pay as composition for this illegal presumption, half of that
price at which that kind of horse is valued, and he shall then return
the horse in good condition to its owner. If the horse is killed or
injured, then he [the man who seized him] shall pay composition
as is read in the earlier edict and, in addition, he shall pay composition as above for the illegal presumption.

[*On contractual agreements made with slaves or aldii belonging
to someone else.*]

87.IIII. If anyone comes to an agreement with the slave or
the aldius or other dependent belonging to someone else concerning
any property whatever without the express consent of his lord—
which [situation] was not provided for in the earlier edict
[Rothair 233–35]—and it is proved that the property of the
[bondsman's] lord has been depleted, then let him who received it
return that property without reward to its possessor, and he shall
then render satisfaction by oath that he did not take more. Afterwards the lord may do that which pleases him concerning his slave
or aldius.

[*Concerning fugitive slaves.*]

88.V. On fugitive slaves. We have already included a law
[dealing with this subject], but it was not expressly stated for

what length of time the lord ought to seek after his slave in order that he may do justice to that one who challenges him. Therefore we decree that if it is in Benevento or in Spoleto [that the slave flees], his lord shall have a period of three months. If it is within Tuscany, he shall have a period of two months. And if it is on this side of the mountains [the Apennines], he shall have a period of one month for seeking after him, and he shall do justice to him who challenges him concerning his slave.

[Concerning the man who wishes to bestow a meta upon his wife.]
89.VI. If anyone wishes to give his wife a marriage portion (meta), it thus seems just to us, that if the man is a judge he may give 400 solidi if he wishes, no more; [he may give] less if desirable. Other noble men may give 300 solidi, not more. If any of these other men wish [to give] less, [let them give] whatever they desire. And the marriage portion to be given shall be appraised according to value in order that at no future time may contention or disagreement proceed thence.

[On the possession of someone else's property with evil intent.]
90.VII. If anyone possesses another man's property—houses or land or cattle or servants (*familias*)—with evil intent and he is convicted and expelled thence by law and justice and judgment, he shall not make composition for any of these things, but he shall under oath render back the time and fruit of the labor up to that day when he was accused and it was proved.

[Concerning scribes and charters.]
91.VIII. In the case of scribes we decree that those who prepare charters should write them either according to the law of the Lombards—which is well known to be open to all—or according to that of the Romans; they shall not do otherwise than is contained in these laws and they shall not write contrary to the law of the Lombards or of the Romans. If they do not know how to do this, let them ask others, and if they cannot know such laws fully, they should not write such charters. He who presumes to do otherwise shall pay his wergeld as composition, except in that case where everything is agreed upon among fellow freemen.

For if men wish to go outside the law and make a pact or

agreement among themselves, and both parties consent, this shall not be regarded as contrary to law since both parties have done it voluntarily, and those who write such charters shall not be found liable to blame. However anything that pertains to inheritance must be written according to law.

That which was added in an earlier edict regarding forged charters shall remain in effect [Rothair 243].

[*Concerning the freeman, living on someone else's property which he holds by* livello, *who commits a homicide.*]

92.VIIII. If any freeman residing on another man's land which he holds by a livello contract (*livellarius*)[10] commits a homicide and flees, then he on whose land the man who committed the homicide lived shall have a period of one month for seeking after that man. And if he finds him, he has the right to seize him, even though he is free, and to hand him over to those [i.e., the family of him] who suffered death. If he does not do this, he ought to give half of all the movable properties, with the exception of the buildings (*tectoras*), which the man who committed the homicide had in that holding (casa). And if he whose land it is does not wish to do this, he ought to give that land by livello agreement to him [i.e., to the family] which suffered the death that it may render [the same service] for it as he returned who committed the homicide. Nevertheless, it is in the power of him whose land it is to choose from these three possibilities and do that one thing which he wishes.

[*Concerning him who puts to oath a woman or girl who is under the legal protection (mundium) of someone else.*]

93.X. If anyone presumes to put to oath a woman or girl or a woman consecrated to religion—any of whom are in someone else's mundium—he shall pay fifty solidi to the treasury.

[*Concerning him who presumes to move another man's ward without the consent of her mundwald (guardian).*]

94.XI. If anyone presumes to move another man's ward from the house where she lives without the consent of her mundwald, and leads her elsewhere, he who is the leader of the band shall pay eighty solidi as composition to her mundwald on account of this illegal presumption. If there were freemen with him, each of them shall pay twenty solidi in composition; however, slaves shall be computed in the composition of their lord. If it is a freeman who took that ward from her house and he marries her, he shall pay composition as established in an earlier edict by King Rothair of glorious memory [Rothair 186, 187].

[*Concerning the woman slave who, for the sake of religion, has been placed in a religious house by her lord.*]

95.XII. If any freeman, because of his piety and devotion, bestows religious garb upon his woman slave and takes her, as is the custom of this land, to some sacred place as an offering, and if it happens that, on account of his sinful nature, any [other] man takes her to wife, wherever they are found, let them be separated and he who took her to wife shall pay forty solidi as composition to her lord and she shall be returned to her former habit.

And if anyone commits adultery with her, which God forbid, in like manner he shall pay forty solidi composition to her lord. An earlier edict provides that twenty solidi should be paid as composition for the unconsecrated woman slave with whom adultery has been committed, and it is just that the composition should be doubled with regard to a handmaiden of God.

These provisions shall apply only if it is proved by a priest or other clergyman that the woman had assumed religious garb. Let there be no blame to any man for the imagined crime but for one certainly true. But if true proof has been established, then composition ought to be paid thus.

Any case involving the matters covered by the present additions to the lawbook shall be adjudicable as here provided. Those cases which have arisen before this time should be determined as the earlier edict provided.

HERE END THE LAWS FROM THE FIFTEENTH YEAR

FROM THE SIXTEENTH YEAR (A.D. 728)

In several previous issues we have added to the ancient lawbook those laws which we regarded as beneficial to our soul and contributing to the salvation of our nation. We now in a like

manner with divine aid in order that perjury may not occur nor
quarrels arise among our faithful people (fideles), acting together
with our judges and with the Lombard fideles, add [these laws] on
this first day of March in the sixteenth year of our reign, Christ
protecting, in the eleventh indiction: we call upon God as our witness [that we do this] not for any vain glory or human praise but
to please Almighty God and remove our subjects from error.

[*Concerning him who has bribed a judge, a local official, or a
sworn follower (fidelis) of the king.*]

96.I. If anyone in the pursuit of his cause hands anything
over [in place of a pledge] to his judge or to any local official
(*locopositus*) or to a fidelis of the king, and if while he [the
official] is still alive he requests its return claiming that it was
never released, then he [the official] shall do justice to him who
seeks it back even after a number of years. If the man [the
official] has died and he [the man who gave the pledge] makes
the claim against his [the official's] children or heirs we decree
that if he brought the charge while the father (i.e., the official) was
still alive or within one year of his death by proclaiming it to the
king or by bringing the charge through such men whose faith is
accepted and if he can produce his petition for recovery, and if it
appears to be true that he who brought the accusation had not been
able to find justice, then his [the official's] children or heirs shall
do justice to him, according to the law.

If, however, he cannot show his petition for recovery and he
allows a year to pass before bringing an accusation, he shall not
have the right to recover it from the children or the heirs, but let
him remain content [without his property]. Because in the matter
of pledges, sureties, and oaths our predecessor Rothair provided in
an earlier law [Rothair 361] that the party who is negligent shall
lose his case after an interval of a year has elapsed. Therefore it
seems fitting to us that he who seeks to reclaim [his property]
without pledges or sureties shall not have the right to reclaim it
after a year has passed.

[*Concerning him who charges that another man's slave or aldius
has committed some theft or homicide.*]

97.II. If anyone charges that another man's slave or aldius

has committed a theft or a homicide or some other evil deed, and if he makes the accusation while that slave or aldius is still living and he brings suit, then the accused shall do justice to him. If he does not accuse the lord [i.e., bring suit against him] while the slave is alive and after the slave's or aldius' death he seeks justice from his lord, we decree that he shall not have the right to make his claim if he has not brought accusation against the lord while his slave or aldius was still alive. For it seems unjust to us that the servant's lord should be required to do justice when he is no longer able to inquire about the matter from the slave or aldius.

[*Concerning the slave of one lord who marries the freed maidservant of another lord.*]

98.III. If any man's slave marries a female slave belonging to another man, and if the woman's lord frees her and makes her amundius, or if he sells her and the man who buys her craftily frees her while her slave husband remains in the status of servitude, then the freed maidservant shall lose her freedom and become a servant of the king; and the man who freed her shall hand over another slave like her to the king as composition or shall pay the price at which she is valued as composition because he entered into collusion [to destroy the marriage since free women could not legally be married to slaves]. The slave shall remain in the power of his lord and the lord shall purchase the maidservant at her value or on such terms as he is able to obtain from the king.

[*Boys under age may not make gifts to the king.*]

99.IIII. Our clemency, together with our judges and the rest of the Lombards, decrees concerning the boy who is under age that, just as he is not able to give any of his property to another man while he is under age, so he cannot give any of his property to the king before he attains his majority. We make this provision because many contentions have arisen from this cause.

[*A man may not allow a woman under his legal protection (mundium) to take the veil within a year after the death of her husband.*]

100.V. No man who holds the mundium of a woman may permit her to take the veil or assume the habit of a nun within a year after the death of her husband. If she wishes to do this on her own authority within a year, let her come to the king's palace and request our clemency; when the matter has been interrogated or investigated diligently by the king, she may receive the religious veil with his permission. If anyone presumes to do this within a year without the king's permission, he [the mundwald] shall pay his wergeld as composition to the king and the mundium of the woman and her property shall pass to the control of the palace. He who attempts to do this within a year [does it] on account of greed or worldly ambition, and not on account of the love of God or for saving her soul; for after the death of her husband, while her grief is new, he is able to incline the woman's mind in any direction he chooses. But when she has returned to herself and the desires of the flesh return, she may fall into adultery and behave as neither nun nor lay woman should. If any man who does not hold the woman's mundium presumes to do this [i.e., permits her to take the veil], he shall pay his wergeld as composition to the royal fisc and the woman and her property shall remain in the control of her mundwald.

[*On the disposition of a woman's property when she takes the veil.*]

101.VI. If a woman takes the religious veil or enters a nunnery, the conditions of the preceding law having been observed, if she has sons or daughters who possess her mundium, she may enter the nunnery with a third part of her own property and after her death this property shall remain in the possession of that monastery which she entered. If she does not have sons or daughters, she may enter the nunnery with half her property and after her death, if she wishes, that half of her property will remain in the possession of the nunnery. If she remains at home, she may have the right to dispose of a third part of her property either for the benefit of her soul or to anyone whom she wishes. Two-thirds of her property will pass to the possession of him who holds her mundium.

[*How a father may dispose of his property by testament if he has legitimate sons and daughters.*]

102.VII. If a Lombard has one legitimate son and one or more daughters and the father dies before he has given his daughter(s) in marriage, he has the right to give a fourth of his property by charter or gift to his daughter(s), if he wishes. If he does this, it shall be valid. If the man has two legitimate sons and one or more daughters, he may leave a seventh part of his property [for the daughters] if he wishes. If indeed there are more sons, [the portion] should be determined according to this principle. If the father has given them [the daughters] in marriage before his death, he shall provide for them as he chooses, according to law.

[*A man may not give his wife more property than the marriage portion (meta) which he gave her at the time of betrothal and the morning gift which he gave her at the time of the marriage.*]

103.VIII. No one may give his wife more of his property through any means than that which he gave on the day of their vows in the marriage portion (*metfio*) and the morning gift (*morgincap*) as is recorded in an earlier edict [Liutprand 7]. Whatever he gives more than this amount shall not be valid.

HERE END THE LAWS FROM THE SIXTEENTH YEAR

FROM THE SEVENTEENTH YEAR (A.D. 729)

We have already before this time taken care to add to our ancient lawbook those provisions which we recognized to be pleasing to God and advantageous for our people. Now, because of a number of controversies which have arisen among our people, we take care to add fitting provisions for these matters. We establish and decree that from this day, the first day of March, in the seventeenth year of our reign, God favoring, in the twelfth indiction, judgment should proceed as follows in these cases; nevertheless that which has been adjudged before should not be altered in any way. These new provisions have been agreed upon with our judges from Austria and Neustria, as well as from the bounds of Tuscany, and with the rest of our Lombard fideles. This law is first.

[*Concerning the married slave who marries another woman slave.*]

104.I. If any man's slave, having a legitimate wife, takes another woman slave over her, then the man slave's lord shall pay composition, according to the edict concerning adultery, to him whose woman slave he afterwards took. The woman herself, for this illegal act, shall receive such punishment from her lord in the presence of the slave's lord that no other slave shall presume to do this.

[*On the offspring of illegal marriages.*]
    105.II. In the case of those who have been born of an illegal marriage before [this] time and their legitimate brothers have voluntarily given them a part of their [property], we decree that they should remain in possession of that property, and they should not be disinherited in the least. However, the father may not establish the illegitimate children as his heirs either by formal act (gairethinx) or by any deceptive agreement.

    We have made this provision so that every man who wishes may receive a legitimate wife but may not contract illegal nuptials. However, in the case where there are no brothers but there are near relatives who can legitimately inherit, if they have been silent up until this time, let them remain silent in the future and have no right to speak against those who have possessed property for thirty years on the charge that they ought to be disinherited [because they were illegitimate]. Those who have been in possession of their property for at least thirty years shall continue to possess it.

[*Concerning the man who marries his own aldia or the aldia belonging to someone else.*]
    106.III. If anyone wishes to marry his own or another man's aldia, he should free her (make her *widerbora*), just as the edict decrees concerning the woman slave [Rothair 222]. But if he marries her without this procedure, her children are not regarded as legitimate but as natural children.

[*On men who make a contractual agreement among themselves.*]
    107.IIII. If a number of men enter into an agreement confirmed by a charter, providing therein a penalty [for breach of the agreement], and if afterwards one or more of the men wish to withdraw from this agreement and break the contract, each of them shall individually pay the full composition as established in the

pact; for all consented unanimously and no one forced them to make such an agreement. Therefore let each man who breaks the agreement pay composition just as each voluntarily consented.

[*Concerning the man who receives a pledge from his surety or debtor and the pledge is not reclaimed.*]

108.V. If any man receives a pledge from a debtor or his surety, and he [the debtor or surety] neglects to recollect that pledge, and if he [the one who received the pledge] gives him notice for twelve days, then that one who holds the pledge (if it is a man or woman slave) shall watch him or her that he or she may not flee, and he or she shall work for him as if his own slave or maidservant.

Furthermore, he [the creditor] shall have the right to take a second pledge, the pledges thus totaling double the amount of the debt. If the debtor or his surety neglects to recollect these pledges for thirty days, if he is in Neustria or Austria, he shall lose his pledges and have no right to seek them back. If he is in Tuscany, he shall have a period of sixty days; but if it is over sixty days, he shall likewise lose his pledges. Furthermore, he who received the pledge shall still have the right to bring and to prosecute his case.

[*Concerning the man who receives permission to take oxen or trained horses as pledges.*]

109.VI. If anyone has been permitted by his debtor or his debtor's surety to take as a pledge domesticated oxen or horses, and he has taken them, and if the debtor or his surety neglect to recollect the pledges within twelve days, then he [the man who took them] shall have the right to keep them and to use them as if they were his own; if the animals die, no [compensation] shall be sought. But if he is accused of deliberately driving the animals harder than his own, he alone shall swear his oath upon the gospels. If they [the debtor or his surety] have delayed for more than thirty days on this side of the mountains [i.e., in Austria or Neustria] or for sixty days on the other side of the mountains [in Tuscany] and have not recollected the pledges, just as above we decreed concerning the slave or the maidservant, so also we decree concerning horses or oxen, gold or silver, clothing, vessels of bronze, iron tools or smaller animals, or any other kind of pledge.

[*Concerning the slave held as a pledge who commits a theft.*]

110.VII. If any man holds another man's male or female slave in place of a pledge and he or she commits theft or homicide or does some other evil deed, the blame shall not be imputed to the slave's lord but to the man who held him or her: because after he takes him or her on account of his debt, he ought to guard him or her in such a way that he or she can do no evil. If indeed it is a woman slave and if either he who took her as a pledge or one of his slaves commits adultery with her before the prescribed thirty or sixty days established above, he shall pay the composition for adultery to the slave's lord. After the elapse of the prescribed thirty or sixty days, if he to whom she belongs neglects to recollect her, she shall remain in the control of him who took her as a pledge.

[*On the seizure of a slave or aldius on some secret understanding.*]

111.VIII. If any man presumes secretly to seize another man's slave or aldius claiming that he took him because he had committed a theft or because he had found him [entering] his courtyard silently at night, and if this collusion is apparent and the truth is certainly proved: then the man who presumed to seize him in any such manner shall pay to him whose slave or aldius it is as much composition as that one [the owner] ought to have paid if he had taken the slave or aldius without collusion or fraud in that crime which he charged—that is, if he claimed theft, [the accuser] shall pay eight times forty solidi for this illegal presumption. If he did not accuse [the slave or aldius] of theft but claimed instead that he took him silently in his courtyard, he shall pay forty solidi as composition, if collusion is apparent.

[*Concerning girls and the legal age at which they may marry.*]

112.VIIII. It has been noted before that the legal age for girls to marry should be twelve years. We now decree that the legal age for marrying ought not to be within the twelfth year but upon its completion. We say this because we know that there have been many controversies over this matter and it appears to us that girls are not mature before they have completed twelve years.

[*How a Lombard may reward his sons for serving him well.*]

113.X. If a Lombard wishes to give his sons something for

serving him well, he may do so in the following manner. If he has two sons, he may reward the one who was especially obedient to him and served him well according to God with a third part of his property. If he has three [sons], he may reward the one whom he wishes with a fourth part; if he has four sons, he may give a fifth part; if he has five sons, a sixth part; if he has six, a seventh; and if he has more sons it should be done according to this same progression: in this way the father always has the right [to bestow his property] accordingly as his sons have obeyed and served him. If all sons serve him equally well, they should have equal parts of the property of the father.

If a man has taken a second or third wife and has children from the former marriage as well as from the subsequent, he may not do better by one of the later children while his mother is still alive lest anyone say that he has done this under the influence of the woman. However, after the woman dies, the father has the right to act as is provided above.

Since slaves who serve well are better rewarded by their lords than those who do not serve well, so much the more should it be right, and we believe according to God's will, that a man be able to recognize and reward the son who serves him better [than the others].

[*Concerning the girl who marries without the consent of her relatives.*]

114.XI. If a girl secretly marries a husband without the consent of her relatives so that a marriage portion (meta) has neither been given nor promised for her, and if the husband then dies before he acquires her mundium, then the woman should be content with no portion nor can she afterwards seek a marriage portion from the heirs of her dead husband since she negligently went to a husband without the consent of her relatives; nor may he who seeks justice for her seek such a portion.

[*On property possessed by false charter.*]

115.XII. If any man possesses movable or immovable property by means of a forged charter and if it is proved that he possesses such property through a false title deed (*monimen*), then possession even though for thirty years shall not defend him nor

will it exclude that one whose property it legally is: but let the man
who possesses by means of a forged charter lose his property—
provided nevertheless, as we have said, that the fact has been
proved. [If the forgery is proved] the man to whom the property
legally belonged before shall receive it again.

[*On the exchange of plowland.*]

116.XIII. If anyone exchanges arable land, meadow, or forest with another man and the latter then works the land and thereafter builds a structure there, or constructs an enclosure or a vineyard, and if thereafter a third man appears who claims that the
land is his own, then if the man who first exchanged the land is
not able to defend his possession, the claimant shall recover the
property that was exchanged. In addition, he who was not able to
defend his possession of the land that he exchanged shall pay damages to him [the man who temporarily held and worked the land]
according to the assessed value of the work he did or the structure
he built. These provisions are to be applied in cases of purchase
as well as exchange. We have made this provision for those cases
where a charter of exchange or sale was not drawn up between
the men; but where they made a charter and it is shown, it should
be as is read in the charter.[11]

HERE END THE LAWS FROM THE SEVENTEENTH YEAR

FROM THE NINETEENTH YEAR (A.D. 731)

Our clemency is constantly beseeched by the unceasing controversies of the superstitious and vain. Since it is our heartfelt purpose to restrain the contentions of evildoers, that which has seemed
proper to our judges and to the rest of our Lombards has been
decreed by us in the foregoing addition to the laws. In like manner
in the present nineteenth year of our reign on the first day of
March in the fourteenth indiction we have taken counsel and
hereby issue certain further additions to our lawbook so that if any
controversy arises at some future time concerning matters covered

in the laws noted below, it shall be adjudicated and completed as we decree here.

[*On the betrothal of boys under eighteen.*]

117.I. If a boy who is a minor wishes to arrange a betrothal before he is eighteen—which is established as the legal age [Liutprand 19]—or if he desires to marry a woman, he shall have the right to provide the marriage portion (meta) and to give the morning gift, as the edict provides [Liutprand 7, 89], and to incur obligations and to offer surety and to sign contracts, if he wishes, for this purpose. The man who acts as surety or the scribe who prepares the charter in this cause shall incur no condemnation for so doing. It is true that we have handled the affairs of children under this age in order that they might not destroy or disperse their property; but in the case of a union blessed by God we agree that it may be done as stated above [this law seems to rescind Liutprand 7 or 19].

[*On using poison to kill a freeman.*]

118.II. In the past we and our judges decreed that he who kills a freeman shall lose all his property [Liutprand 20, 62]. As a result there have been some men who sought to prove by combat —as provided by the earlier law—that one of their relatives who had suffered some illness and died in his bed was actually deliberately killed. However, it seems to us to be a very serious thing that a man should lose his entire substance as the result of a duel fought by one man. Therefore we now decree that if in the future such a case arises, he who wishes to prove by means of a duel that the death of one of his relatives was caused deliberately, then, those things having been observed which were prescribed in the earlier edict [Liutprand 71], he should take oath on the gospels that he does not press his suit with evil intent, but as the result of a definite suspicion. Then he shall have the right to prove his charge by duel, as has been provided before. If the blow falls upon that man who was charged with the crime or upon the champion whom he secured, he shall not lose all of his property but shall pay composition to [his accuser] according to the quality of the person [who had died] just as the earlier law of compositions provided. For we are uncertain concerning the judgment of God [in this matter] and we have heard that many men have unjustly lost their cause through combat; however, on account of the customs of the Lombard people we are unable to abolish this law.[12]

[*To whom one may betroth his daughter or sister.*]

119.III. He who wishes to arrange a betrothal for his daughter or his sister has the right to betroth her to anyone whom he chooses, provided he is a freeman, as an earlier edict established [Rothair 178]. After he has arranged the betrothal, he may not give her to any other man as her husband within two years. If he presumes to give her to anyone else or wishes to break the betrothal agreement (*spunsalia*) he shall pay such a composition to the man to whom she was betrothed as was set out in the agreement between themselves, as provided in the earlier law; in addition he shall pay his wergeld as composition to the king's treasury, and the man who presumes to take her shall likewise pay his wergeld as composition to the treasury. If a man presumes to take a woman who is already betrothed to someone else without the consent of her father or brother, he shall pay double the marriage portion as composition to her betrothed, just as the earlier edict contains, and he shall pay his wergeld as composition to the king's treasury. The father or brother who did not consent in this case shall be absolved from blame.

As for the girl who presumed to do this voluntarily, if any portion of the inheritance of her relatives is due to her, she shall lose that portion: she shall receive none of the property of her relatives but those who are legally able to do so shall succeed to her share. Nor can her father or brother give or transfer any part of the inheritance to her by any means because she sinned against our people in doing this because of her desire for gain. We do this in order that enmity may cease and there may be no feud (faida).

If, however, God forbid, after such a betrothal agreement has been made, some hostility develops between the relatives of those betrothed and they are in enmity for any reason—such as, for example, the killing of one of their relatives—then he who neglects to give or to take [the bride] shall pay as composition the sum which they [the prospective bridegroom and the girl's mundwald]

had agreed upon between themselves, and he shall then be absolved
of further blame: because it is not good that a man should give his
daughter or his sister or some other relative where hostility caused
by a homicide is proven to exist.

[*He who mistreats his ward shall lose her mundium.*]

120.IIII. An earlier law provides that he who mistreats his
ward shall lose her mundium, but the law does not define such mistreatment [Rothair 182]. We now state that it is mistreatment if
he lets her go hungry or does not give her clothes or shoes according to the quality of his wealth, or if he presumes to give her as a
wife to someone else's slave or aldius, or if he strikes her dishonorably (unless she is still a child and in honest discipline he is trying
to show her a woman's work or is correcting her evil ways just as
he would do with his own daughter), or if he sets her forcefully to
indecent work, or if he has intercourse with her. If anyone presumes to do any of these things, we say that it is ill treatment. In
addition, the guardian may not presume to marry his ward to a
freeman without her consent, because there can be no worse treatment than that she be forced to marry a man whom she does not
want. Therefore we decree that in the case of such treatment or
injury or intercourse, the mundwald shall pay composition to that
woman and he shall lose her mundium, as the edict states [Rothair
43–74].

[*Concerning the man who talks dishonorably with another man's
wife.*]

121.V. He who converses shamefully with someone else's
wife—that is, if he places his hands on her bosom or on some other
shameful place and it is proved that the woman consented, he who
commits such an evil deed shall pay his wergeld as composition to
the woman's husband. If, however, the case is not proved but some
man, suspecting another man of so treating his wife, accuses him of
doing this, then he who accuses shall have the right to challenge the
other man to combat or put him to the oath, as he chooses. If the
woman had consented to such an illicit deed, her husband has the
right to take vengeance on her or to discipline her in vindication as
he wishes; nevertheless, however, she may not be killed nor may
any mutilation be inflicted on her body. If perchance the man

proved guilty is a freeman who does not have enough to pay the
composition, then a public official shall hand him over to the
woman's husband, and the husband may take vengeance on him or
discipline him in vindication, but he may not kill him or inflict any
mutilation on his body.

If, moreover, someone else's aldius or slave presumes to do
this to a free woman, then his lord shall pay sixty solidi as composition to the woman's husband and hand over his person to the husband. If indeed someone else's slave or aldius commits such an evil
deed as is stated above with the consent of his lord and it is proved
that his lord consented, then the lord shall pay his own wergeld as
composition and, moreover, the slave must also be handed over
with the composition. If the case is not proved concerning the
lord's consent, then the lord of that slave or aldius may clear himself by oath taken with his legitimate oathhelpers to the effect that
he had not consented to this evil deed. He shall then be absolved
and he shall carry out the provisions established above concerning
his slave or aldius.

[*Concerning the man who betroths a woman who already has a
husband.*]

122.VI. If any poor foolish man dares to betroth a woman
who already has a husband, whether her husband is sick or well—
as in that case just reported to us—and this is proved, then the
man who did this shall pay his wergeld as composition to the husband, and the woman shall receive such a treatment as we provided
above for her who permits herself to be basely treated [Liutprand
121].

[*On what shall be done if a free woman or girl is struck after she
had come to observe a brawl.*]

123.VII. If some man in rage has hit a freeman or a free-
woman or a girl who had come to a brawl (*in scandalum*) where
men were fighting and if his blows were as weighty and ponderous
as we have just heard, then he [who struck the blows] shall pay
composition, in the case of striking a man, half of the value of such
a man as if he had killed him, and in the case of a woman he shall
pay as composition a similar half value (*pretium*) as if he had
killed her brother. But in those cases where he has caused wounds

or injuries he must then pay composition as provided in an earlier edict [Rothair 40–137].

[Concerning him who cripples a male or female slave, aldius or aldia.]

124.VIII. He who strikes an aldius or aldia, or a male or female slave, and they are crippled as a result of the blow shall pay to their lord or patron as composition half of the price (pretium) which he would have paid had he killed them. If he causes wounds or injuries he shall pay composition as is provided in an earlier edict [Rothair 78–127].

[Concerning him who strikes a free woman or girl while she is crouching.]

125.VIIII. If anyone maliciously or through spite, just as we are aware that it has been done, presumes to hit or stab a free woman or girl as she crouches to relieve herself or on any other occasion when her need requires her to remove her clothes, he shall pay eighty solidi as composition to her mundwald. If it is an aldius or slave who presumes to do this, his lord shall pay sixty solidi as composition and hand over the person who committed this evil deed to the woman's mundwald.

[Concerning the aldius who marries an aldia belonging to another lord.]

126.X. If the aldius of one man takes to wife the aldia of another man and begets children of her but does not acquire her mundium, then the children shall belong to the lord of the aldia mother. But if the aldius acquired her mundium and children were born thereafter, the children shall follow their father, as the earlier edict provided [Rothair 218], and they shall enjoy the same status in relation to their patron as had their father.

[On Romans who marry Lombard women.]

127.XI. If a Roman man marries a Lombard woman and acquires her mundium, and if after his death the widow marries another man without the consent of the heirs of her first husband, feud and the penalty for illegal intercourse shall not be required; for after she married a Roman man and he acquired her mundium, she became a Roman and the children born of such a marriage shall be Roman and shall live according to the law of their Roman father. Therefore the man who marries her after the death of her first husband ought not to pay composition for illegal intercourse just as he would not pay it for another Roman woman.

[*What sort of surety should be provided to enable a man to redeem his pledges.*]

128.XII. In an earlier edict we issued a law [Liutprand 36, 38] providing that if any freeman produced three sureties (freemen) to guarantee his pledge, and if the man who had received the pledge neglects to return it, then he [who refused to return the pledge] should pay composition as that one who does not have prepared sureties. Now since we realize that evil men offer as sureties those who possess nothing but their persons alone so that through them justice cannot be done at all, we decree that sureties should have as much property, if not more, as is the amount of the obligation so that if necessary they can give pledges on behalf of him who owes the debt for which sureties were required. If the sureties do not have this much, the creditor who does not wish to accept them ought not to be blamed, nor can the debtor offering the surety excuse himself from blame by saying that he had ready sureties; for it is not possible that a man be compelled to accept as a surety someone who does not own as much, if not more, than is the amount of the debt which can be taken in place of the pledge. If from those men at hand the debtor can find sureties who possess enough to cover the pledge and who ought therefore to be accepted, it is well. If, however, the debtor does not find such persons immediately, he has three days without penalty to find such sureties who possess enough wealth that they can pay whatever the debtor owes. If there is more delay in providing such a surety, the debtor shall pay composition as decreed before.

[*On women who seek to marry boys who are minors.*]

129.XIII. A most vain and grasping suasion and perversion has appeared in these times which seems to us, in conjunction with the rest of our judges, to be illegal: women, adult and mature in age, have joined themselves in union with small boys who are under the legal age and claim them as their legitimate husbands— [all this seems illegal to us] since at this time the boys are not strong enough to have intercourse with women. Therefore we now decree that in the future no woman shall presume to do this thing unless the boy's father or grandfather has made provision for this with the woman's relatives. But if a boy remains under age after his father's death and a woman presumes to marry him before the boy has completed thirteen years, saying that he ought to be her legal husband, that union shall not be valid and they shall be separated from one another. Indeed the woman shall return empty-handed with reproach and she may not marry any other man until the boy reaches the above age. If on reaching this age the boy himself wishes to have her as wife, he may do so. If he does not want her, he may marry any other woman whom he wishes and is able to acquire. And if the boy does not want her and she marries another man, the man who marries her may not give a full marriage portion (metfio) for her as he would for another girl but he may give only half, as if for a widow [cf. Rothair 182, 183]. The man who persuades a boy [to enter such a union], whether he is a relative or a stranger, shall pay 100 solidi as composition, half to the king and half to the boy himself.

HERE END THE LAWS FROM THE NINETEENTH YEAR

FROM THE TWENTY-FIRST YEAR (A.D. 733)

[*Concerning the man who urges his wife to lie with another man.*]

130.I. In the case where a man gives his wife permission to do evil by saying to his wife, "Go, sleep with such a man," or by saying to the man, "Come sleep with my wife," and where such an evil deed has been carried out and it is proved that it was done through the advice of the husband himself, we decree as follows. The woman who consents to and commits such an evil thing shall be killed, in accordance with an earlier edict, because she ought not to commit nor to hide such a case [Rothair 212]. For if a woman's husband commits adultery with his maidservant or with another woman, the wife herself should proclaim this to the king's court or to the judges; therefore she ought by no means to be silent when he first says such a thing to her. Therefore, as we have said, she shall die in accordance with the earlier edict.

The husband, moreover, who offered such evil counsel to her or to the other man, and who gave authority to his wife to commit such an evil deed, shall pay as composition to the wife's relatives such an amount as would be paid if she were killed in a brawl (scandalum) [Rothair 378], since, because of her evil nature, she participated in scandalum when she consented to commit this deed —indeed, she could not participate in greater scandalum if she were killed in a brawl. Therefore, as said before, the husband shall pay her wergeld as composition. If the woman has children, the children shall have her property. If she does not have children, her property shall return to her relatives. We do this because we believe that the wretched man who sought to do this thing [did it] so that he might get rid of his wife and have her property.

The man who commits adultery with another man's wife, even though he had the consent of her husband, shall be handed over to the woman's relatives and not to the husband who consented to such an evil deed or gave his illegal advice.

Further in such cases as outlined above, if the husband gives counsel or permission to his wife and she does not consent and if it is clear that she did not do this evil thing, then the husband who gave her such privilege and advice shall pay composition just as noted above in the edict in the case of the man who gives evil advice to another [see Rothair 10, where the composition set is twenty solidi], that is he shall pay fifty solidi, because it is a greater evil for a man to give illegal counsel to his wife than to give evil counsel to another man.

[*Concerning the man who commends his property to another man and it is then stolen.*]

131.II. If a freeman places his property in the house of any of his fellow freemen and it happens that a thief comes along and steals that property, the man in whose house the property was placed shall repay it, or, if he has not repaid it, he should do so. If afterwards the thief is found, then the thief shall pay composition to the man from whose house he seized or stole that property. We make this provision because if the thief pays composition for the theft to the man to whom the property belongs, then afterward the man whose house he broke into may charge him for the violation of his house, and we cannot impose two penalties in one case.[13] Therefore it seems just to us that he who commended his property shall have it repaid by that man from whose house it was lost, and the man from whose house it was lost or where the theft occurred shall seek composition for the theft; he shall receive that composition as the law provides and the thief, even though he is a malefactor, will not be held to two penalties for one offense.

[*Concerning the man who fraudulently claims someone else's female slave as the wife of his slave or aldius.*]

132.III. If any man fraudulently seizes another man's woman slave saying that she is married to his own slave or aldius, and if afterwards it becomes clear that the slave or aldius had not married her, then first of all he shall return that bondswoman to her lord and she shall be his servant as she was before. The man who perpetrates such a fraud shall also give another such female slave or aldia to that man who suffered from the fraud and he shall pay for the work done by that woman servant whom he fraudulently took for as long as he had her with him.

[*On freemen who reside in another man's house.*]

133.IIII. If a freeman enters the house of another man for the purpose of residing there in return for a rent, and if thereafter he purchases anything with the property which he brought with him when he entered that holding, or if he purchases anything with his wife's property and it is proved, then [when he quits the holding] he shall leave his purchase with the holding and receive its value in return. Proof should be established in this way. When the man buys anything with the property of his wife, he should have in attendance men who know what the value of his wife's property is in order that his case may not come to perjury and so that when he needs to offer oath that the purchase was made with his wife's property these witnesses will know and can swear that they were present at the time the purchase was made with the wife's property. After this the man shall receive the value of the purchase and the acquired item shall remain with the holding.

If a man makes the purchase with [the proceeds of] the work which he performed or did after he entered the holding which he held in return for a rent, he shall leave it in that house where he worked.

We are adding this provision because such a case was always adjudged in this manner both in the time of our predecessors and in our own in accordance with tribal custom, but it has not been recorded in our lawbook.

[*Concerning the men living in a village who arrange some agreement among themselves regarding a field or vineyard, meadow or forest.*]

134.V. If men living in the same village are involved in a controversy over their fields or vineyards, meadow or forest, or some other property and one party of them collect themselves together for the purpose of driving their opponent forth by force from that place, and if they go and commit violence (scandalum) there or inflict wounds or injuries or kill the man, we decree that they shall pay composition for the wounds or injuries or for killing the man in accordance with the earlier edict which our glorious King Rothair established and which we [have supplemented] ourselves [Rothair 43–73]. Moreover, for their illegal presumption in collecting themselves together thus, they shall pay twenty solidi as composition to that party who labored in the field or vineyard or meadow or forest.

We establish this in order that no one may presume to incite or perform such evil deeds in any place and, since this case does not correspond to breach of the peace with an armed band (*arischild*) [Rothair 19; Liutprand 35, 141] or to the banding together of rustics [Rothair 279] or to the sedition of rustics [Rothair 280], it seems more fitting to us to regard it as the same as giving evil counsel, or plotting a death [Rothair 11]. When men, driven by their evil nature, collect themselves together and proceed against another man, they do this in order to commit some evil deed: they may even kill the man or inflict wounds or injuries upon him. Therefore, as we have said, we associate this case with that of counselling death [the penalty for which] is twenty solidi, as set forth above.[14]

[*Concerning the woman, bathing in a river, whose clothes are stolen.*]

135.VI. It has been made known to us that a certain perverse man took all of a woman's clothes while she was bathing in the river; as a result the woman was naked and everyone who walked or passed through that place considered her condition to be the result of her sinful nature. She could not, moreover, remain forever in the river and, blushing with shame, returned naked to her home. Therefore we decree that the man who presumes to do such an illicit act shall pay his wergeld as composition to that woman to whom he did this shameful thing. We say this because if the father or husband or near relatives of the woman had found him, they would have entered into a violent fray (scandalum) with him and he who was the stronger would have killed the other man. Therefore it is better that the culprit, living, should pay his wergeld as composition than that a feud develop over a death and produce such deeds that the eventual composition be greater still.

[*What shall be done if a man is killed while water is being raised from a well.*]

136.VII. It has likewise been made known to us that a certain man has a well in his courtyard and, according to custom, it has a prop (*furca*) and lift (*tolenum*) for raising the water. Another man who came along stood under that lift and, when yet another man came to draw water from the well and incautiously released the lift, the weight came down on the man who stood under it and he was killed. The question then arose over who should pay composition for this death and it has been referred to us. It seems right to us and to our judges that the man who was killed, since he was not an animal but had the power of reason like other men, should have noticed where he stood or what weight was above his head. Therefore two-thirds of the amount of his composition shall be assessed to him [the dead man] and one-third of the amount at which he was valued according to law shall be paid as composition by the man who incautiously drew the water. He shall pay the composition to the children or to the near relatives who are the heirs of the dead man and the case shall be ended without any feud or grievance since it was done unintentionally. Moreover, no blame should be placed on the man who owns the well because if we placed the blame on him, no one hereafter would permit other men to raise water from their wells and since all men cannot have a

well, those who are poor would die and those who are traveling
through would also suffer need.[15]

[*On borrowed animals which cause damage.*]
   137.VIII. It has likewise been brought to our attention that a
certain man had borrowed a beast of burden from another man for
his own use, and an unbroken colt followed its mother. While the
man who had borrowed the animal for hauling was walking along
the road, it happened that a child standing in a certain place was
struck by a blow from the hoof of the colt and the child was killed.
The relatives then sought retribution for the death of that infant
and the case was referred to us. We, with our judges, decree that
two-thirds of the amount at which the infant was valued shall be
paid as composition by the man who owned the colt and the man
who had borrowed the beast of burden shall pay a third. Indeed we
know that it is written in an earlier edict that if a horse causes
damage with its hoof, then its owner shall pay composition for that
damage [Rothair 325, 326], but because this horse was borrowed
and the man who received it in loan was a rational being and able
to warn the child, if he had not neglected it, to watch out for itself,
then this accident would not have occurred. For this reason we say
that he who borrowed the horse should pay as composition a third
part of the value (pretium) because of his negligence.

[*Concerning the man who urges a slave to strike his lord.*]
   138.VIIII. It has been brought to our attention that a certain
man, inspired by the devil, said to another man's slave: "Come and
kill your lord and I will give you the bounty you wish." The boy,
persuaded by that one, entered into this evil affair and allowed
himself to be so led that when presently he was further told, "Strike
your lord," he struck him as for his sins. And yet again the man
said to the boy: "Strike him again now for if you do not strike him,
I shall strike you." The boy then turned to his lord [and struck]
another blow and he was killed. Assessment of the composition for
this death must be made. Some men say that the man who persuaded the boy and told him to strike his lord in his presence
should pay such a composition as the earlier edict provides for
those who give counsel of death [cf. Rothair 10, 11]. But this is

in no way pleasing to us and to our judges since the counsel of death is arranged in secret and sometimes carried out and sometimes not carried out; but this homicide was committed in the presence [of the instigator] and we say that it is not counsel when a man points out another man with his own words and in his own presence and says, "Strike this man." Therefore he who commits such an evil deed and it is proved shall not pay the composition assessed for the counsel of death but he shall pay composition as we have added to the code in our own time [Liutprand 20]: he shall lose all of his substance and the dead man's heirs shall receive half of it and the king's fisc half—however, the heirs of the man killed shall have the amount of the old composition before [the property is divided], as has been added to the edict in our own time.

HERE END THE LAWS FROM THE TWENTY-FIRST YEAR

FROM THE TWENTY-SECOND YEAR (A.D. 734)

It is now our concern to add to the body of our lawbook laws covering a few cases which have recently arisen and were found not to be covered in the edict before this time as a result of which our judges have found themselves in doubt when rendering a decision. On this the first day of March, I, Liutprand, in the name of God, king of the Lombard nation, in the twenty-second year of my reign, God favoring, in the second indiction [establish the following laws].

[*Concerning the aldius of one lord married to the aldia of another, or the slave of one man married to the female slave of another.*]

139.I. If any man's aldius marries the aldia of another man, or a man slave marries a woman slave, and if before their lords have made some agreement between themselves concerning this marriage it happens that some miserable man commits adultery with that aldia or woman slave who is the wife of another, we decree that he who committed this evil deed be subjected for this

offense to him with whose wife he committed adultery. And the
wife's lord shall receive such a mundium for her, if she is an aldia,
as the law provides; and if she is a woman slave, he shall receive
her value (pretium) or a substitute [slave] in this case, as he
chooses. We have made this provision concerning the wife of a
slave or of an aldius because if some wretched man commits adultery with the wife of a freeman, he pays composition to her husband, not to her relatives, even though the husband does not hold
her mundium [Liutprand 122].

[*Concerning the man who commits adultery with his married
aldia or woman slave.*]
140.II. If a freeman has a man and woman slave, or aldius
and aldia, who are married, and, inspired by hatred of the human
race, he has intercourse with that woman whose husband is the
slave or with the aldia whose husband is the aldius, he has committed
adultery and we decree that he shall lose that slave or aldius with
whose wife he committed adultery and the woman as well. They
shall go free where they wish and shall be as much folkfree (*ful-
freal*) as if they had been released by the formal procedure for
alienation (gairethinx)—for it is not pleasing to God that any man
should have intercourse with the wife of another. Nevertheless concerning this liberty we say that since they cannot be freemen without true manumission as the edict provides [Rothair 224] through
the formal act of thingation [by leading them] around the altar as
we have established, let them come to us at our palace or to whomever is prince of the land at that time, and he shall free them and
give them their charter. Afterwards they will most certainly be free
and legally manumitted.

[*On the collecting together of a band of women and sending them
into a village or house.*]
141.III. It has been related to us that certain perfidious and
evil-minded men, not presuming themselves to enter armed into a
village or into the house of another man in a violent manner since
they fear the composition which has been set up in an earlier law
[Rothair 279, 280], gather together as many women as they have
both free and bond, and set them upon weaker men. Seizing these

men the women rain blows upon them and commit other evil deeds
in a violent manner more cruelly than men might do.

Since this has been brought to our attention and these less
strong men have entered an accusation on account of this violence,
we add to the edict that if, in the future, women presume to do this,
if they receive any injury or dishonor, wounds or injuries, or even
death there, those who, in defending themselves, inflicted this
injury or caused destruction to them shall pay no composition to
the women themselves or to their husbands or to their mundwalds.
And in addition the public agent who is established in that place
shall seize those women and shave (decalvere) [see note 8 above]
them and drive (frustare) them through the neighboring villages of
that region in order that other women shall not presume to commit
such evil deeds. If the women in this situation inflict wounds or
cause other injuries to any man, their husbands shall pay composition for the wounds or injuries they inflicted according to the
provisions of the code.

We have decreed this rather on account of the discipline than
for the composition because we cannot equate the collecting
together of women with a breach of the peace with an armed band
(arschild) [Rothair 19; Liutprand 35, 134] nor with the sedition
of rustics [Rothair 280], because these are things that men do,
not women; therefore it shall be done concerning such women as
provided above. If a woman rushes into a brawl (scandalum) and
receives there death or a blow or injury, justice shall be done her as
our predecessor King Rothair provided and adjudged [Rothair
378].

[*Concerning the man who knows that his aldius or aldia, male or
female slave, is in another man's house.*]

142.IIII. If a man knows that his aldius or aldia, his man
slave or his woman slave, either married or otherwise, is in another
man's house and does not seek him or her back either through the
judge or through another public official, and if he does not bring
him or her back and allows him or her to remain in the house of
that other man for a longer time, then he [the master] may not
seek compensation for his servant's work because he knowingly
neglected to seek back his man slave or woman slave, his aldius or

aldia. But if their lord seeks them back and he who has them neglects to return them or blocks the way [to their lord], then he shall pay compensation for their work as the law provides [Rothair 275; see also Rothair 27 and Liutprand 132].

[HERE END THE LAWS FROM THE TWENTY-SECOND YEAR]

FROM THE TWENTY-THIRD YEAR (A.D. 735)

In the name of our Lord Jesus Christ, I, Liutprand, most excellent Christian and Catholic king of the Lombard nation, together with our judges and our fideles, have undertaken to add to the lawbook in the twenty-third year of my reign, God favoring, on the first day of March in the third indiction, those laws which have not been set down before and concerning which we recognize that there has been contention. [We do this] so that in the future there may be no doubt in the minds of our judges but they may be able to issue their decisions with confidence in accordance with the provisions added here with the favor of God. This is the first law.

[*Concerning the male or female slave, aldius or aldia, who seeks refuge in a church.*]

143.I. If a man's male or female slave, aldius or aldia while fleeing seeks refuge in one of God's churches and his or her lord or patron either acting by himself or through one of his agents drags the dependent forth violently, then the lord or patron shall pay his wergeld as composition to the abovementioned church. If the slave or aldius commits some evil deed without his lord's consent, then his lord shall hand over that slave or aldius to the custodian of the church in recompense for the evil deed; if the lord or patron can offer satisfaction that this was done without his consent, he shall then not pay his wergeld as composition.

[*On men who commit perjury.*]

144.II. That man who, disdaining the fear of God and acting out of a materialistic desire for property, intentionally offers a false oath and this is found out and it is proved that he perjured himself, shall lose that property concerning which he swore falsely and the man to whom he offered oath contrary to reason shall have it. And in addition—because this man has sinned against himself and, what is more, against God and has denied his faith and perjured himself before God and has not saved himself—he shall pay half his wergeld as composition to the man to whom he gave the false oath.

[*On succession to the property of an unmarried niece.*]
145.III. We call to mind that provision has already been made [Liutprand 4] concerning the man who dies and leaves one or more daughters as well as one or more unmarried sisters, that both the sisters and daughters ought to succeed him in similar fashion and equally; if one of the sisters dies unmarried, her surviving sister(s) shall equally succeed her. But now a controversy has arisen between brothers and sisters over a niece who died unmarried, the question being who should succeed her: we decree that the paternal uncles who held her mundium ought to succeed to her share. The sisters of the dead girl's father shall receive none of her portion, but they shall have such a share as they would have had if their niece had continued to live.

[*Concerning the man who finds a free woman or girl walking through his sowed field.*]
146.IIII. The man who finds a free woman or girl walking through his seeded field and leaving a path shall take pledges from her, and her relatives or mundwald shall pay six solidi as composition for her as the law provides [Rothair 357]. However, if he presumes to seize her and lead her bound in manacles to his house, he shall pay 100 solidi as composition, half to the king and half to her relatives or mundwald—the composition of six solidi being counted in this [latter] composition.

If the holder of the woman's or girl's mundium is accused of deliberately causing that woman to walk through the other man's cultivated field in order that he might receive composition for her, he shall offer oath that the woman did not deliberately walk through that man's cultivated field in order to collect composition or to cause any damage. If he so offers oath, then the man who presumed to seize the girl shall pay the 100 solidi composition, as above. If he does not dare so to swear, then the woman's relatives or mundwald shall pay six solidi as composition for beating a path [through his field] as said above, and as also said above, the man who seized her shall be absolved from any blame.

[*Concerning the male slave or aldius, female slave or aldia, who has been caught in the act of theft.*]

147.V. If any man's slave or aldius, woman slave or aldia, has been taken in theft and if his or her lord neglects to free him after being sent to for thirty days, the slave or aldius shall be regarded as taken in the act of theft (figanges) and he against whom the theft was committed shall keep him in settlement for himself. Afterwards his lord shall pay composition to the aggrieved man as the law provides and the edict sets forth [Rothair 253–76, 281–99].

[*On those who claim another man's land.*]

148.VI. If a man encloses (*wifaverit*) another man's land without his consent or without [the order of] a public official saying that [the land] ought to be his own, and if he is not then able to prove that it is his own, he shall pay six solidi as composition in the way that a man who places a stake on another man's land must pay [Liutprand 47].

[*On minor children who are found to be in need.*]

149.VII. This law concerns children who are under age and who are in great need and are dying from hunger. It seems right to us that, since it is a time of hunger, they should have the right to sell part of their land or of their other property with [the advice of] a representative of the king or one of his judges in such an amount that they are enabled to live and to free themselves from hunger and will not die. The judge who presides in that place ought to make provision for this if the minor does it because of his hunger—but it should be done in the judge's presence with the help of God. If the judge does otherwise, God will be his judge. In the charter of sale it should be noted that this sale was made on account of the necessity created by hunger; and the man who conducts this proceeding must not presume to buy from such children. After the period of famine is over, minor children may not dispose of their property or their substance except in accordance with the provision of the earlier edict for we have made this exception on account of necessity alone and not, heaven forbid, to correct the earlier edict [Liutprand 19, 58].

[*On him who digs a ditch along the road.*]

150.VIII. That man who digs a ditch along the road and is not able to prove that the land is his own shall pay six solidi as composition and shall fill in the ditch. And if he causes some damage to vineyard or to wood in digging such a ditch, he shall pay composition as the earlier law provides [Rothair 281, 283, 292, 294, 295].

[*On him who sends his pigs into another man's defended forest.*]

151.VIIII. In the case where a man sends his pigs into another man's defended forest and there are fewer than ten pigs, then if the owner of the forest kills one of the pigs, it shall be as provided by an earlier edict [Rothair 349, 350]. If he finds ten pigs and kills more than one, he shall pay an eightfold composition just as if he had taken another man's property with evil intent. But if the man who controls the pigs sends more than ten of his own pigs or of someone else's pigs into the defended forest, and if the owner of the forest kills more of the pigs than the edict allows, nothing shall be required of him.

If the man who sent the pigs into the forest can offer oath that he did not send them with evil intent but they went without his consent, then the man who killed the pigs shall pay singlefold for those pigs. And if [the owner] swears likewise concerning his swineherd, the pigs shall likewise be repaid singlefold. But if he cannot offer such oath concerning the evil intent of his swineherd, only half of the pigs shall be repaid singlefold and the other half shall be charged to himself because he had an undisciplined slave.

[*Concerning the prodigal man who has sold or dissipated his substance so that he is unable to pay composition.*]

152.X. If the man who is prodigal or ruined, or who has sold or dissipated his substance, or for other reasons does not have that with which to pay composition, commits theft or adultery or a breach of the peace (scandalum) or injures another man and the composition for this is twenty solidi or more, then a public representative ought to hand him over as a slave to the man who suf-

fered such illegal acts.[16] If the composition is less than twenty
solidi, if, as often happens, it is six to twelve solidi, then the public
representative ought to hand the offender over to the man who suffered the deed to be a slave and to serve him for as many years as
is required to redeem the fine for his crime. Afterwards he is free to
go where he wishes.

[*Concerning the children of a man who becomes a priest.*]

153.XI. If a Lombard is married and has sons or daughters,
and if afterwards, compelled by divine guidance, he becomes a
priest, then the sons or daughters who were born before his conse-
cration shall live by that law as their father lived when he begot
them, and they ought to settle their lawsuits according to this
law.[17]

HERE ENDS THE EDICT ISSUED BY LIUTPRAND

IV. The Laws of King Ratchis

(I). In the name of our Lord Jesus Christ and in such manner as is according to God, for the salvation of our own souls and the souls of all our people, it seems right to us, together with our judges, [to issue these laws] in order that all men, the powerful as well as the poor, who seek justice, may not be put off at all. (A.D. 745 or 746)

HERE BEGIN THE TITLES OF THE LAWS

I. 1. Every judge shall hold court every day and shall not receive bribes.

[2. All men should first seek justice from their own judge.]

[3. No man may bring suit on behalf of another man without the consent of his judge.]

[4. Every freeman should provide himself with certain military equipment.]

II. 5. On pledges and how they shall be given in the future.

6. A new provision concerning free women who marry slaves.

7. Concerning those who acquire a slave or aldius with consent of the king.

8. On bills of sale and claims of nonpayment.
9. Concerning those who send their agents outside the boundaries of the country.
10. Concerning those who cause an uprising or raise sedition against their judge.
11. Concerning the man who attempts to prosecute another man's suit without the consent of the judge.
12. Concerning those who investigate and reveal the secrets of the king.

III. [13. On protection of the frontiers.]
    [14. On gasinds (gasindii) and their men.]

[HERE BEGIN THE LAWS]

[Every judge shall hold court every day and shall not receive bribes.]

1. Each judge shall hold court every day in his district (civitas) and he should not attend to his own emulation or devote himself to any other worldly vanity, but he should preside there himself and assure justice for all in such way that he receive reward from no man, just as our judges have already promised us in writing. He who acts otherwise shall lose his right to render justice. If, in the future, any judge neglects to do justice for a freeman (arimannus), rich or poor, or for any other man, he shall lose his office and pay his wergeld as composition to the king's treasury; and he shall likewise pay composition to the man for whom he neglected to judge justly in accordance with the provisions of our lawbook [Liutprand 25-28]. Indeed, we have said this, as God is our witness, because we cannot go anywhere or attend any celebration or ride anywhere without being besieged by the appeals of many men. Therefore it is our wish and we decree that every judge shall behave as stated here that we may not be offensive in the eyes of God.

It is our desire that our judges should in like manner admonish their schultheises, their hundred-men (centini), the other local officials (locopositi), or those men directly under their own control, that they should perform in the same way and that they should promise their judge, just as the judges themselves have promised us, that they will be obedient and worthy of confidence. And if one of these does not observe and carry out these orders as written above from the present day on the Kalends of March, and if appeals against such instances come to us, then let him in whose judgment district (*iudicalis*) the man lives who did not obtain justice and who appealed to us know that we shall expel him from office and no patron will be able to intercede to prevent his losing that office. And him to whom he [the judge] neglected to do justice shall not pay composition to us and to them [the judges] as we have established above [Liutprand 28] because we recognize that he [the judge] is faithful neither to God nor to ourselves, nor does he seek the welfare of this land but, as we have said, he seeks to act against God and against ourselves.

[*All men should first seek justice from their own judge.*]

2. If a freeman (arimannus) or someone else does not first go to his judge for a judgment but, in seeking justice, appeals first to us, he shall pay fifty solidi as composition to his judge. For we make known to all that anyone who has a case should first go to the judge of his district (civitas) and make his complaint known to that judge; and then if he does not receive justice he may come to us. But if anyone presumes to come to us before he goes first to his judge, he shall pay fifty solidi as composition if he has that much money; if he does not have enough to pay this composition we order him to be beaten [see the laws of Liutprand, note 9]. It is thus our wish that everyone go first to his judge for justice as the law provides.

[*No man may bring suit on behalf of another man without the consent of his judge.*]

3. We order that no man shall presume to take up or introduce by speaking another man's suit except with the consent of his judge, and then he may speak only on behalf of a widow or of an orphan. The man who dares to take up or introduce a suit for one of his fellow freemen shall pay his wergeld as composition, half to the king and half to his judge. And if the judge before whom the case is argued permits this to be done or consents to it, he shall pay his wergeld as composition to the king.

[*Every freeman should provide himself with certain military equipment.*]

4. We decree that every freeman (arimannus) should carry a shield and lance for himself when he rides out with his judge. And when he comes to the palace with his judge, he shall be likewise equipped. We order this to be done so because the times are uncertain and it cannot be known what orders he will receive from us or where they will be asked to ride. The man who fails to do this shall pay twenty solidi as composition to his judge. If the judge whose freeman (arimannus) delays to comply with this order does not compel [him to do so], as we have said above, he shall pay his wergeld as composition to the king's court. With regard to iron weapons and other arms or horses, let it be done as commanded before in our decree.

(II) THE PROLOGUE OF KING RATCHIS (A.D. 746)

It is fitting that we issue these laws with the aid of Christ Jesus our Saviour under whose guidance we have attained to the height of our rule: with his compassion to aid us we have undertaken to establish such laws as are fitting for our people, the Catholic Lombards, chosen of God. When the most glorious and lofty King Rothair, king of the Lombard nation, with royal care and under the inspiration of God recorded and established laws to eliminate all controversies and disputes in contentious matters, he recommended that his successors, also acting under the inspiration of God, recognize that some unjust and harsh things remained and that they should seek divine guidance to remedy them. And so Rothair's successor, the most excellent King Grimwald, with great care and vigilance studied the needs of individual matters and brought together certain laws and added to or condensed them for the furtherance of our well-being. Later that most glorious and orthodox supporter of the faith and ruler of this nation and, through the mercy of omnipotent God, our instructor, the exceptional and lofty Liutprand, this most wise prince, persisting in divine works and daily vigils, adorned with all modesty and sobriety, acting with divine aid and with divine inspiration issued and confirmed with his judges and the rest of the Lombards all those laws which he added to the law-book.

Through the providence of our redeemer, I, Ratchis, with divine aid a most excellent and lofty ruler, in the second year of my reign, on the first day of March, in the fourteenth indiction, acting together with the judges of the Lombard nation, those from Austria and from Neustria as well as from the bounds of Tuscany, considering carefully, have found that certain things should be removed.

Evil men do not consider the things which belong to God; they care more for the things of this world than for the redemption of their souls and never cease to oppress the weak and needy with the cleverness of man. We recognize that, because of their sinful nature, many men either negligently and compelled by human cupidity are guilty of perjury because our glorious King Rothair established in his laws [Rothair 366] how pledges should be given; he provided that if a debtor wished to deny the procedure of an established case, he might deny that procedure either by taking oath or by an appeal to arms. But it seems just to us and to our judges and to the Lombards present that the cause of this perjury be eliminated.[1]

[*On pledges and how they shall be given in the future.*]

5.I. If in the future a man gives pledges in any manner in the presence of the king or of the judges or of other freemen and if afterwards he wishes to deny that he had given pledges in such manner as that one maintains who received the pledges: if [the case] is between freemen whose faith is credited, no man may claim by offering oath that he had not given pledges in such a manner. But according as the judge who sits in judgment recalls or as the men who were present when the pledges were given testify, he shall fulfill such things and their testimony shall be believed. Because if simple declarations which a man makes before his freemen ought to stand, so much the more ought those cases [to be valid] which are confirmed by pledges in the presence of freemen: in such a case, no form of denial is permitted. If men whose faith can be credited were not present when those pledges were given, then judgment shall proceed as was established by King Rothair [Rothair 366].

[*A new provision concerning free women who marry slaves.*]

6.II. We are aware that the earlier edict provided that free women who have married slaves should be reduced to servitude whenever they are found [Liutprand 24]. Although King Grimwald ordered that those who had lived in liberty for as much as thirty years should not be returned to servitude [Grimwald 2], nevertheless we note that the possession of the royal court is not impaired except after the passage of sixty years, as lord King Liutprand provided [Liutprand 78]; therefore we say this. If in the future any women are found who have married slaves and they have remained at liberty at least sixty years, no one shall presume to return them or their sons or their daughters or any others who are descended from them into servitude, but they shall continue in their liberty as they have been for sixty years. If in the future any slave presumes to take a free woman (arimanna) to wife, however, judgment shall be rendered as the earlier edict provides [Rothair 221].

[*Concerning those who acquire a slave or aldius with consent of the king.*]

7.III. If any Lombard wishes to make a man his slave or aldius and he comes to the king's court and makes this known, he may take the man away with him provided he has received permission from either the king himself or one of the justices who have jurisdiction at the king's court. If he neglects to do this and in fury strikes his man or, may God forbid, kills him (as has just now been made known to us), he shall pay his wergeld as composition to the royal court. If the man lives and already was a slave or aldius, his master shall lose him together with his property and he and his children shall remain at liberty. If he was a freeman, the man who struck him shall pay his wergeld as composition to the king and also pay composition to the man struck according to the penalties set for injuries to freemen. If he kills him in anger he shall pay composition for the death of that one as is read above [Liutprand 20] and likewise for this presumption he shall pay his wergeld as composition to the king. If it was an aldius or slave [whom he killed], he shall lose that one's children and property and shall pay his wergeld as composition to the palace.

[*On bills of sale and claims of nonpayment.*]

8.IIII. It is well known that because of their cupidity, evil men have been willing to swear that a sales price has not yet been fully paid even though the buyer had obtained a charter confirming that sale; as a result, the buyers must be able to offer oath that they have paid the full price. This seems harsh to us and to our judges because those who do not wish to take oath because of their convictions must offer a pledge in place of their oath or make payment for damages without cause: thus men may be ruined by such an accusation since anything can be taken away by such an oath. Therefore we decree that if anyone has negotiated a charter of sale concerning any property, and this has been confirmed by the mark of a public scribe or by suitable witnesses, and the witnesses sign the charter which contains the details of the sale and the charter makes it clear that the seller has received the agreed price: if afterward the buyer is accused of not having paid the full price, he shall not be required to give oath, unless by chance he has obligated himself by pledges; the seller may then take pledges from the surety.

[*Concerning those who send their agents outside the boundaries of the country.*]

9.V. If a judge or any other man, without the king's permission, presumes to send his representative to Rome, Ravenna, Spoleto, Benevento, France, Bavaria, Alamannia, Raetia, or to the land of the Avars, he shall lose his life and his property shall be confiscated.

[*Concerning those who cause an uprising or raise sedition against their judge.*]

10.VI. It is known to us that in some districts (civitates) evil men have brought about tumults and insurrections (*zavas et adunationes*)² against their judge. Therefore we order that if in the future any man raises an insurrection with four or five or more men saying that they will not allow their judge to render justice for them and they will not accept his judgment but will seek the patronage of someone else, and if they attempt to get other men to do the same thing, they shall pay composition as the earlier edict provides for those who raise sedition against their judge [Liutprand 35]. If anyone has anything to say about a case which involves the king, he may come to the palace. If he proves that his charges are true, the man against whom he spoke [i.e., the judicial official] shall be condemned and he shall receive sentence according to the nature of the case as an earlier law provides.

If he is not able to prove his charge, then he and his property shall be handed over to the judge to do with as he chooses. If a man suffers any violence either from his judge or from any other man and the judge neglects to render justice because he is waiting on (*adtenderit*) one of his followers (gasindius) or upon a relative or upon a friend, or he [is doing something] for his own profit rather than adjudicating a complaint, then the man suffering this injustice shall come to the palace and make known this abuse. If the charge is proved, then the man making the claim shall not be regarded as guilty of insurrection, but the judge himself shall pay his wergeld as composition, half to the king and half to the man to whom he denied justice; and the judge shall lose his position of honor [i.e., his office].

If the freeman (arimannus) deliberately lies about this matter and appeals to the king before he goes to his judge for justice: if he has enough to pay composition, he shall pay fifty solidi as composition, half to the king and half to his judge. And if he does not have enough to pay composition, he shall be punished so that he himself may be corrected and others will not presume to do such a thing.

[*Concerning the man who attempts to prosecute another man's suit without the consent of the judge.*]

11.VII. He who presumes on behalf of someone else to bring suit and argue a case in the presence of the king or of a judge, unless the king or the judge has given him permission to do so for a widow or an orphan or some man who is unable to prosecute his own cause, shall pay his wergeld as composition, half to the king and half to him against whom he brought the case.

If anyone through lack of knowledge does not know how to prosecute his own case, let him come to the palace, and if the king or a judge sees that this is true, then he [the king or judge] shall provide him with a man who will direct his cause. If a judge permits this in any case except in such situations as these and does not correct it, he shall likewise pay his wergeld as composition to the king. If any freeman enters the service (*servitium*) of a follower (gasindius) of the king or of one of his fideles, and the judge under whom he lives seeks to oppress him grievously because he has entered someone else's service and judges harshly and unjustly against him on this account so that he is not able to obtain justice from his judge, the judge shall pay composition as is noted above and the man whose service the freeman entered shall have the privilege of taking his case and leading it to law—provided nevertheless that the freeman went first to his judge in order to obtain justice for his suit.

[*Concerning those who investigate and reveal the secrets of the king.*]

12.VIII. It has been made known to us that there are some evil men who have penetrated our court to learn our secrets, seeking either through the cellerar (*dilicioso*) or the chancellor (*hostiario*) or some other deceitful hidden man to find out something about what we are doing. What they have learned by questioning such men they release or announce as our secrets and thus they make known our orders even outside the country. It seems to us that he who presumes to do such a thing is not rightly in our faith, but should be held under suspicion of having done evil. Wherefore we decree that he who in the future is tempted in such a cause, both the man who subverts as well as the man who has been subverted, shall suffer the loss of his life and his property shall be confiscated. Because thus the scriptures say: although it is honorable to reveal the works of God, it is good to conceal the secrets of the king [Tobit 12:7].

(III) THE LAWS OF KING RATCHIS IN BRIEF

PROLOGUE

Let the laws found written above be included in our lawbook. In addition we add these two brief titles.

[*On protection of the frontiers.*]

13. It is our command that, with the help of Christ, our

boundaries will be maintained and guarded in order that neither our enemies nor our people can send spies through them or allow fugitives to go out and in order that no man can enter them without a letter sealed by the king. Every judge should use such care and vigilance with regard to the frontier committed to him both in his own actions as well as in those of his local officials and gate wardens that no man can go out without a letter sealed by the king. When strangers who plan to go to Rome come to our borders, the judge shall inquire diligently whence they come. If he recognizes that they come without evil intent, the judge or the gate warden shall issue a passport placing it on a wax tablet and setting his seal to it in order that afterward the travelers may show this notice to our appointed agents. After this notice has been sent to us, our agents shall give the travelers a letter to enable them to go to Rome; and when they return from Rome, the judges shall collect these letters that bear the seal of the king's ring.

But if the judges recognize that the travelers have come fraudulently, they shall send them to us and make this cause known to us through our agents.

The judge who delays to do this and, though God forbid, allows someone to go out without his notice shall suffer the loss of his life and his property shall be confiscated. If he dares swear that it was done without his permission, he shall be absolved from blame: he may clear himself of guilt, but nevertheless he shall pay his wergeld as composition to the palace for his neglect.

Each judge in the bounds of Tuscany shall take such care throughout his judicial district that no man may go out without the king's consent or without his seal. If it is found that anyone has gone out without such an order, or without the seal, and if he cannot clear himself, the judge shall pay his wergeld as composition.

[*On gasinds (gasindii) and their men.*]

14. Concerning our sworn followers (gasindii) [see Rothair's Edict, note 62], we decree that no judge shall oppress them since we should defend our followers. If these followers do anything contrary to law to a freeman (arimannus) and he cries out against him to the judge, the judge shall either through letter or by his own voice warn our gasind that he may judge for himself.

And if he does not know how to judge, other fellow freemen who know how to judge having been called together, he shall judge the case according to law and judgment shall be made in order that the freeman shall not suffer wrong. But before he [the judge] has warned him [the gasind], he [the gasind] shall not presume to act with regard to possession (*wifa*) or pledge without our command.

Indeed, if the gasind himself delays to judge and does not judge according to law, then the judge shall force him likewise to do justice to the freeman (arimannus): provided nevertheless that it be done without intent [when] the gasind stands in the judgment of the judge, [otherwise] the judge himself shall lose his office. And if afterward it appears to him [the gasind] that he [the judge] has not judged according to the laws, he shall come into our presence with his judgment.

HERE END THE LAWS OF KING RATCHIS

V. The Laws of King Aistulf

[I. FROM THE FIRST YEAR, A.D. 750][1]

. . . As agreed by generations of earlier Lombards, the dispositions of our predecessors have served up to the present time. Now, however, with the aid of our Lord Jesus Christ, in whose name Aistulf is king of the Lombard nation, [a position] confirmed to us by the Lord of the Roman people [i.e., by the Pope], in the first year of my reign, in the third indiction, together with the rest of our judges and Lombards from all our provinces, from our residence at Ticinum (Pavia) we recognize that, since the Lombard lawbook has been issued by act of earlier kings, our predecessors, it is fitting that we add to the code the following titles on this first day of March.

[TITLES]

1. On gifts made by King Ratchis and his wife Tassia.
2. Concerning those men who can afford armor.
3. Concerning merchants.
4. Also concerning merchants.
5. On broken boundaries.

6. On sea and land merchants.
7. On judges who send men away from the army.
8. On illegal marriages.
9. On theft.

[LAWS]

[On gifts made by King Ratchis and his wife Tassia.]
1. First of all let it be established concerning those gifts which were made by King Ratchis and his wife Tassia that all gifts made after Aistulf became king shall not be valid unless they were conceded again by King Aistulf to the man to whom they were originally given.[2]

[Concerning those men who can afford armor.]
2. All men who can afford it should at least have a coat of mail. Lesser men (minores homines) who can afford it should at least have a horse, shield, and lance. Men who do not have an animal to ride and cannot afford one should at least have a shield and quiver.

The man who holds seven manses (*casas massarias*) [see Rothair's Edict, note 30] should have a coat of mail and the other military equipment, in addition to horses. If he has more than this number [of manses], he should also have horses and the remaining armament. Those men who do not hold manses but who hold forty iugera of land should have horse, shield, and lance. With regard to lesser men, it is pleasing to us that if they can afford it, they should have a shield as well as a quiver and bow and arrows.

[Concerning merchants.]
3. Let it be observed likewise with regard to those men who are merchants and have money wealth (*pecunias*): those who are the greater and more powerful should have a coat of mail and horses, shield, and lance. Those who come next should have horses, shield, and lance. And those who are the lesser men should have a quiver and bow and arrows.

[Also concerning merchants.]
4. Let this be observed concerning those men who conduct business with a Roman[3] without the king's consent: if it was a

judge who presumed to do this, he shall pay his wergeld as composition and shall lose his position of honor [his office]. If it was a freeman, he shall lose his property and, having been shaved (decalvatus), he must go about crying out: "Those who conduct business with a Roman contrary to the king's wish, as long as the Romans are our enemies, suffer thus." The judge who neglected to investigate this matter, if it had come to his attention that one of his freemen or any other man in his judicial district planned to do this, shall likewise pay composition: he shall pay his wergeld as composition but shall not lose his office. If the judge claims that the matter had not come to his attention, he may clear himself by swearing on the holy gospels that he did not know of it.

[*On broken boundaries.*]

5. Let broken boundaries be restored and a guard placed there so that our men will not be able to cross without the king's consent, nor will strangers be able to enter our country without the king's wish or command. If anyone is found within the walls, the gate warden who neglected to guard them shall be subjected to such a punishment by his judge as his judge has been notified of earlier by the king, unless the judge had sent away his man to serve the king or had received a stranger on the king's business.

[*On sea and land merchants.*]

6. On sea and land merchants. No man may travel around to carry on business or for any other purpose unless he has a letter from the king or the consent of his judge. He who does this shall pay his wergeld as composition.

[*On judges who send men away from the army.*]

7. Any judge or schultheis or other official who sends powerful men home from the army shall pay composition as the edict provides [Liutprand 83; Ratchis 4].

[*On illegal marriages.*]

8. It is pleasing to us that any illegal marriage prohibited by canon or secular law be ended immediately. Any judge in the present indiction who neglects or delays to adjudicate such a case shall pay his wergeld as composition: for it seems to us and to everyone that he who consents to such a marriage acts against God and against his own soul and allows evil to increase.

[*On theft.*]

9. With regard to thieves, whoever neglects to investigate or seek them out or allows them to go outside the borders shall be subjected to such penalty as the edict provides [Rothair 264] and an investigation shall be made within the present indiction. We further decree that if the theft is learned of by any judge after it has been committed in a place under the jurisdiction of another judge, and if the judge who learned of the theft sends notice to the other judge and that one neglects to take the thief: that judge to whom the theft was made known shall pay composition because he neglected to apprehend the thief. And if the thief was the slave of some man, the judge shall make it known to his lord, and the lord shall seek his slave and do justice to the man who accused him. If the lord neglects to apprehend or seek the slave, he shall pay composition to the man who suffered the theft since he neglected to apprehend his servant.

[II. FROM THE FIFTH YEAR, A.D. 755]

PROLOGUE

We heed the words of that prophet who has said, "Let the sons of man render judgment with justice," and "Learn justice, you who possess land, since the good Lord loves that which is just." It is fitting indeed that we observe this sacred injunction in order that the nation entrusted to us be not burdened in judgment and that we may strive to please Almighty God with whose aid we reign. In this we follow the example of our predecessors, who, courageously desiring to please the Redeemer of the world with their concern for the care of the people entrusted to them that they might be ruled by a true government, have issued laws. Therefore with the aid of Almighty God, I, Aistulf, the most excellent king of the Catholic Lombard nation, after studying those provisions established by our predecessors, have ordered such laws to be added to the edict as we have found not to be included there and concerning which our judges have been involved in great error when rendering justice. This we do in the name of God in the fifth most happy year of our reign, on the first day of March, in the seventh indiction, together with our common council, the judges serving us having been called together from the different parts of our realm. We have added those laws which seem just to our most excellent self and to God so that justice may be established and that which has been obscure may be made clear for the rendering of judgment by our judges.

[TITLES]

10. Concerning the disposition of property if a brother dies without sons or daughters and leaves sisters.
11. How a slave may be freed and his services still retained.
12. Concerning the man who, while ill, wishes to dispose of his property.
13. In what way a man may reward his daughters as well as his sons.
14. On the widow's usufruct.
15. Concerning those who throw dirty water on a wedding party.
16. On agreements made with bishops and abbots.
17. Churches which belong to the crown may not exact a double composition.
18. Concerning the man who possesses church property for more than thirty years.
19. Concerning the oaths of judges, abbots, or presbyters of churches.
20. Concerning oaths given by the king's agents.
21. Pledges may not be demanded from a man after he has been ordered to military service.
22. Concerning the man who voluntarily enters the service of someone else.

[LAWS]

[*Concerning the disposition of property if a brother dies without sons or daughters and leaves sisters.*]

10.I. We note that it is provided in an earlier law [Liutprand 3] that if a brother dies without sons or daughters and leaves sisters, the sisters shall succeed him as his heirs, but any aunts may have none of the property of their nephew: only sisters or near [male] relatives may succeed. We also note that since the aunts remain at home unmarried and unprovided for, suffering need, they marry slaves. Therefore, with God inspiring us, we now provide that if a Lombard dies leaving one or more sisters at home unmarried and one or more sons, his sons ought to consider in what manner their aunts can live according to the quality of their status that they will not suffer need from lack of food, or clothing, or even service. And if one of the aunts wishes to live in a holy convent under an established rule, let it be arranged by the nephews as desired by her or as is suitable. If a nephew dies without sons or daughters or intestate and leaves sisters, the aunts who remain at home unmarried together with their nieces [the sisters of the deceased] shall succeed equally to the entire property of their nephew and brother.

[*How a slave may be freed and his services still retained.*]

11.II. The provisions of an earlier law [Rothair 224; Liutprand 23] read that if a Lombard hands one of his slaves through four hands and thus makes him legally competent (amundius), or if he hands his slave over to a priest to lead around the altar, then the former slave shall remain absolved from all condition of servitude. But since some perverse men, having thus received their freedom, esteem their benefactors less thereafter and are by no means willing to serve them as patrons, many men, fearing lest their freedmen will serve them less in the future, do not give them their freedom. Therefore we decree that if a Lombard wishes to give one of his slaves into a fourth hand by the formal alienation procedure (gairethinx), he may give him a charter and thus reserve the service of that one so long as he lives; after his lord's death the servant shall be completely free. It shall be observed as noted in the text of that charter which the lord gave his former slave; for it seems fitting to us that a man not leave his benefactor while he is alive. However, if the slave is handed to the priest and set free by him in a church, he shall retain his liberty as the earlier law provides.

[*Concerning the man who, while ill, wishes to dispose of his property.*]

12.III. We know that many unscrupulous men have acted contrary to the wishes of their dead relatives who, for the well-being of their souls, distributed their property to sacred places and gave outright liberty together with some property to their dependents. Acting with cleverness, the heirs remove [the freed slaves] from their huts and replace them in servitude, so that they lose their liberty as well as their property. Therefore we decree, in order to correct this evil practice, that the desire and command of the dead shall be carried out: if any Lombard, whether in sickness or in health, arranged by charter that holy places shall have his property and that the household servants by whom that property is served are to be free in order that they may make a return [i.e., pay rent] to those holy places, these things shall be observed to all time by a man's heirs as was established. And those who were freed shall be free in their persons just as their lord established, and they shall not be recalled by his heirs, nor shall they be removed from their huts, but they shall be protected by those sacred places [who received the gift]. And if they wish to leave of their own free will, they shall have the right to leave with their freedom and to live wherever they choose.

If a man has hastened to his end so that he, on account of his sudden death, was not able to free one of his men by the formal procedure (gairethinx) and could not hand him over to a priest to set him free before an altar, but he did order that after his death the slave whom he designated should be led around the sacred altar by the hand of the priest: because of our compassion we decree that it shall be done as the slave's lord ordered and the priest shall free that man whom his lord designated without any contradiction, and this man shall then remain free: because it seems to us to be a good thing that slaves be given their freedom from servitude since our Redeemer himself deigned to become a slave in order that He might make us free.

If a lord gives anything to his slave at the end of his life or orders it to be given him, that gift shall remain valid: because that great authority, the apostle Paul, has commanded us to reward our servants for their loyalty. The slave's service shall be counted as a return gift (launigild) since as a slave he would not have anything else from which he could give a launigild to his lord.

[*In what way a man may reward his daughters as well as his sons.*]

13.IIII. It has been established before by our predecessors

[Liutprand 113] that a Lombard may reward that son who serves him well from his property; the law does not say anything about daughters. Therefore we now decree that if a man has two daughters, and does not leave a son, he may reward one of the daughters if he wishes with a third part of his property. If he has three daughters he may reward one of them with a fourth of his property; if there are more the portion shall be determined according to this principle.

[*On the widow's usufruct.*]

14.V. That Lombard who on dying wishes to grant to his wife a usufruct from his property, if he leaves sons or daughters by her, cannot grant more to her for her usufruct than a half of his property since he has already given her a morning gift (morgincap) and a marriage portion (meta) according to law [Liutprand 7]. And if he leaves one or two sons or daughters from a previous wife, he can leave only a third portion of his property for the usufruct of his surviving wife; if there are three [children from the previous marriage, he can leave her] a fourth part; if there are more children, her share shall be determined according to this progression. But she shall have the complete morning gift and marriage portion which her husband gave her according to law. If she marries again or if she dies, the usufruct [of her portion] shall revert in entirety to the heirs and, concerning the marriage portion and the morning gift, let it be observed as provided in the earlier law [Rothair 182].

[*Concerning those who throw dirty water on a wedding party.*]

15.VI. It has been made known to us that when a number of men walked along with a wedding party (*paranimpha et troctingis*)[4] that was taking a bride to her bridegroom certain perverse men threw down polluted and unclean water upon them. Since this evil has been committed in several different places, we decree, lest a breach of the peace (scandalum) [Rothair 35–40, 273, 378; Liutprand 37, 122, and 135] or homicide occur from this cause, that if any freeman tries to do such a thing, he shall pay 900 solidi as composition, half to the king and half to [the woman's] mundwald. If they are men who belong to someone else and they do this thing without their lord's consent, and if their lord dares to offer oath that the thing was not done at his desire or with his counsel or advice and thus clears himself: the slaves shall be handed over to [the woman's] mundwald, and he may do with them as it pleases him. In this case their patron shall bear no further blame. But if their lord does not dare so to swear, he shall pay 900 solidi as composition, as read above.

[*On agreements made with bishops and abbots.*]

16.VII. If a Lombard makes an agreement involving any property whatsoever with a bishop, abbot, or other guardian of a church or with the director of a hospital, and if the parties agree between themselves on a penalty [for breach of contract], and if the Lombard's heirs or successors give their consent and suitable men are present as witnesses, the agreement cannot afterwards be nullified by the man's successors, just as it may not be nullified by the man himself unless he pays composition according to the penalty established for breaking his agreement. If the transfer of property involves servile holdings (*casis terris*) or household servants (familiis), and representatives of the king or of the priest, or judges or three other such men whose faith is accepted were present; if it seemed a better thing to the giver at the time of the exchange that the religious place should have that property, at no time afterward may the giver's successors cancel it, but the exchange shall always remain in effect. If the man himself wishes to nullify his act he shall pay as composition the penalty set out in the agreement.

[*Churches which belong to the crown may not exact a double composition.*]

17.VIII. It has been made known to us that up until this time it has been customary for monasteries or other holy places, known to be under the protection of the sacred palace, to exact a double composition from those who owe them composition, just as the royal court exacts. We now decree that in the future monasteries, churches, or hospitals which are under the protection of the palace shall, when the occasion arises, collect composition in the same manner as those holy places that do not belong to the palace.

[*Concerning the man who possesses church property for more than thirty years.*]

18.VIIII. If a Lombard possesses any property whatever and the guardians of a holy place challenge his possession of that property, if he can authenticate his possession for thirty years and this is manifest, he shall possess that property in the future. Holy places shall act in the same way concerning the property that they possess if they are accused by a Lombard. The earlier edict provides that if a man has possessed his property for five years or less and someone challenges his right of possession, he must defend himself according to law [Rothair 228]. In disputes between holy places, the right to continued possession is created by possession for a period of forty years.[5] And we here state that it is just that the man who possesses his property for at least thirty years ought to continue to possess it in the future.

[*Concerning the oaths of judges, abbots, or presbyters of churches.*]

19.X. If a Lombard is involved in a case with a holy place which is known to be under the protection of the palace and if it is a case in which an oath must be given: if a judge accuses an abbot, guardian, or provost, he alone [the abbot, guardian, or provost] shall offer satisfaction to him. If an abbot, guardian, or provost accuses a judge and an oath ought to be given, the judge alone shall likewise offer the oath to him. If any other Lombard has a case with an abbot whence an oath ought to be given, the abbot alone shall be accused [and offer oath]; the Lombard [if accused by an abbot] shall choose such other men as are required by law to support his oath—provided nevertheless that the abbot himself is one who lives by rule according to God and has fifty or more monks subject to him who live according to rule. If the Lombard has a case with some other guardian or provost of a sacred place, the guardian or provost shall offer oath alone [and the Lombard must provide the usual number of oathhelpers as required by law].

[*Concerning oaths given by the king's agents.*]

20.XI. If anyone has a suit with the royal court and it is a case where a party of the royal court should take oath: if it is a major case [i.e., twenty solidi—Rothair 359], the oath shall be taken by the *ovescarioni* together with the agents.[6] If it is a lesser cause, the agent of the place shall take oath together with as many other agents as the nature of the case requires.

[*Pledges may not be demanded from a man after he has been ordered to military service.*]
21.XII. After the king has ordered the army to march and a day for movement has been set, no one may take pledges from his surety or debtor for any reason within a period of twelve days before that surety or debtor leaves for the army, if the parties are from the same judicial district, but he shall be immune for twelve days before he goes and for twelve days after he returns from the army. If the parties are from different judicial districts, the time period shall be twenty days. And if anyone takes pledges within this time, he shall pay composition for those pledges just as does the man who steals pledges contrary to reason [Rothair 246, 248-52].

[*Concerning the man who voluntarily enters the service of someone else.*]
22.XIII. If a man out of his own goodness enters the service of a judge or of some other man and serves him or his sons or his nephews and if it is manifestly true that his own relatives are all free, if afterward he [whose service the man entered] wishes to keep him in servitude claiming that he has served him or his relatives for as much as thirty years, he cannot keep him by this kind of possession; for it is unreasonable and contrary to the commands of God that, while all his relatives are free, he alone who served voluntarily should be retained in servitude for possession alone. But if a man has been handed over to someone to serve on account of theft or for any other offense, and this is proved, then he shall continue to serve, as the law provides [Liutprand 80, 152]. If a man's relatives belong to someone and he alone wishes to establish his liberty, unless he can prove his liberty by charter or through the witness of freemen or through possession [of liberty] according to law, he shall continue to serve in the future.

HERE END THE LAWS

SPURIOUS LAWS OF THE SAME KING AISTULF[7]

23.XIIII. It is pleasing to us that no priest presume to enter into the property of any Lombard on his own authority without seeking the adjudication of those who judge, nor may any Lombard because of his greater strength presume to enter the property of a church, a priest, or a clerk. If anyone in the future, Lombard as well as clerk, presumes to take anything due to him without seeking a judgment first, he who is convicted of having done this shall be bound by this stipulation: he must restore the property that he seized together with another of the same value to him against whom he used force [rather than seek judgment].

HERE END THE LAWS ———————

24. [From the corrected reading.]
The villa and the fortifications of the villa (*castro villarum*) and the fish pool which has been made by hand, and anything which is partially (*mediocrem*) surrounded by ditches or fences, or any other kind of fortified enclosure, is called a territory with immunity (*inmunitate et terretorius*); but the field and forest that are without works (*laborationibus*) and not surrounded by any fortification are no more included in the name of immunity than is the enclosure of a monastery.

HERE END THE EARLIER AND LATER EDICTS ISSUED
BY CERTAIN OF THE LOMBARD KINGS

NOTES

I. Rothair's edict

[1] This translation follows the edition of the laws by F. Bluhme, *Leges Langobardorum, Leges, Monumenta Germaniae Historica,* Vol. IV (Hanover, 1869). The edition and translation prepared by Franz Beyerle, *Die Gesetze der Langobarden* (Weimar, 1947) and 2nd ed., 3 vols. (Witzenhausen, 1962–1963) has been consulted.

[2] Since the blood feud (*faida*) was prohibited among the Lombards, the hostility of an aggrieved party or family was to be allayed by receipt of a payment known as "composition." The amount of composition varied with the seriousness of the offense and in general the code sets out in elaborate detail just which composition is to apply in any of a large number of cases.

[3] *Scandalum* seems to have been the offense of disturbing the public peace, depending in seriousness on the nature of this "peace breaking." If the peace were broken in a nonphysical manner, the offense was much less serious than if physical violence were involved. Similarly, the place where the public peace was broken also affected the seriousness of the offense, for scandalum in the presence of the king or even in the district (civitas) where the king was present was much more serious than scandalum in that district where the king was not present. Cf. Rothair 35–40, 273, 378; Liutprand 37, 122 and 135.

[4] The Lombards knew two kinds of judicial proof: that by compurgation and that of trial by battle. The term *camfio* refers to this latter type of proof, the word being used both for the combat itself and for those who participate in such duels. See note 41 below.

[5] The wergeld was the juridical value placed on a man's life and hence represented the amount to be paid in case of homicide or other grievous offenses in order to avert the blood feud.

[6] For the meanings of these Germanic words, see the Glossary.

[7] From a comparison with other laws of the code, this probably

means that half of this sum is to be paid to the family of the victim, the other half to the king·as his share of the proceeds of justice.

[8] There are quite a number of laws in the code, especially in *Rothair's Edict*, which deal with curious cases involving some kind of personal affront. Evidently the Lombards encountered no Latin equivalent for these offenses and hence kept the Germanic word to describe them. Cf. *crapworfin* in this law and *rairaub* in the following one. Note that these laws carry extremely high penalties.

[9] The gastald (gastaldius) was the chief administrative, judicial, and military representative of the Lombard king, presiding over an administrative district called *civitas* in the laws. This official is the "judge" referred to in many of the laws and was the chief instrument of the royal power in Lombard Italy.

[10] The schultheis (*sculdahis*) was a royal representative lower in rank than the gastald and responsible to him. This official also had administrative and judicial duties but in all his work he was subject to the immediate supervision of his gastald. He presided over a subdivision of the civitas sometimes called *sculdascia*.

[11] When the Lombards first entered Italy, the dukes were the most powerful of Lombard officials, being in some respects almost independent of the king. As the power of the Lombard monarchy increased to provide for the survival of the Lombard state, the power of the dukes had to be limited by the appointment of officials who were dependent only upon the king. Hence there resulted a kind of dual jurisdiction in the Lombard state: that of the dukes on the one hand and that of the king represented by his royal officials on the other. This dual jurisdiction is apparent in *Rothair's Edict* but is not mentioned in any of the later issues of the laws where only the king's officials are named.

[12] *Wegworin* was the offense of placing oneself in the road before another person and thus blocking the way to him. This is another of the "personal affront" offenses and carries a correspondingly high penalty.

[13] Women, minor children, and certain other incompetent persons in the Lombard kingdom did not enjoy the right to represent themselves in legal affairs. The right of representing such persons is called the *mundium*, an extremely valuable privilege among the Lombards as well as among other Germanic peoples. Hence the disposition of the mundium is carefully provided for in the Laws.

[14] *Marahworfin* was the act of throwing a man from his horse, another insulting offense to the free Lombard. See notes 8 and 12 above.

[15] Here again the seriousness of this offense (walopaus) seems to depend to a large extent on the secretiveness of the action causing a more serious personal affront than if the crime were committed openly.

[16] A man's peace, which entitled him to certain protective rights so far as his person was concerned, was also extended to include his house and courtyard. A man enjoyed, in a sense, certain sovereign rights so far as his house was concerned and hence any violation of his "boundaries" was a very serious offense.

[17] The chief territorial unit of Lombard administration was the civitas, an institution probably taken over from an earlier period of Italian history. As to the exact nature of the civitas, there is no clue in the *Leges Langobardorum*, and it must simply be assumed that it included some urban center as the seat of the administration together with the surrounding rural regions. The civitas was the area presided over by the gastald (gastaldius), the chief royal representative. In some cases it may have also coincided with the boundaries of the duchy.

[18] The Latin term used in this and comparable places is literally the "palace of the king," the "court of the king" or the "sacred palace." Cf. W. K. Williams, *The Communes of Lombardy from the VI. to the X. Century, Johns Hopkins University Studies in Historical and Political Science* (Baltimore, 1891), and James Westfall Thompson, *The Dissolution of the Carolingian Fisc* (Berkeley, 1935).

[19] Rothair 43–128. In many cases, the laws simply state that composition is to be paid by the slave, although this is probably not to be taken literally. Unless specifically stated to the contrary, it was the slave's lord who was to pay or to receive the composition since the slave's lord was his legal representative.

[20] *Faida* is the Lombard term for the blood feud or vendetta. Theoretically the faida was prohibited among the Lombards and money compositions had been substituted, but the rather numerous occasions upon which the lawgiver expressly mentioned that the faida was to be abolished causes one to suspect that actual pursuit of the blood feud was not unknown among this people.

[21] Germanic law in general makes frequent use of plastic expressions which have little if any literal meaning. "Men were especially prone to express provisions relating to time and space in such a naive and inexact way as left room for chance in particular cases. It is often declared that something shall be the rule as far as a cock walks, or flies, a cat springs, as a stone or hammer is thrown, as one can reach with a sickle. A law shall endure so long as the Main flows into the Rhine, etc." Rudolf Huebner, *A History of Germanic Private Law, The Continental Legal History Series* (London, 1918), p. 10.

[22] This law indicates that the lawgiver felt that his reduction to writing of the laws would go far toward the discouragement of the faida and the chief means used seems to have been an increase in the "fine" assessed to each offense.

[23] All Lombard freemen enjoyed the same legal rights but that eco-

nomically there was some differentiation is indicated by the different wergelds assigned to the various classes. The value of these wergelds is never mentioned in the laws of Rothair, but is clearly stated in Liutprand 62. As for women, technically they had no wergeld since they were not legally competent as persons, but in actual fact, a woman's value was computed to be the same as that of a male member of her social rank.

[24] Somewhere between the free in status and the slaves were the aldii—free in their persons, presumably, but legally dependent on a patron or lord. Cf. Carlo Calisse, *A History of Italian Law, The Continental Legal History Series* (London, 1928), pp. 73–74.

[25] The servi ministeriales were the household slaves who had been specially trained for their work, their value (pretium) being greater than that of the field slaves (servi rustici). Note the survival of the expression servi ministeriales among the lesser knights ("slave knights") of the Holy Roman Empire.

[26] The "physicians" mentioned in these laws are a little difficult to identify. The histories of science and medicine do not refer to any physicians or doctors in Lombard Italy. We can only infer from these laws that there was a class of doctors in the seventh and eighth centuries whose services were required for the treatment of wounds.

[27] Technically, the aldius was not a juridical person and as such he could have no wergeld, nor could he pay or receive composition. In such a case, the "value" of the aldius would be expressed by the term "pretium" rather than "wergeld" and his lord or patron would represent him in the paying and receiving of compositions. In actual practice, however, the legal position of the aldius seems to have been somewhat better. Occasionally his value is loosely described as a wergeld and he seems on some occasions—especially those implying personal affront—to have received composition in his own right.

[28] At the bottom of the Lombard social structure were the slaves who seem to have been divided into two major groups: the servi ministeriales (see note 25 above) and the servi rustici or *rusticani*. The ministeriales were household slaves and their value (pretium) was greater than that of the rusticani, the agrarian or field slaves, although as can be seen from this and the succeeding laws, the value of the field slaves might differ greatly depending upon their training.

[29] See Glossary.

[30] The servus massarius was the most valuable of the Lombard agrarian or field slaves. It seems that he held land, a manse, from which he got his name, massarius (mansarius), (on what terms is never stated), with a hut upon it, and it is possible that the economic condition of such slaves might be fairly high. The pretium or value of the massarius was twenty solidi. Rothair 134, 137, 234, 352.

[31] Cf. Rothair 136 below. The distinguishing characteristic of the slaves mentioned in Rothair 133 and 136 is that they occupied some kind of a holding of their own and were not housed in the household of their lord.

[32] The magistri comacini are difficult to identify. They seem to have been a group, perhaps a guild, of builders or construction workers. Whether they were Lombards or a remnant of the former Roman population is not clear. Their services were evidently in great demand, however, for Liutprand or Grimwald issued a special memorial or group of regulations governing the type of construction and the pay to be received for each: *Memoratorium de Mercedibus Commacinorum* in F. Bluhme, *Leges Langobardorum*, pp. 176–80.

[33] Rothair 147, 175, 330, 337, 349; Liutprand 43, 151. See Glossary for meaning.

[34] See Glossary for meaning.

[35] The Lombard inheritance laws are among the most detailed of the code. The Lombard conception of inheritance was strongly Germanic, an heir being born and not made. Inheritance was governed by the custom of the people; wills and testaments were unknown except those in favor of the church. A man might modify the rules of succession in favor of one son or daughter who had served him better than the others, but even the amount of such extraordinary gifts was strictly regulated by law.

[36] As noted before, the Lombards used two methods of judicial proof, that by compurgation and that by judicial duel, proof by compurgation being by far the more usual one. Such a method of proof rested primarily upon the oath, and hence every freeman had a number of oathhelpers (sacramentales), usually members of his own family or at least neighbors, who would be willing to take oath concerning the credibility of their oath kin in court. In general, the value of a man's oath seems to have depended upon his social class. The lesser freemen, for example, would have to provide up to twelve oathhelpers in court (depending on the seriousness of the charge) whereas men of the upper classes would have to provide fewer oathhelpers. Some extremely credible persons—especially the king's judges—might be sufficient in their own oath to be believed and hence these men would have to offer no oath except their own in case of a judicial suit.

[37] As among almost all of the barbarians, so among the Lombards the notion of publicity was extremely important for the validity of contracts. At one time such contracts were completed before the assembly of the people (*thinx*) by the handing over of a spear (*gaire*) as a symbol of the tradition or transfer of property. By the time of the Lombard kingdom, the popular assembly no longer met, at least under ordinary circumstances, and hence it would have been impossible to

confirm acts before the assembly of the entire people. But the notion of publicity remained and the *gairethinx* remained an act of tradition performed in the presence of witnesses. The number of witnesses necessary to validate such acts is never mentioned in the Lombard Laws, but presumably some symbol of the possession was handed over to the new "owner" since it is stated that the recipient of any gift had to make a "return gift" (launigild)—if not the transfer was invalid. So presumably symbols of the gift and of the return gift were exchanged during the course of the gairethinx ceremony.

[38] See Glossary.

[39] See Note 13 above. The mundium of women represented an extremely valuable legal privilege, for its possession gave the mundwald, or possessor, the right to represent the woman in legal matters including the handling of her finances or property (although the mundwald could not alienate his ward's property). The possession of the mundium then was a valuable right and very elaborate provision was made in the laws concerning its inheritance.

[40] This is a rather strange provision—that the property of natural brothers should pass only to the legitimate brothers. It would seem that the natural sons should be reckoned in the family of the mother, and yet in that case it would be the mother's family which should inherit (and not the legitimate brothers as here provided). Are the natural sons reckoned in the family of the mother but discriminated against in this particular case of inheritance by the fact that only legitimate sons were capable of raising the faida?

[41] Proof by combat or battle was a recognized form of proof among the Lombards although it was not so frequently used as compurgation. It seems to have been a form of proof available to freemen in certain very serious offenses at the choice of the defendant. Women and minors, of course, did not fight themselves but selected a "champion" (not so-called in the Lombard Laws) to defend their rights. This dueller (*camphio*) was ordinarily selected from the family and was usually, no doubt, the mundwald. But should the mundwald not be a very strong fighter, someone else—even from outside the family— might be selected. Evidently the Lombard kings had some doubts as to the validity of the proof by combat and such is even stated by Liutprand (Liutprand 118), although he adds that due to the time-honored nature of the duel he does not feel that he can abolish it entirely. See note 4 above.

[42] The *meta* was the price agreed upon between a prospective bridegroom and his future father-in-law to be paid by the man in exchange for the mundium of the woman he expected to marry. The meta might be paid at the time of the betrothal or an agreement to pay guaranteed by the giving of pledges or the naming of a surety might be made. At

the time of the marriage, if the meta were complete, the woman and her mundium were handed over to the new husband. Such was the ordinary procedure. In some cases, however, it seems to have been agreed that no meta would be paid, in which case the mundium remained in the possession of the father or previous mundwald. There is some indication (see Rothair 199 and Liutprand 89) that following the marriage the meta was turned over to the woman and became a part of her personal property. See notes 51 and 52 below.

[43] The thinx was, properly speaking, the public assembly, *ding*, of the Lombards. After the settlement in Italy, however, the wide scattering of the Lombard people would have made such a general assembly impossible. Hence the witnessing of contracts—an important function of the assembly—was transferred to a smaller group of witnesses. The gairethinx ("spear assembly") name remained, however, and from this word the shorter form *thinx* was often used to refer to the formal contractual procedure of gairethinx, or even to the gift, the object of the transfer, itself.

[44] Literally, "he who receives the lash"—a symbol of ownership. Cf. Rothair 224.

[45] See Glossary.

[46] The family was all-important among the early Germans, and in Lombard law we find rather typically Germanic provisions for the preservation of the family's property. Individual alienation of property seems to have been completely forbidden at one time in order to keep the family property intact—hence testamentary succession was not known and alienation of property could be achieved only through compliance with set regulations, the most important aspect of which was the publicity of the act. Since any alienation of property must bring a diminution of the family holdings—and hence implied the alienation of that which did not entirely "belong" to the disposer of the property—outright gifts were practically prohibited and any transfer of property must be an exchange of property. At one time then, the making of a gift required a return gift of approximately equal value in order that a man's family or his heirs might not be unjustly deprived. The requirement of such "return gifts" (launigild) is still a part of the Lombard code although it would seem that such "return gifts" have become merely symbolic things, so that a gift is really a gift but the fiction of the return gift is retained. (Cf. Rothair 184, Liutprand 43 and 54.) Calisse, *op. cit.*, pp. 782–83; Huebner, *op. cit.*, pp. 545–46.

[47] The farae seem to have been expanded kin groups or clans found among all the early Germanic people. However, since the Lombard family, although larger than the modern nuclear family (husband, wife, children), was smaller than the old clan, it would seem likely that the Lombard farae were smaller related groups than existed among some

of the early Germans. At any rate, the Lombards were organized in farae when they entered Italy and the conquered territory of the peninsula was bestowed on the farae and not upon individuals.

[48] When the Lombards entered Italy they were established on the land in much the fashion of the late imperial system of hospitality whereby a former Roman possessor (now become the "host") retained part of his land (perhaps a third) and the new Lombard "guest" secured the rest (perhaps two-thirds). In addition to the original distribution of land made at the first conquest, the Lombard kings seem to have had sizable personal estates which were constantly augmented by conquest and escheat—and from which the Lombard king (through himself or through his representatives, the gastalds) might make grants to such persons as he deemed fit. The original distributions were probably to family groups (farae) but later distributions were on an individual basis to such persons as the king desired to reward.

[49] Upon contracting a debt—whether in the form of a payment of composition or some contractual agreement—the debtor might not wish or might be unable to pay at once. In such case, the creditor was authorized to take pledges (under certain legal restrictions) from the debtor's property to serve as a guarantee for the eventual payment of the debt. If the debtor wanted the pledges (*wadia*) back before he paid off his debt, he would have to furnish a surety, again with certain legal restrictions. The surety would guarantee in his own person or property the ultimate disposal of the debt and might be required to give pledges to guarantee this. (Cf. Rothair 360, 361; Liutprand 38, 128.)

[50] When property was transferred from one possessor to another—whether it was physical property or some property right such as the mundium of a woman—Germanic custom laid heavy emphasis on the actual physical fact of the change of possession. In the case of marriage, the bride's father or mundwald actually passed the girl from his hand over to the hand of the groom to signify the "tradition" or the delivery of possession. In the case of the delivery of other forms of property, where the nature of the property manifestly made it impossible to hand the property itself over, symbols of the property were given —e.g., a clod of earth for a piece of land, a rod or staff for the disposition of some legally incompetent person, etc. By the time the Lombard laws were reduced to writing, the influence of Roman law had modified this concept somewhat. In place of the thing itself or a symbol of the thing, the man making the gift handed over a charter (detailing the terms of the gift or sale) as a symbol of the possessory exchange. Although the details of the charter might be important as legally defining the terms of the exchange, it was the physical fact of the handing over of the charter (as a symbol of the thing) which first led the Lombards to adopt it.

[51] The morning gift (*morgengab, morgincap*) was a gift made by the husband to his wife on the morning after the wedding night. Originally this gift seems to have been public acknowledgment on the part of the groom that he was satisfied with the virginity of the woman he had married. Among the Lombards the morning gift had become a bestowal of property by the husband upon his wife and became a part of her personal property. After the husband's death, this amount was always subtracted before the property as a whole was divided among the heirs, the widow receiving her share (or rather the usufruct of her share) in addition to her morning gift.

[52] Upon the marriage of his daughter, the father made her a gift, the *faderfio*, which became a part of her personal property and which seems to have taken the place of what would have been her share of the division of the family estate on the death of the father if she had remained in her father's home. It may have included part or all of the meta paid by the bridegroom.

[53] In other words, if the arrangement is acceptable to both parties, he may then take steps to acquire her mundium legally by negotiation with the woman's mundwald.

[54] See Glossary for meaning. Cf. Rothair 188–90, 214.

[55] A belief in witchcraft must, at one time, have been widespread among the Lombards or among the native population of the Italian peninsula. The Lombard kings approached the subject in an enlightened manner, practically denying the existence of this occult science and providing protection against random accusations of witchcraft or sorcery which might bring death or outlawry to the person accused. Such would seem to be the intent of the present law. On the other hand, there are laws in the code (Liutprand 84, 85) which specifically state that it is the duty of royal officials to seek out sorcerers and such like and apply the penalty of the law—sale outside the country (Liutprand 85).

[56] Beyerle, *op. cit.*, edits this law to read, "to one who was born of a freed woman," and that does make better sense, for there is some indication in the laws (Rothair 224) that an aldius is a partially freed slave.

[57] Note that the composition for rape of an aldia is greater than for rape of a freed woman. Perhaps this is an indication of the fact that an aldia is still classed as a man's property and hence an injury to her is more an injury to her lord than in the case of the freed woman where the legal tie would not have been so close.

[58] I.e., free according to the law of the folk. Cf. F. Bluhme, *Leges Langobardorum*, p. 52, n. 26. Also cf. Rothair 224, 1, 3; 225; 257; and Liutprand 9 and 142.

[59] A similar provision with regard to aldiae is found in Liutprand 106.

[60] When a man formerly dependent on another in a legal sense—that is, in the mundium of someone—was emancipated by his lord or patron and thus became a freeman, he was described as "a-mundius," meaning that he was no longer in the mundium of someone else.

[61] I.e., the slave being emancipated is handed the symbols of his freedom.

[62] The institution of the *comitatus* had not disappeared completely under the Lombards for the gasindium seems to have consisted of a leader and his pledged band of followers. The most important of these personal groups was the gasindium of the king himself, the members of which group were probably the fideles mentioned in a number of Liutprand's prologues and laws (Prologue to years 721 (9th), 724 (12th), 726–729 (14–17th), 735 (23rd)). These followers of the king obviously owed the obligation of court service to their lord and, by the time of Liutprand, the assembly—or more accurately, the court—consulted by the king upon the issuance of the laws was a court attended by the major royal officials (the judges or gastalds) and the fideles. Whether a man could be a royal official and belong to the king's gasindium at the same time is not clear.

[63] Perhaps this might better be translated "commended."

[64] For more serious thefts (those above twenty siliquae), the ordinary penalty was the rather high one of eightfold the value of the property stolen.

[65] The penalty prescribed in case of serious theft is sometimes called an eightfold payment and sometimes a ninefold payment. The two amounts are the same. In the latter case the reasoning follows the fact that the article itself must be returned plus an eightfold payment of the value of the article—making a ninefold payment in all.

[66] The right of coinage seems to have been a royal prerogative among the Lombards, a right not delegated to the local lords or dukes. Punishment for illegally minting coins—as well as for falsifying charters—was the cutting off of the right hand, presumably the offending member. In this penalty the Lombard law closely resembles that of some of the other Germanic peoples as well as the Byzantine.

[67] The usual Lombard mode of enforcing the payment of debts was that of distraint—usually private distraint but occasionally distraint enforced by a public official. According to the theory of distraint, the creditor assured himself of the repayment of the debt by receiving or taking pledges from the property of the debtor, pledges which remained in his possession until a surety for the debt was provided or (as most frequently happened) until the debt itself was paid. If the

debt were never paid, then the pledges remained in the permanent possession of the creditor. The keeping of the pledge by the creditor, however, did not relieve the debtor of his obligation, and specific provision is made for the taking of second pledges from the debtor (while keeping the first) in an additional attempt to secure payment of the debt (Liutprand 108).

[68] The meaning of the Lombard expression *fegangit* or *fegangi* is not clear. Carlo Calisse, *A History of Italian Law,* favors the interpretation that it corresponded to the Roman *furtum manifestum* as opposed to *furtum nec manifestum,* and that it was related to the customary proceeding of "outlawry" which had already passed out of the code by the time the *Leges* were reduced to writing. In this earlier period before the written *Leges* and before any police power was claimed and asserted by the state, a man might kill him whom he surprised in the act of theft. By the period of the *Leges,* however, this practice had been modified to allow the thief to purchase his life (eighty solidi in the case of a freeman and forty solidi in the case of a slave) in addition to making a ninefold payment of the thing stolen. A woman was defined as not being able to be fegangi (Rothair 257), so her penalty would not include the redemption payment in addition to the ninefold payment (cf. the fact that a woman also could not be outlawed according to Germanic custom), and slaves of the king also could not be fegangi. Furthermore the object stolen must be above the value of twenty silequae or more to justify the payment of the ninefold composition (Rothair 253). Cf. Calisse, *op. cit.,* 342–43. Cf. also Huebner, *op. cit.,* 410–11, and Eduard Osenbrüggen, *Das Strafrecht der Langobarden* (Schaffhausen, 1863).

[69] The value of Lombard coins is a little difficult to determine. In general, the barbarian kingdoms adopted the gold coinage of the Empire as it had been established by Constantine early in the fourth century. The gold solidus of Constantine was worth about twenty-five *denarii* (silver "pennies"). Having need of a smaller gold coin, the barbarian kings minted half-solidi (*semissis*) and third-solidi (*tremissis*). The basis of the Lombard coinage was also the solidus—presumably the same Constantinian gold solidus used by the other barbarians. The minting of these coins was a royal monopoly. The lesser coins cause the difficulty however for the Lombard Laws mention only one coin less in value than the solidus: seliquas (Rothair 254), siliquae (Rothair 253). Perhaps this coin corresponds to the half solidus (semissis), but this is not clear.

[70] The *proditor* seems to have been a semiofficial informer or "way-pointer" whose services were rendered chiefly in connection with strayed livestock. Among some of the barbarians this individual seems to have been almost a diviner. That the proditor's usefulness was

acquired by occult arts is not implied in the Lombard laws, however. Cf. *vegius* in the Burgunidan laws. Cf. Rothair 235.

[71] And therefore not under the immediate control of his lord.

[72] See Glossary.

[73] Those offenses involving personal affront (cf. notes 12, 14, and 15 above) included the violation of a man's house or courtyard. Such an offense was a breach of the peace and hence entitled him to compensation. Since a breach of the peace implied violence (although it did not necessarily bring violence), it was assumed that a woman, not carrying arms, could not break the peace of a man's courtyard.

[74] Bluhme, *Leges Langobardorum*, p. 69, n. 42, argues that the three kinds of fence are a pole fence, a twig fence, and a "natural" fence.

[75] In general, the Lombard code was a territorial code and applied equally to all residing in the Lombard kingdom. There were, however, some developments in the direction of the principle of personality of law, a principle which would be widespread upon the establishment of the Carolingian empire. The present law is one example of this trend for here it is indicated that the Lombard king, at his own discretion, might concede to non-Lombard individuals and their families the right to be tried by their own national law. The application of anything but Lombard law within the kingdom, however, was on an unofficial basis and did not come before the public courts at all during the period of an independent Lombard kingdom.

II. The Laws of King Grimwald

[1] Rothair 254, 258; also cf. Liutprand 147. See Rothair's Edict, note 68.

III. The Laws of King Liutprand

[1] When the Lombards entered Italy, they conquered the land as they proceeded southward. While the major portion of the Lombard nation remained together and proceeded on to further conquests, it was the custom from the beginning to leave behind a local leader and a group of families (farae) to organize the newly conquered territories. These local leaders were called dukes and hence one may call the territory assigned to each one his duchy. By the time the Lombard conquest of Italy was complete, the peninsula was divided up into a number of duchies, each under the control of its duke who presumably responsible to the king but who more likely acted in an almost independent manner. The most easily identifiable of these duchies were Friuli in the northeast, Brescia in the north-central section, and Spoleto

and Benevento in the south. The Lombard administrative system was organized on the basis of the civitas which may or may not have been coterminous with the duchy. The civitates were grouped into three main geographical areas—Austria, Neustria, and Tuscany—for the Lombard lawgiver often refers to the advice and counsel rendered by the judges of Austria, Neustria, and Tuscany. Furthermore the time limit in certain kinds of cases depended upon whether both parties lived in the same section. These three geographical areas do not seem to have corresponded with the duchies. The names of the sections come from the area's location with respect to Pavia, the Lombard capital— east Lombardy would be Austria, west Lombardy Neustria, and the region on the other side of the Apennines, the northern part of the peninsula proper, Tuscany.

[2] The term *fideles* is sometimes used to refer to all the faithful members of the Lombard nation or, as here, it is used to denote those members of the king's gasindium (see Rothair's Edict, note 62) who were bound by an oath of loyalty to the king. The relationship between the king and these latter fideles seems to be essentially that of a lord and his vassals, but the term "vassal" does not appear in the Lombard laws.

[3] The term *in capillo* is used to refer to unmarried women. The phrase means literally "with their hair." It seems that before the Germanic girl was wed she wore her hair hanging down her back, but on the occasion of her marriage part of the ceremony required the doing up of her hair. Evidently German matrons wore their hair up while unmarried girls wore their hair down in more informal fashion. Huebner, *op. cit.,* pp. 600–603.

[4] One Jewish scholar has argued that the increasingly greater emphasis on the property aspect of the morning gift reflected some Jewish influence, the Lombard *morgengab* coming to have some of the same characteristics as the Jewish *Ketuba*. Jacob J. Rabinowitz, "Jewish and Lombard Law," *Jewish Social Studies* 12 (October, 1950), no. 4.

[5] Since a slave was property, he had no true need of legal representation and hence it is not correct to say that slaves were in the mundium of their lords. Lords could, however, emancipate their slaves in various ways, some forms of emancipation bringing complete freedom, some only partial freedom (see Rothair 224). If a lord gave his slave only partial freedom, the slave might become an aldius and remain in the service of his lord. Although the economic and physical condition of the slave may not have changed, his legal position had, for the aldius was not property and belonged among the dependents of the lord's family. Hence partially freed slaves (aldii) were in the mundium of their lords.

[6] The Lombard freeman is sometimes called by the Latin word *exercitalis*, sometimes by the Germanic term *arimannus*. Both these expressions indicate the original military nature of the Lombard organization

and it was both a duty and a privilege which made the ordinary free-man a soldier of the nation. By the time of the Lombard Laws, how-ever, this original organization is in the process of transition and although the freeman is invariably called exercitalis or arimannus the terms no longer mean anything except just "freeman." By the eighth century military service had become more closely associated with one's economic condition rather than with one's social status and not all free-men were expected to answer the call to arms. Ratchis 4; Aistulf 2, 3.

⁷ "Across the mountains" from the standpoint of the Lombard capi-tal, Pavia, in the Po Valley. See note 1 above.

⁸ The Germanic people looked upon the hair as being a mark of free or noble birth. The punishment known as "decalvation" seems to have meant the shaving of the head—a mark of supreme disgrace for the physically proud German. There has, however, been some dispute as to the exact nature of this punishment among other Germanic peoples, in some cases the explanation tending in the direction of scalping rather than shaving. For a consideration of these various explanations, see F. S. Lear, "The Public Law of the Visigothic Code," *Speculum* (January, 1951), Appendix C. For an explanation which emphasizes eastern influences in Germanic law, see R. S. Lopez, "Byzantine Law in the Seventh Century and Its Reception by the Germans and Arabs," *Byzantion,* XVI for 1942–43 (1955). Also see Liutprand 141.

⁹ Mutilating punishments were relatively infrequent in Lombard law. Amputation of the hand was prescribed in the case of the false moneyer as well as for the writer of false charters. Shaving of the head (decalvation—see preceding note) was prescribed in certain cases so that the personal humiliation caused by shaving off the highly prized hair might serve as a deterrent to such offenders in the future. In this same law, the branding of a thief on the forehead was provided. Aside from these few exceptions, however, mutilating penalties are lacking in the Lombard Laws. Cf. Lopez, *op. cit.* Also cf. Liutprand 141; Ratchis 2. Carlo Calisse argues that this lack of "horrible" punishments was due to the still weak position of the state where punishment was still associated with the family and the state has stepped in only to prevent the blood feud by the requiring of money payments. It was not until the state could punish in its own name and for offenses against the state (or society) that physical penalties were inflicted in order to create fear in the hearts of those who would violate a state law. Calisse, *op. cit.,* p. 95.

¹⁰ Holding land by "book" or charter (*livellum*) is one of the few methods of landholding specifically called by name in the code. The holder of land by the kind of charter called livellum was a freeman who might work the soil himself or have it worked by dependents. The terms under which such land was held differed from place to place, depending upon the particular terms agreed upon between the landlord and his tenant and set down in the contract. The Italian livellum was

usually made for twenty-nine years ("one life") but was renewable for an indefinite number of times.

[11] When the Lombards entered Italy, the conquered land was distributed among the Lombard families or *farae* which thus came to have a kind of common ownership of the land. As a result of this family ownership, such family estates were inalienable except with the express consent of all the heirs involved. Consequently gifts and sales of such land were practically impossible although they became possible during the interval between the issuance of the laws of Rothair in the seventh century and those of his successors in the eighth century. Although outright gifts and sales were mistrusted, the same did not hold true of the exchange which was presumably an exchange of equal value and hence did not diminish the patrimony of the family. These considerations, of course, applied only to the family lands. Lands acquired by the individual as a result of royal gift or in some other way were the individual's alone and could be disposed of at will.

[12] This law is a good example of the dilemma facing the Lombard lawgivers—the clash between custom and the needs of the time. Insofar as the Lombard laws were the reduction to writing of time honored Lombard customs, the code is one of customary law. But the Lombard kings from time to time introduced modifications of the old customs, and occasionally they issued laws based upon a particular case which had come to the attention of the king and his advisers. Such laws would seem to be true legislation and the Lombard code is at least in part a legislative enactment. Even so, however, the force of custom was strong and enjoyed a kind of sanctity illustrated here by Liutprand's reluctance to abolish an old custom which no longer seemed to insure perfect justice.

[13] This rather sophisticated legal reasoning is a marked advance over the short laws of Rothair where no attempt at analysis was made —the offense was stated followed by the fine or punishment with little or no regard for ameliorating or aggravating circumstances. In general, all the laws of Liutprand, but especially the later ones, are marked by a considerable amount of legal reflection.

[14] "In the legislation of the purely Lombard epoch at the beginning of the eighth century, we find already traces of jurisprudential analysis. There is, for instance, an enactment of Liutprand (c. 134) treating the ejectment of a landed proprietor by his neighbors. If, in the course of these violent proceedings, he suffers bodily harm, the offenders must, of course, pay the fine for homicide or wounding, but the legislator declares in addition that they are guilty of conspiracy, and must be fined twenty solidi on that account. In analyzing the case, Liutprand, or his legal advisers, explains why they decree such a fine and not another. They state their reasons for not considering the transgression to be one of *arischild*, that is, of forming an armed band (cf. Roth. 19,

Liutpr. 35, 141), not a case of unlawful organization of country folk (*consilium rusticanorum*, Roth. 279), not of riot (*rusticanorum seditio*). It seems to the legislator that the material point in the case lies in the preparation to commit murderous assault. It is this intention which constitutes the criminal element in the conspiracy, and which may lead to the perpetration of the crime. In spite of the barbarous language, the mode of reasoning testifies to a rising level of juridical thought; and, though a direct connection with Roman rules is not traceable, yet this and similar cases of legal analysis in Lombard legislation suggest that Lombard justice was progressing from a naive application of barbarian rules to a reflective jurisprudence, and this undoubtedly opened the way for a consideration of Roman doctrine." Paul Vinogradoff, *Roman Law in Medieval Europe*, 2nd ed. (London, 1929), pp. 21–24.

[15] This is another example of the rather advanced legal reasoning referred to in notes 13 and 14 above.

[16] Among all the early Germanic peoples it seems to have been accepted that in the last analysis a man would guarantee the payment of debts with his own person. Such is clear even in the work of Tacitus for Tacitus remarks on the Germanic prediliction for gambling which did not stop with the wagering of a man's property but would extend to the wager of his own person. The Lombards knew both temporary and permanent debt servitude. For all unpaid debts over twenty solidi, the debtor delivered himself or was delivered into the permanent service of the creditor. For the nonpayment of lesser debts—from six solidi to twenty solidi—temporary servitude was required until the labor of the debt slave should be equivalent to the amount of his debt. When one considers the extremely high compositions involved in almost all personal offenses (varying to amounts as high as 900 or 1200 solidi) it seems pretty clear that the intent of the law was to turn the offender (obviously unable to pay such a fine) over to the person or family injured. The offended party might then take vengeance as he pleased, a vengeance which undoubtedly was exacted to the death in some cases.

[17] This law is good proof that by the end of the Lombard monarchy the principle of personality of law was making headway in Italy. Although other Germanic laws might have no official existence in Lombard Italy and although secular Roman law likewise had no official existence, it is clear that the influence of the Roman canon law was spreading rapidly and although Roman canon law might have no official existence so far as the Lombard law courts were concerned, there is little doubt about the existence of ecclesiastical courts where such a law should be applied. That a Lombard freeman should be released from the application of Lombard law while still resident within the Lombard kingdom, even though now subject to the jurisdiction of the Church, is a major inroad on the Lombard conception of the superiority of the territorial Lombard law. Note however that this law is

concerned with limiting the extension of the claim to be subject to Church law.

IV. The Laws of King Ratchis

[1] See the Laws of Liutprand, note 12. This is the only instance in the entire code where the lawgiver went so far as actually to "repeal" an earlier law.

[2] See Glossary. Also see Bluhme, *Leges Langobardorum*, p. 190, n. 17.

V. The Laws of King Aistulf

[1] For the relationship between these first laws with their incomplete prologue and the laws from Aistulf's fifth year, see Bluhme, *Leges Langobardorum*, p. 195, n. 1.

[2] A monk's chronicle repeats the story that Ratchis took to wife a woman from the city of Rome and the traditional Lombard marriage contract was not made. Furthermore, Ratchis and his Roman queen, Tassia, proceeded to make a number of grants of land by charter according to Roman law. The Lombards were aroused and when Aistulf sought to become king, they petitioned him to undo the gifts of Ratchis. Aistulf promised he would so do if he became king, and the Lombards elected him. Bluhme, *Leges Langobardorum*, p. 196, n. 2.

[3] Bluhme suggests that the term "Roman" here refers to a man from Ravenna with which the Lombards were at war. However, since the Lombard relationship with the city of Rome was almost as strained as its relationship with the Exarchate, the term "Roman" might well refer to an inhabitant of the city of Rome.

[4] For probable derivation see Bluhme, *Leges Langobardorum*, p. 201, n. 12.

[5] Bluhme, *Leges Langobardorum*, p. 203, n. 14, suggests that this law is based upon Justinian's novel 111 and novel 131, cap. 6.

[6] Cf. Rothair 278, 373, 380. Presumably one of the royal officials in the kingdom—perhaps one of the centini, degani, or missi.

[7] These "spurious" titles appear in only one of the manuscripts. See Bluhme, *Leges Langobardorum*, pp. 204–5, notes 21–23.

GLOSSARY

adunationes. See *zavas et adunationes.*

aidos. "Aids," oathhelpers. Cf. the modern German *Eid.* See Bluhme, *Leges Langobardorum*, p. 82, n. 53.

(h)aistan. With enraged soul, vehement, violent. For Anglo-Saxon parallels see Meyer, p. 290; Bruckner, p. 206.

aldius. One who is half-free, who stands between the freeman and the slave in the Lombard economic and social scale. The derivation of this word is most uncertain and no very reasonable analogies have been suggested. Cf. Carl Meyer, *Sprache und Sprachdenkmaler der Langobarden* (Paderborn, 1877), p. 277 (cited hereafter as Meyer), and Wilhelm Bruckner, *Die Sprache der Langobarden* (Strassburg, 1895), p. 201 (cited hereafter as Bruckner).

amundius. An adjective meaning not under the protection or guardianship (mundium) of anyone; legally independent. See *mundium* below.

anagrip. Illegal sexual intercourse with a woman. Cf. modern German *angreifen.* Most of the modern German equivalents cited in this glossary are taken from Meyer or Bruckner.

(h)andegawerc (andegawere). Hand tools, implements which one uses in his ordinary daily work. Cf. modern German *Hand* and *Gerät.*

angargathungi. The "worth," that is, wergeld or pretium, of a person. From the Gothic *gethungen,* "to be worthy," and *angar,* which is obscure, perhaps referring to the possession of land. Cf. modern German *Anger*.

arga. Both Meyer and Bruckner translate "coward" without giving derivation (Meyer, p. 279; Bruckner, p. 202). But compare the rendering given by C. D. DuCange, *Glossarium Mediae et Infimae Latinitatis* (Paris, 1840–50), I, p. 387 (cited hereafter as DuCange).

(h)arigawerc (arigawere). Weapon or implement forming part of a soldier's armament. Cf. the modern German *Heer* and *Gerät* ("army tool"). Cf. *arimannus* below.

(h)arimannus. The ordinary Lombard soldier who was a freeman—hence the word is used interchangeably with "freeman." Cf. the modern German *Heer* and *Mann*. Meyer, p. 290 and Bruckner, p. 206. Note the Gothic derivation given in Sigmund Feist, *Etymologisches Wörterbuch der Gotischen Sprache*, 2nd ed. (Halle, 1923), p. 182 (cited hereafter as Feist).

(h)ariscild. Cf. modern German *Heer-Schild*. In the laws this word seems to mean breach of the peace with an armed band.

(h)aritraib. A group of soldiers (or freemen) gathered together for the purpose of forcing armed entry into or destroying a house. Cf. the modern German *Heer* and *treiban*.

(h)asto. Intentionally, on purpose. For early Germanic analogies, see Meyer, p. 291.

camphio (camfio). A fighter or champion, one who participates in a judicial duel. Also used for the fight or duel itself. Cf. the modern German *Kämpfer*.

cawarfida. Tax, duty. Note the rather circuitous explanation in Meyer, p. 293.

crapworfin (grapuuorf). The act of throwing a dead body out of the grave. Cf. the modern German *Grab* and *werfen*. For Gothic analogies, see Meyer, p. 294.

faderfio. A payment or money gift made by the father at the time of the marriage of his daughter. Cf. the modern German *Vater* and *Vieh*.

faida. Vendetta, feud. Cf. the modern German *Fehde*.

fara. Family, clan, even race or nation—those bound together by the bond of relationship. This word appears in a number of the Germanic codes, but has disappeared from the modern language. For early analogies, see Meyer, p. 285; Bruckner, p. 203.

fereha, fagia. Oak tree.

ferquido. Like, similar. For Gothic form, see Feist, p. 107.

fornaccar. A field after the harvest has been gathered. The prefix is obscure, but cf. the modern German *Acker* for the second element.

fraida. Flight. Cf. *fr-ei-th* with Latin *eo*. Julius Pokorny, ed., *Alois Walde Vergleichendes Wörterbuch der Indogermanisch Sprache*, Vol. I (Berlin and Leipzig, 1932), p. 103.

fulborn. Legitimate, legal birth according to the law of the tribe—used only in connection with persons of free birth. Cf. the modern German *Fulle* and *geboren*.

fulcfree. "Folkfree," i.e., free according to the law of the folk. An adjective used to refer to the ordinary freeman. Cf. the modern German *Volk* and *frei*.

gafand. A co-heir.

Gahagium. An enclosure, forest, used in the laws to refer to the preserve of the king.

gaida. An arrow. For Anglo-Saxon equivalent, see Meyer, p. 286.

gairethinx. The procedure whereby a contract became legally binding. Literally, "spear assembly" before which contractual proceedings (as well as the other business of the tribe) were transacted, the procedure had, by the time of the writing down of the Lombard Laws, become any publicly witnessed act. Cf. the modern German *Ding*. For derivation see Meyer, p. 287; Bruckner, p. 205.

gamahalos. The legitimate relatives—the *confabulatis*—those born of a *fabula*, i.e., a legal marriage pact or agreement (*foedus*). DuCange, III, p. 469.

gasindium (casindius). An attendant, servant, hence a follower or "man" in the medieval sense, a member of the early Germanic *comitatus*. The word can also refer to the group of attendants or followers of a man. Cf. the modern German *Gesinde*.

gastaldius. The royal administrative and judicial officer in each district (*civitas*) immediately subordinate to the king. For derivation see Meyer, p. 288; Bruckner, p. 205.

gisel. Whip. Cf. modern German *Geisel*. For the translation "witness," see Franz Beyerle, *Die Gesetze der Langobarden* (Weimar, 1947), Glossary, p. 503.

idertzon (eterzon). The fence around a courtyard. Derivation not clear.

lagi. The thigh or upper leg. Cf. the modern English "leg."

langobardi. Evidently a translation of the Lombard *Winili* by which name the Lombards called themselves. Literally, the "long beards," contracted to Lombards. DuCange, IV, p. 25. Cf. the Anglo-Saxon *Longbearden*.

launigild. A return gift, literally "reward money." Cf. the modern German *Lohn* and *Geld*.

lidinlaib. *Laib* equals "remains," "inheritance." *Leith* is an Indo-Germanic root equalling *forthgehen* or *sterben* (to die). Hence "death remains."

marahworfin. To throw or drag off a horse. Cf. the modern German *werfen*.

medula. Oak tree.

meta. "Purchase price," the sum paid by a man to the father of his affianced bride. Cf. the modern English "meed."

metfio. A payment in cattle originally, but later any payment made by a man for his prospective bride. The word is a combination of *meta* (see above) and *fio* (cf. the modern German *Vieh*).

mordh. Murder. Cf. the modern German *Mord*.

morgingap (morgincap, morgengab). The "morning gift." A gift made by the groom to his bride the morning after the wedding. Cf. the modern German *Morgen* and *Gabe*.

mundium. The power or right of guardianship. Cf. the modern German *Vormund* and *Vormundschaft*. See *amundius* above, and *mundwald, selpmundius* below.

mundwald (munduuald). A protector, guardian, one who holds the *mundium* of some dependent person. Cf. the modern Italian *mondwaldo*.

murioth. The upper arm. See Meyer, p. 297 and Bruckner, p. 210 for parallels.

nazzas. Nets. Cf. the modern German *Netz*. For parallels, see Meyer, p. 298 and Feist, p. 279.

(h)oberos (hoberos). Breach or violation of a man's courtyard. Cf. the modern German *Hof*. For parallels see Meyer, p. 292.

octogild (ahtugild). An eightfold payment. Cf. the modern German *acht* and *Geld*.

pans. Royal favor.

pisele. *Pisalis* (cf. *gynaecium*). Originally the women's apartments in a house or palace, but eventually those rooms where the weaving was done.

plodraub. Robbery of the dead. Cf. the modern German *Tod* and *Raub*.

pulslahi. A blow which causes a bump. Cf. the modern German *Pulschlag*.

rairaub. Robbery of dead bodies or of the grave. Cf. the modern German *Grab* (Gothic *hraiv*) and *Raub*.

sala. Property, perhaps that property which is to be transferred by will or testament.

scamaras. Blasphemer. Cf. Indo-Germanic *Kem, Hem,* modern English "shame."

sculdahis (sculdhaizo). A local official representing the king, responsible to the gastald (gastaldius). Cf. the modern *Schuld* and *heiszen*.

selpmundius. Legally independent, in the guardianship of oneself. Cf. the modern German prefix *selb* and see *mundium* above.

snaida. Identification marks cut on trees in a wood. For parallels see Meyer, p. 304; Feist, p. 332.

sonorpair. The strongest boar of the herd. For parallels, see Meyer, p. 304 and Bruckner, p. 212. Also see Bluhme, *Leges Langobardorum*, pp. 80–81, n. 52.

stolesazo. One of the king's officials of uncertain rank, perhaps a household official. Cf. the modern German *Stuhl* and *sitzen*. For parallels, see Meyer, p. 304; Bruckner, p. 212.

stupla. Stubble, stalk. From the Latin *stipula*.

thingare. To conclude a contractual agreement legally before a court or witnesses. Literally, a legal action concluded before the assembly (*thing*). For parallels, see Meyer, p. 306; Bruckner, p. 212.

thinx. Either the procedure whereby a contract becomes legally binding, or the object about which the contract was made. An abbreviation of *gairethinx* (see above).

threus. A word comparable to Anglo-Saxon "thrall," varying in meaning almost as widely as the term "boy," "cniht."

triuuas. A pledge or security. Cf. modern German *treuga.*

wadium (uuadium). A legal pledge. For parallels see Meyer, p. 307; Feist, p. 410.

walopaus (uualapaux). One who has disguised himself for some ulterior purpose. For parallels, see Meyer, p. 307.

waregang (uuaregang). Immigrants or recent arrivals. Cf. the Anglo-Saxon *Vaergenga.* For parallels see Meyer, p. 308; Bruckner, p. 213.

wegworin (wecwori). Road blocking, a personal offense in the Germanic laws. Cf. the modern German *Weg* and *werfen.*

wergeld (uuergild, werigeld). The value affixed to a man's life which varied with his social status. Cf. the modern German prefix *wer* and *geltan.*

zava. Division. Meyer, p. 310. But for *zavas et adunationes*, Beyerle translates "outcry and alliance." Beyerle, *Die Gesetze der Langobarden* (1947 edition), p. 349. DuCange, on the other hand, equates *zavas* with *lorica* (armor or weapon), and translates *adunationes* as an assembly. DuCange, VI, p. 928; I, p. 103.

BIBLIOGRAPHY

PRIMARY SOURCES

Legal

The most convenient edition of the various barbarian law codes is to be found in the *Leges* volumes of the *Monumenta Germaniae Historica*, while a more up-to-date edition together with German translation of the most important of the codes is to be found in the *Germanenrechte* series published by the Akademie für deutsches Rechtsgeschichte in Weimar. For the Lombard Laws, the specific reference to these editions is as follows:

For the *Germanenrechte* series:

Beyerle, Franz, *Die Gesetze der Langobarden* (Weimar, 1947).

Beyerle, Franz, *Leges Langobardorum, 643–866, Germanenrechte Neue Folge* (Witzenhausen, 1962).

Beyerle, Franz, *Die Gesetze der Langobarden, Germanenrechte Texte und Übersetzungen*, Bd. 3, 2nd ed. (in 3 parts) (Witzenhausen, 1962–1963).

For the *Monumenta* edition:

Bluhme, F., ed., *Leges Langobardorum, Leges, Monumenta Germaniae Historica*, Vol. IV (Hanover, 1869).

There are a number of older editions of the Lombard Laws, the most important of which follow:

Baudi a Vesme, Caroli, *Edicta Regum Langobardorum, Historia Patriae Monumenta* (Turin, 1855); 2nd ed. by J. F. Neigebaur (Munich, 1856).

Canciani, Paul, *Leges Langobardicae, Barbarorum Leges Antiquae* (Venice, 1771), Vol. I.

Muratorius, L. A., *Leges Langobardorum, Rerum Italicarum Scriptores* (Milan, 1725), Vol. I, Pt. 2.

Walter, Ferdinand, *Corpus Juris Germanici Antiqui* (Berlin, 1824), Vol. I.

The most impressive translations into a modern language of

the barbarian codes appear in the *Germanenrechte* series of the Akademie für deutsches Rechtsgeschichte cited above, but the following should also be noted:

Attenborough, F. L., *The Laws of the Earliest English Kings* (New York, 1922).

Drew, Katherine Fischer, *The Burgundian Code* (Philadelphia, 1949); reprinted, with introduction by Edward Peters, Philadelphia, 1972.

Liebermann, F., ed. and trans., *Die Gesetze der Angelsachsen*, 3 vols. (Halle, 1903–1916).

Robertson, A. J., *The Laws of the Kings of England from Edmund to Henry I* (New York, 1925).

Scott, S. P., *The Visigothic Code* (Boston, 1910).

For use with the barbarian codes, the following is indispensable:

Pharr, Clyde, *et al.*, *The Theodosian Code* (Princeton, N.J., 1952).

Historiographic

The most important contemporary source written with a view to providing the Lombards with a "history" is an account written by the Lombard known as Paul the Deacon. The edition of Paul usually referred to is that in the *Monumenta Germaniae Historica*:

Bethman, L., and G. Waitz, eds., *Pauli Historia Langobardorum, Scriptores Rerum Langobardicarum et Italicarum Saec. VI-IX, Monumenta Germaniae Historica* (Hanover, 1878).

There are several modern translations:

Foulke, William Dudley, *History of the Langobards by Paul the Deacon* (Philadelphia, 1907; reprinted, with introduction by Edward Peters, Philadelphia, 1972), under the title, *History of the Lombards*.

Roncoroni, Federico (with introduction by Enzo Fabiani), *Storia dei Longobardi* (Milan, 1970).

Of other contemporary sources with material about the Lombards, the most significant are:

Gregor von Tours, *Zehn Bücher Geschichten*, trans. by W. Giesebrechts and Rudolf Buchner (Latin edition with German translation) (Berlin: Rutten & Loening, n.d.), 2 vols.

Gregoire de Tours, *Histoire des Francs*, trans. by Robert Latouche, 2 vols. (Paris, 1963–1965).

Gregory of Tours, *History of the Franks*, trans. by O. M. Dalton, 2 vols. (London, 1927).

Le Liber Pontificalis; texte, introduction et commentaire par l'abbé Duchesne (Paris, 1886–1892), 2 vols.

Loomis, Louise Ropes, trans., *The Book of the Popes (Liber Pontificalis) to the Pontificate of Gregory I* (New York, 1916).

Procopius, *The History of the Wars*, trans. by H. B. Dewing, 5 vols. (London, 1914–1938).

Waitz, G., ed., *Origo Gentis Langobardorum, Scriptores Rerum Langobardicarum et Italicarum Saec. VI–IX. Monumenta Germaniae Historica* (Hanover, 1878).

Cartularies

Charters from the Lombard period are not numerous; nonetheless there are several extremely valuable collections for the Lombards generally as well as a number of collections of documents for various ecclesiastical bodies that contain material from the Lombard period. The general collections and only a few of the more interesting ecclesiastical collections are cited here:

Cipolla, Carlo, ed., *Codice diplomatico del Monastero di S. Colombano di Bobbio, Fonti per la Storia d'Italia*, 52–54 (Rome, 1918).

Giorgi, I., and U. Balzani, eds., *Il Registo di Farfa compilato da Gregorio di Catino, Biblioteca della R. Società romana di Storia patria*, 5 vols. in 4 (Rome, 1883–1892).

Leccisotti, T. D., ed., *Abbazia di Montecassino: I Regesti dell' Archivio* (Rome, 1964).

Codex Diplomaticus Langobardiae, Historiae Patriae Monumentae, Vol. XIII (1873).

Schiaparelli, Luigi, *Codice Diplomatico Langobardo, Fonti per la Storia d'Italia*, Parte Secolo VIII (Rome, 1929).

Troya, Carlo, *Codice Diplomatico Langobardo* (Naples, 1845).

SECONDARY MATERIALS

The Germanic Migrations and Germanic Kingdoms

Amira, K. von, *Grundriss des germanischen Rechte*, 3rd ed. (Strassburg, 1913).

Bethmann-Hollweg, M.A. von, *Der Civilprozess des gemeinen Rechts in geschichtlicher Entwickelung* (Bonn, 1867-74), 6 vols. Vol. IV:

Der Germanisch-romanische Civilprozess im Mittelalter (Bonn, 1868).

Brunner, H., *Deutsche Rechtsgeschichte* (Leipzig, 1906), 2 vols. Vol. II, 2nd ed. by Claudius Frh. von Schwerin (Munich and Leipzig, 1928).

Conrad, Hermann, *Deutsche Rechtsgeschichte*, Vol. I: *Frühzeit und Mittelalter* (Karlsruhe, 1954).

Courcelle, Pierre, *Histoire littéraire des grandes invasions germaniques*, 3rd ed. (Paris, 1964).

Dahn, F., *Die Könige der Germanen*, 11 vols. (Würzburg and Leipzig, 1870–1910).

Dahn, Felix, *Die Völkerwanderung* (Berlin, 1960).

Davoud-Oghlou, G.A., *Histoire de la législation des anciens Germains* (Berlin, 1845), 2 vols.

DuCange, C.D., *Glossarium Mediae et Infimae Latinitatis* (Paris, 1840–1850), 7 vols.

Eichhorn, K.F., *Deutsche Staats- und Rechtsgeschichte*, 5th ed., Vol. I (Göttingen, 1843).

Feist, Sigmund, *Etymologisches Wörterbuch der Gotischen Sprache*, 2nd ed. (Halle, 1923).

Gamillscheg, E., *Romania Germanica* (Berlin-Leipzig, 1935).

Goebel, Julius, Jr., *Felony and Misdemeanor* (New York, 1939).

Grierson, P., "Election and Inheritance in Early Germanic Kingship," *The Cambridge Historical Journal*, VII, 1 (1941).

Grimm, Jacob, *Deutsche Rechts-Alterthümer* (Göttingen, 1838).

Halphen, L., *Les barbares des grandes invasions aux conquêtes turques du XIᵉ siècle*, 2nd ed. rev. (Paris, 1930).

Hayes, Carlton J. H., *An Introduction to the Sources Relating to the Germanic Invasions* (New York, 1909).

Hillgarth, J.N., ed., *The Conversion of Western Europe, 350–750* (Englewood Cliffs, N.J., 1969).

His, Rudolf, *Geschichte des deutschen Strafrechts bis zur Karolina* (Munich and Berlin, 1928).

Hodgkin, R.H., *A History of the Anglo-Saxons*, 3rd ed. (London, 1952), 2 vols.

Hübner, Rudolf, *A History of Germanic Private Law*, trans. by Francis S. Philbrick, *The Continental Legal History Series* (Boston, 1918).

Kern, Fritz, *Kingship and Law in the Middle Ages*, trans. by S. B. Chrimes (Oxford, 1939).

Latouche, R., *Les grandes invasions et la crise de l'Occident au Vᵉ siècle* (Paris, 1946).

Lavisse, Ernst, and Alfred Rambaud, *Histoire général du IVᵉ siècle jusqu'à nos jours*, 12 vols. (Paris, 1896).

Lear, F. S., *Treason in Roman and Germanic Law* (Austin, Texas, 1965).

Lopez, R. S., "Byzantine Law in the Seventh Century and its Reception by the Germans and the Arabs," *Byzantion*, XVI, 2 (1942–1943).

Lot, Ferdinand, *The End of the Ancient World and the Beginning of the Middle Ages* (New York, 1931).

Lot, Ferdinand, *Les invasions barbares et le peuplement de l'Europe*, 2 vols. (Paris, 1937).

Lot, F., Christian Pfister and F. L. Ganshof, *Les destinées de l'Empire en Occident de 393 à 888* (Paris, 1935).

McNeal, Edgar Holmes, *Minores and Mediocres in the Germanic Tribal Laws* (Columbus, Ohio, 1905).

Musset, Lucien, *Les invasions: les vagues germaniques* (Paris, 1965).

Niermeyer, J.F., *Mediae Latinitatis lexicon minus* (Leiden, 1954–19   ).

Odegaard, C.E., *Vassi and Fideles in the Carolingian Empire* (Cambridge, Mass., 1945).

Pepe, Gabriele, *Le moyen âge barbare en italie* (Paris, 1956).

Pepe, Gabriele, *Il Medioevo Barbarico in Europa* (Verona, 1949).

Pirenne, Henri, *Histoire de l'Europe des invasions au XVIe siècle* (Brussels, 1936).

Pokorny, Julius, ed., *Alois Walde Vergleichendes Wörterbuch der Indogermanischen Sprache* (Berlin and Leipzig, 1927–1932), 3 vols.

Pontieri, Ernesto, *Le Invasioni Barbariche e l'Italia del V e VI Secolo* (Naples, 1960).

Riché, Pierre, *Education et culture dans l'Occident barbare VIe–VIIIe siècles* (Paris, 1962).

Riché, Pierre, *Les invasions barbares* (Paris, 1964).

Romano, Giacinto, *Le Dominazioni Barbariche in Italia (395–888)*, rev. ed. by Arrigo Solmi (Milan, 1940).

Savigny, F. C. von, *Geschichte des römischen Rechts im Mittelalter*, 2nd ed., Vol. II (Heidelberg, 1934).

Schroder, Richard, and Eberhard Frh. von Kunssberg, *Lehrbuch der deutschen Rechtsgeschichte*, 6th ed. (Berlin and Leipzig, 1922).

Schubert, Hans von, *Staat und Kirche in den Arianischen Königreichen und im Reiche Chlodwigs, Historische Bibliothek*, Vol. 26 (Munich and Berlin, 1912).

Stenton, F. E., *Anglo-Saxon England*, 3rd ed. (Oxford, 1971).

Thompson, E. A., *The Early Germans* (London, 1956).

Thompson, E. A., *The Goths in Spain* (London, 1969).

Villari, P., *Le Invasioni Barbariche in Italia*, 4th ed. (Milan, 1928).

Vinogradoff, Paul, *Roman Law in Medieval Europe*, 2nd ed. (London, 1939).

Wallace-Hadrill, J. M., *The Barbarian West, 400–1000* (London, 1952).

Wallace-Hadrill, J. M., *The Long-Haired Kings* (London, 1962).

Wattenbach-Levison, *Deutschlands Geschichtsquellen im Mittelalter, Vorzeit und Karolinger: Die Rechtsquellen* (by Rudolf Buchner) (Weimar, 1953).

The Lombards and the Lombard Kingdom

Bognetti, Gian Piero, *L'Età Longobarda*, 4 vols. (Milan, 1966–1970).

Bruckner, Wilhelm, *Die Sprache der Langobarden* (Strassburg, 1895).

Bruhl, Carlrichard, *Studien zu den Langobardischen Königsurkunden* (Tübingen, 1970).

Calisse, Carlo, *A History of Italian Law, The Continental Legal History Series*, Vol. VIII (Boston, 1929).

Centro Italiano di Studi sull'alto Medioevo, all volumes but especially Vol. V: *Caratteri del Secolo VII in Occidente* (Spoleto, 1958); Vol. VI: *La Città nell'alto Medioevo* (Spoleto, 1959); Vol. VII: *Le Chiese nei Regni dell'Europa Occidentale e i loro Rapporti con Roma sino all'800* (Spoleto, 1960); Vol. VIII: *Moneta e Scambi nell'alto Medioevo* (Spoleto, 1960); Vol. IX: *Il Passaggio dall' Antichità al Medioevo in Occidente* (Spoleto, 1962); Vol. XIII: *Agricoltura e Mondo Rurale in Occidente nell'alto Medioevo* (Spoleto, 1966); and Vol. XIV: *La Conversione al Cristianesimo nell'Europa dell'alto Medioevo* (Spoleto, 1967).

Cilento, Nicola, *Italia Meridionale Longobarda* (Milan, 1966).

Darmstadter, P., *Das Reichsgut in der Lombardei und Piemont 568–1250* (Strassburg, 1896).

Devoto, G., *Profilo di Storia Linguistica* (Firenze, 1960).

Diehl, Ch., *Études sur l'administration byzantine dans l'exarchat de Ravenne (568–751)* (Paris, 1888).

Drew, K. F., "Class Distinctions in Eighth Century Italy," *The Rice Institute Pamphlet*, XXXIX, 3 (October, 1952).

Drew, K. F., *Notes on Lombard Institutions, The Rice Institute Pamphlet*, XLVIII, 2 (July, 1956).

Fasoli, Gina, *I Longobardi in Italia* (Bologna, 1965).

Fiorelli, Piero, *La tortura giudiziaria nel diritto comune (Ius Nostrum, Studi e testi pubblicati dall'Istituto de Storia del Diritto Italiano dell'Universite di Roma)* (Rome, 1953–1954), 2 vols.

Hartmann, L. M., *Geschichte Italiens im Mittelalter* (Gotha, 1900), 4 vols.

Hodgkin, T., *Italy and her Invaders*, Vol. VI (Oxford, 1896).

Jacobi, R., *Die Quellen der Langobardengeschichte des Paulus Diaconus* (Halle, 1877).

Leicht, Pier Silverio, "King Ahistulfs Heeresgesetze," *Miscellanea Academica Berolinensia*, II, 1 (Berlin, 1950).

Leicht, Pier Silverio, numerous articles reprinted in *Scritti vari di Storia del Diritto Italiano*, 2 vols. in 3 (Milan, 1943–1948).

Leicht, Pier Silverio, *Breve storia del Friuli* (Udine, 1931).

Löfstedt, "Studien über die Sprache der langobardischen Gesetz," *Acta Universitatis Upsaliensis, Studia Latina* 1 (Stockholm, 1961).

Manacorda, Francesco, *Ricerche sugli Inizii della Dominazione dei Carolingi in Italia* (Rome, 1968).

Meyer, Carl, *Sprache und Sprachdenkmäler der Langobarden* (Paderborn, 1877).

Migliorini, B., *Storia della lingua italiana* (Firenze, 1961).

Mor, Carlo Guido, *L'età Feudale* (Milan, 1952), 2 vols.

Mor, Carlo Guido, "Modificazioni strutturali dell'Assemblea nazionale longobarda nel sec. VIII," *Album Helen Maud Cam*, II (Louvain-Paris, 1961).

Paschini, P., *Storia del Friuli* (Udine, 1953).

Pochettino, Giuseppe, *I Langobardi nell'Italia meridionale (570–1080)* (Naples, n.d.).

Politzer, Robert L., *A Study of the Language of Eighth Century Lombardic Documents* (New York, 1949).

Rabinowitz, Jacob J., "Jewish and Lombard Law," *Jewish Social Studies*, XII, 4 (October, 1950).

Schupfer, F., *Il Diritto Privato dei Popoli Germanici con Speciale Riguardo all'Italia*, 2nd ed. (Città di Castello-Roma, 1913–1915).

Tagliaferri, A., *I Longobardi nella civiltà e nell'economia italiana del primo Medioevo* (Milan, 1965).

Vaccari, Pietro, *Introduzione Storica al Vigente Diritto Privato Italiano* (Milan, 1957).

Vaccari, Pietro, *Profilo Storico di Pavia* (Pavia, 1956).

Williams, William K., *The Communes of Lombardy from the VI. to the X. Century, Johns Hopkins University Studies in Historical and Political Science* (Baltimore, 1891).

Zeiller, J., "Étude sur l'arianisme en Italie à l'époque ostrogothique et à l'époque lombarde," *Mélanges de l'école française de Rome*, XXI (1905), 127–146.

Works Based on Archeology—Both General and Lombard

Students of archeology are very active in working on materials connected with the Germanic migrations and the Germanic kingdoms. Only a brief sampling of these works (and only those dealing with the continent) are mentioned here, but the bibliographies of these volumes will carry the interested student deeper into the subject.

Åberg, Nils, *Die Goten und Langobarden in Italien* (Uppsala, 1923).

Bernareggi, E., *Le Monete dei Longobardi nell'Italia Padana e nella Tuscia* (Milan, 1963).

Bognetti, G. P., *S. Maria di Castelseprio* (Milan, 1966).

Brozzi, M. and A. Tagliafcrri, *Arte Longobarda* (Cividalc, 1961).

Fuchs, S., *Die Langobardische Goldblattkreuze* (Berlin, 1928).

Haseloff, A., *Die vorromanische Plastik in Italien* (Berlin, 1930).

Owen, Francis, *The Germanic People, their Origin, Expansion and Culture* (New York, 1960).

Porter, A. K., *Lombard Architecture* (New Haven, 1917).

Rice, David Talbot, ed., *The Dawn of European Civilization: The Dark Ages* (section on Lombard art by Donald Bullough) (London, 1965).

Salin, Édouard, *La civilisation mérovingienne d'après les sépultures, les textes et le laboratoire*, 4 vols. (Paris, 1950–1959).

Salin, Édouard, "L'épée longue des grandes invasions," *Comptes Rendus dé l'Académie des Inscriptions et Belles-lettres* (1946), 586–595.

Schaffran, E., *Die Kunst der Langobarden* (Jena, 1941).

Tagliaferri, Amelio, ed., *Problemi della Civiltà e dell'Economia Longobarda, Scritti in memoria di Gian Piero Bognetti* (Milan, 1946).

Barbarian Law, Cultural Anthropology, and the Sociology of Law

The evolution of law and the interrelationship between the legal systems of various peoples became in the late nineteenth century a subject of interest to students of historical jurisprudence. The works of these early writers have now been taken up by contemporary scholars interested in cultural anthropology and in the sociology of law. The barbarian codes are cited for the analogies that they provide with the legal institutions of other "primitive" peoples. But the modern behavioral scientist is hampered in his work by the necessity for the most part of approaching barbarian law through the eyes of nineteenth-century commentators since few of the codes are available in modern translation. Nonetheless much stimulating work has been done in this field and a few important titles are cited here.

Diamond, A. S., *The Evolution of Law and Order* (London, 1951).

Diamond, A. S., *Primitive Law* (London, 1935).

Gluckman, Max, *Politics, Law and Ritual in Tribal Society* (Chicago, 1965).

Hoebel, E. Adamson, *The Law of Primitive Man* (Cambridge, Mass., 1954).

Jenks, Edward, *Law and Politics in the Middle Ages* (New York, 1913).

Krader, Lawrence, ed., *Anthropology and Early Law* (New York, 1966).

Lee, Guy Carleton, *Historical Jurisprudence* (New York, 1922).

Maine, Sir Henry Sumner, *On Early Law and Custom* (London, 1890).

Nader, Laura, ed., *Law in Culture and Society* (Chicago, 1969).

Sawer, Geoffrey, *Law in Society* (Oxford, 1965).

Schur, Edwin M., *Law and Society, A Sociological View* (New York, 1968).

Stone, Julius, *The Province and Function of Law* (Cambridge, Mass., 1960).

Stone, Julius, *Social Dimensions of Law and Justice* (Stanford, 1966).

Vinogradoff, Sir Paul, *Outlines of Historical Jurisprudence* (London, 1920).

INDEX